The Very Breast of

RUSS MEYER

edited by Paul A. Woods

Plexus, London

Published by Plexus Publishing Limited
55a Clapham Common Southside
London SW4 9BX
www.plexusbooks.com
First printing 2004

British Library Cataloguing in Publication Data

The very breast of Russ Meyer - (ultra screen; no. 4)
   1.Meyer, Russ - Interviews 2.Exploitation films -
   United States
   3.Motion pictures - United States - Production
   and direction
   I.Woods, Paul A.
   791.4'3'0233092

ISBN 0 85965 309 9

Cover design by Phil Gambrill
Book design by Phil Gambrill and Rebecca Martin
Printed in Great Britain by Cromwell Press

Acknowledgements
We would like to make special acknowledgement to the following
for their contributions and permission to reproduce material in this
book: 'Mondo Russo' by Dale Ashmun, from Film Threat, 1988.
'Uncertain Innocence Part One' by Kenneth Turan and Stephen F.
Zito, from Sinema: American Pornographic Films and the People
Who Make Them, Praeger Publishers, 1974. 'The Immoral Mr.
Teas' from Variety, 27 January 1960. 'Eve and the Handyman'
from Variety, 10 May 1961. 'Uncertain Innocence Part Two' by
Kenneth Turan and Stephen F. Zito, from Sinema: American
Pornographic Films and the People Who Make Them, Praeger
Publishers, 1974. 'Lorna' from Variety, 25 August 1965. 'Russ
Meyer vs. the Italian Masters: A Discussion of Lorna with "King
Leer"' interview by David K. Frasier, from Cinefocus 1.2, Fall 1990.

'Fanny Hill: Memoirs of a Woman of Pleasure' from Variety, 17
March 1965. 'Rope of Flesh (aka Mudhoney)' from Variety, 25
August 1965. 'Motor Psycho!' by Kim Newman, from City Limits,
31 May 1985. 'Faster Pussycat, Unpleasant Film' by James Powers,
from The Hollywood Reporter, 8 February 1966. 'Russ Meyer:
Master' by John Waters, from Shock Value, Bantam Doubleday
Dell, 1981. 'Mondo Topless' by Jimmy McDonough, from Film
Comment, July 1986. 'Uncertain Innocence Part Three' by
Kenneth Turan and Stephen F. Zito, from Sinema: American
Pornographic Films and the People Who Make Them, Praeger
Publishers, 1974. 'Russ Meyer 1967!' by Moose McGill, from
Ungawa!, early 1990s. 'Finders Keepers, Lovers Weepers' by
Vincent Canby, from The New York Times, 15 May 1968. 'Vixen'
by David McGillivray, from Monthly Film Bulletin, May 1981.
'From Vixen to Vindication' interview by Dannis Peary, from
Velvet Light Trap No.16, University of Texas Press, 1976. 'Cherry,
Harry & Raquel' from Film Bulletin, 26 January 1970. 'Beyond
the Valley of the Dolls' by Nick Yanni, from Motion Picture
Herald, 15 July 1970. 'Russ Meyer: King of the Nudies' by Roger
Ebert, from Film Comment, 1972. 'Interview with Russ Meyer and
Edy Williams' interview by Maureen Koch, from Interview,
February 1972. 'The Seven Minutes' from Filmfacts, 1971. 'Sex,
Violence and Drugs: All in Good Fun!' by Stan Berkowitz, from
Film Comment, January 1973. 'Slaves (aka Blacksnake!)' by Tom
Milne, from Monthly Film Bulletin, March 1978. 'Supervixens:
Meyer Uber Alles' by T. K. McMahon, from Take One, May/June
1974. 'Russ Meyer's The Supervixens' in his own words, from
Brightlights, Spring 1975. 'Up!' from Filmfacts, 1976. 'Beyond the
Big Breast: Can Russ Meyer Keep it Up?' by Dan Yakir and Bruce
Davis, from The Thousand Eyes Magazine, December 1976. 'Rock
is Sick and Living in London' by Charles M. Young, from Rolling
Stone Magazine. 'Russ Meyer on Who Killed Bambi?' interview by
Ed Lowry and Louis Black, from Film Comment. 'Portrait of the
Pornographer with his Ass to the Wall' by Tony Rayns, from Time
Out. 'Beneath the Valley of the Ultravixens' by Tony Rayns, from
Monthly Film Bulletin, January 1980. 'Return of the Ultravixens!'
by Jessica Berens, from The Observer, 22 July 2001. 'Russ Meyer at
the National Film Theatre' interview by Jonathan Ross,
Guardian/National Film Theatre lecture, 17 February 1995. The
Guardian.

   Many people therefore have helped to bring this book together
and special thanks are due to Jonathan Ross; Roger Ebert; David
Flint; Pete Tombs; British Film Institute; Hollywood Book and
Poster Company; Lucas Balbo/Artschiv; All Action; Justin
Thomas; Ellis O'Brien; RM International; 20th Century-Fox. It
has not been possible in all cases to trace the copyright sources and
we would be pleased to hear from any such unacknowledged copyright holders.

Contents

MEYER BOUNCES BACK!

A CLEAN BREAST

Introduction
by Paul A. Woods

'My films are outrageous, with cantilevered, pneumatic women as aggressors (that happens to be my taste) and a kind, dumb, industrious male with an IQ of around 38 who, by and large, has some kind of sex problem.' – Russ Meyer

Russ Meyer's best defence was always to own up to everything. Observing how people who apologise for their own work and their personal tastes 'really show the chink in their own armour,' he explained, 'That's why years ago I stopped defending myself, and I could deal then with almost any kind of interview by agreeing.'

It's a matter of record that his doting mother, Lydia, who brought him up alone in 1920s Oakland, CA, breastfed her only son. It doesn't take much cod-Freudian conjecture to work out that Mom had alluringly large breasts – as Meyer confirmed, though he insisted his self-diagnosed (and celebrated) 'bosom mania' was not strictly oedipal. 'I was about thirteen,' he remembered with fondness. 'I had taken up with a stripper from a distance in San Francisco, Marjorie Sullivan was her name. I thought that to spend the rest of my life cradled in her arms would have been the best.' The obsession would turn into a mammalian worldview that Meyer regarded through a viewfinder, as well as through the curve of a D-cup.

Meyer may owe his obsession to Mom, but it was down to her that he developed the skills to showcase it. Lydia Meyer pawned her engagement ring to buy fourteen-year-old Russ his first camera, which he used to take pictures of Oakland's 'neighbourhood children, pets, and town drunks'. But the next most formative experience of his life would begin at age nineteen, when he enlisted for the Signal Corps and served throughout World War Two, up until age 23, as a cameraman.

'It was a very romantic, very exciting moment,' Meyer explained of his treasured wartime experiences. His footage of a Free French division entering Paris during liberation appears in the military biopic *Patton* (1970), and he describes the war as the defining moment of his life, admitting, 'I've gone back [to France] many times, always trying to seek out my youth.' Most crucial of all, perhaps, he also lost his virginity, aged twenty, to a buxom French whore.

It was the Signal Corps that taught him all the basic skills he'd later hone to a fine point on industrial films, as a stills photographer on James Dean's last movie, the Texan oilfields drama *Giant* (1956), and as a centrefold photographer for the early *Playboy* and its rivals. World War Two also developed within him the all-American individualist's taste for risk-taking – as Meyer has always been at pains to point out, he nearly always risked his 'own nut' with the sexploitation films he self-financed and self-produced, as well as self-directed.

The Very Breast of Russ Meyer

The military precision with which Meyer attacked his film projects was born of a similar gung-ho enthusiasm – and from an insistence on diverting sexual energy, recalling sexologist Wilhelm Reich's theory that suppressing the orgasm in able-bodied youth allowed the Nazis to re-channel all that vitality into the Third Reich. If Russ had anything to do with it, then no one was going to screw around on any of his movies. 'We're just not gonna sleep together when we make the picture,' he insisted to his alluring young trophy wife, Edy Williams, at the time of his 1969 Hollywood breakthrough. 'I think we're gonna make a better picture if we don't.'

While lesser pornographers would make do with the jiggling boobs or simulated screwing of softcore, or devote all their attention to the penetrative 'money shot' when, post-*Deep Throat*, the censorship barriers came rapidly down, Meyer was always painting on a bigger canvas.

'No matter how I try it would appear that the only thing I can make is some kind of half-assed comedy or satire or parody.'

'Russ Meyer, the original King of the Nudies,' acclaimed the *LA Times* in the mid-Seventies, 'typically projects sex fantasies that reveal as much of the male psyche as they do female skin.' That his cartoon campiness and overblown melodrama earned him a reputation as an American auteur is testament to his painstaking craftmanship.

Meyer's quick-cutting, salacious surrealism created an absurd universe, haunted by the exaggerated presence of the male libido. Insisting his films are 'really pro-female, in the sense that they very definitely put a woman in control,' Meyer emphasises their (all too obvious) lack of realism: 'My whole thing is to try to make sex *so ridiculous* and, oh, almost like qualifying for the Olympics . . . I deal with women who are . . . *beyond women.* They're caricatures of ladies.'

He also observes of his male characters, 'the men are all their willing tools, klutzes. Women are the ones after their own physical pleasure.' Indeed, despite the softcore t&a trappings, Meyer's chaotic but moral universe is far from being a male wish-fulfillment fantasy. When impotency rears its head (so to speak), its stigma denotes the sufferer is out of kilter with a world where the cantilevered female form is a religious icon.

Clint, the hero of *Supervixens* (1975), is denied an alibi for the murder of his wife when he can't make love to barmaid SuperHaji, and is beaten up after failing to get it up with SuperCherry; the real killer, evil Harry Sledge, stomps, slashes and electrocutes SuperAngel in the bath, in Meyer's most extreme (and misogynistic) scene of violence, on account of mocking him for his own lack of vertical enthusiasm.

Lamar Shedd, the hero of *Beneath the Valley of the Ultravixens* (1979), is put through an absurd personal crisis by missionary man Meyer on account of his anal fixation, unable to 'look a good fuck in the eye'. Ultimately, Lamar is saved by the saintly Sister Eufaula Roop (the unbelievably stacked Anne Marie). Like the good momma's boy he is, Meyer regards a semi-maternal nuzzling between two huge tits as the answer to any sexual hang-up. (As if in testimony to his infantilism, the squelching erotic sound effects of *Ultravixens* are actually Meyer's own synchronised farts.) In the 1990s, one of his numerous unmade projects – *Up the Valley of the Beyond*, co-written with collaborator and early champion Roger Ebert – featured the ultimate deviant combination: Nazis and non-vaginal sex. 'Hitler was into rear admiral action, if you're familiar with that term,' claimed Meyer, a clear enthusiast for wartime propaganda. 'He liked it up the old wazoo.'

In their knockabout manner, many of Meyer's films are haunted by a past in which he and his young comrades had a common enemy: Martin Bormann – the Secretary of the Nazi Party, widely believed to have taken on a new identity at the end of WWII – appears in *Beyond the Valley of the Dolls* (1970) and returns in *Supervixens* as the proprietor of Bormann's Super Service garage; in *Ultravixens*, he reflects the sexually deviant milieu of Smalltown USA by indulging in necrophilia. In *Up!* (1976), Hitler has survived in 1970s America, under the name Adolph Schwartz (in a typically unsubtle Meyer touch, the Fuhrer poses as a Jew and enjoys a multi-racial harem of female sex slaves), only to be castrated by piranhas in his bathtub.

As Ebert ironically commented on Meyer's style, after the collapse of the Sex Pistols movie they were scheduled to make in 1977, 'we were both a little nonplussed, I think, to hear Johnny Rotten explain that he liked *Beyond the Valley of the Dolls* because it was so true to life.'

'It's a blending of violence, melodrama, hoke, parody, satire, really unbridled sex, the kind of sex that people fantasise about.'

Starting with the so-called 'roughies' that began with *Lorna* (1964), violence became an integral element of Meyer's movies, occasionally equal to the sex. From the lynch law of *Lorna* and *Mudhoney* (1965), through the feminine gender terrorism of the sublime *Faster Pussycat, Kill! Kill!* (1966), the climactic murder orgy of *BVD*, the much-censored bathtub murder of *Supervixens* and the ultraviolence of *Up!*, Meyer's best films are as much carnography as pornography. While Shari Eubank's demise in *Supervixens* is more than some viewers can take, Meyer expressed surprise at how seriously the slapstick carnage was taken in *Up!*: 'I always felt that they would take it in the manner I presented it. That if a man got a double-bitted axe buried in his chest, he could still wrench it out, run 100 yards and kill a giant with a chainsaw.' By the time of his unintented swansong, *Ultravixens*, Meyer was playing down the violence to the extent where participants in a fight bleed garish green or yellow, anything but blood-red.

Male sexuality too, when not represented by props like giant dildos, or, rarer still, the exposed member of the aptly-named character Leonard Box in *Up!*, was very coyly signified: erupting fountains or showers; bananas; phallic-shaped buildings or rock formations.

'If nothing else has happened in my life, I've known some great women, exciting beautiful women, and I wouldn't have had it if I hadn't been in this business.'

The Very Breast of Russ Meyer

'I've had the pleasure of marrying or living with eight to ten ladies who are really special,' the thrice-married Meyer reminisced while in his seventies. His most valued companion remained Eve Meyer, his second wife and star of his second nudie feature, *Eve and the Handyman* (1960), who died in the 1977 jumbo jet collision at Tenerife Airport. Though they divorced due to Meyer's adultery late in the 1960s, they remained close, and Meyer worked with Eve Productions until hitting mainstream Hollywood to make *BVD*.

The last of his three weddings, to Edy Williams, the full-maned starlet Meyer dubbed 'the last of the lust queens', was attended by old associate and *Playboy* proprietor Hugh Hefner, Mr. Good Living himself. Having previously shot several centrefolds for *Playboy*, including some with Eve, in many ways Meyer epitomised the martini-sipping ethos of the regular *Playboy* reader. 'You *can* have it all: the lifestyle, the new car, the nubile young chick,' the magazine seemed to tell the would-be urbane American male. That Meyer seemed more personally removed from the Swinging Sixties generation than 'Hef' was peculiarly apt, bringing him closer to the unsophisticated young drive-in audiences – the 'Joe Sixpacks', as he approvingly called them – who embraced his exaggerated fantasies.

In later years, the strippers Kitten Natividad and Melissa Mounds would come closest to becoming the fourth Mrs Meyer. 'I like strippers,' Meyer freely admitted, 'you don't have to reduce any resistance to taking their clothes off; they are, in a sense, actresses.' Indeed, Francesca 'Kitten' Natividad, winner of the Miss Nude Universe contest, was discovered by Meyer in a stripjoint – while his last longterm partner, the formidable Ms Mounds, is a full four decades his junior.

'I feel pretty strongly about people getting their just desserts, if you do something bad you gotta pay for it.'

Ultimately, while the exploitation films of Russ Meyer are not held together by consistent themes or concepts (just the iconography of big boobs and square jaws), they're the work of an auteur in that they present the idiosyncratic view of one man. His all-Americanism and (not always jokey) Horatio Alger-esque belief in doing the right thing were exemplified in his business dealings. Meyer explained how he could never let an investor lose money on a film, claiming they would always be paid back from the next if the previous one failed to turn a profit. 'It's easier to walk away from them and say, "Oh, fuck it,"' he admitted, 'but it's a thing, a code I have . . .'

Julien Temple, the young director who took over from Meyer on the Sex Pistols film, described him as 'very Californian . . . a mixture of complete sentiment as well as bizarrely bad taste. His mother [then in her dotage] is a cripple and every Sunday he wheels her across the road into this topless restaurant to have brunch.'

But while Meyer was always ready to denounce himself as a hopeless mammary maniac before anyone else – 'They've got be gravity-defying . . . And she's got to be wasp-waisted and with small hips' – he still insisted on his place in the American cinematic canon. His final completed film, *Ultravixens*, features a reinforcement of the Meyer universe in Smalltown, USA – where sexual problems, fugitive Nazis, even incestuous relations between Kitten Natividad and her (onscreen) fourteen-year-old son, carry an *Our Town*-type familiarity when described in the mock-sentimental tones of narrator Stuart Lancaster.

The subsequent two decades have seen Meyer announce pet projects like *The Jaws of Vixen* – previewed in a trailer at the end of *Ultravixens*, and intended to star Kitten 'and a whole new batch of bosom buddies' – or the self-parodic *Blitzen, Vixen and Harry*. But the days of him being able to shoot an *Ultravixens* for $300,000, filming the interiors in his own house in the Hollywood hills, were long gone. Neither did Meyer need to work, boasting, 'I could probably lay my hands on seven, eight million dollars,' as testament to his hard-won status as the world's most successful independent film director.

Ensconced in the home that doubles as a business office and a memorabilia storehouse, he devoted himself instead to an audacious, not to say narcissistic, autobiographical film project, *The Breast of Russ Meyer*. Reputedly running to a total of seventeen hours over nine videocassettes, it was periodically announced, from the beginning of the 1980s onwards, as containing a four-hour segment on World War Two alone and twenty-minute truncations of each of Meyer's independent features. New footage was to feature such buxotic strippers as the delectable Ms Mounds and Pandora Peaks.

By the latter half of the 1990s, however, as old age and ill health began to bite, Meyer backslid on *The Breast of . . .* Instead, he insisted, his life was best channelled into the equally long-awaited book *A Clean Breast: The Lives and Loves of Russ Meyer*. Finally published in the autumn of 2000, this extensive (and expensive) two-volume set was, as its author-subject promised, 'a fuck and tell', with postage stamp-sized reproductions of all the different vixens in the Meyer universe.

Despite the door closing on his film career, the grossly caricatured supperreality of Russ Meyer's best films – *Lorna, Mudhoney, Faster Pussycat, BVD*, underrated sex-and-violence exploiter *Blacksnake!* (1973), *Supervixens, Up!* – delineates the oeuvre of an original American stylist, at its best as enveloping and idiosyncratic as that of John Ford, Sam Peckinpah or David Lynch. He is, as the *Washington Post* noted several decades ago, 'practically an American institution'. The unashamed pornographer, glad to take credit for America's moral decline, can be credited with a handful of truly classic films – no matter whose sensibilities he offended along the way.

Sadly as this book was going to press Russ Meyer died. He was 82 years old and had suffered from dementia; he died of complications from pneumonia at his Hollywood home on September 18th 2004.

'In the final analysis you have to be a man . . . Otherwise you ain't worth shit if you don't really finally stand up to something, to something you believe in' – Russ Meyer.

THE NUDIES

Mondo Russo

by Dale Ashmun

Russ Meyer was born March 21, 1922, in San Leandro, California. He has made 29 features, most of which have been box-office hits. Those familiar with Meyer's work know his trademarks: hilariously ludicrous plots, outrageous narration, bizarre camera angles, hefty doses of violence, degradation, and of course, women who sport mountainous mammaries.

I recently interviewed the King of D-Cup Cinema in his luxurious home high in the Hollywood Hills. Meyer was resistant to being interviewed when first called. 'I just spent half the day with a writer from *Newsday* and I've heard they axed the feature,' he told me.

When I arrived at the Meyer Museum, he had just returned from buying some groceries. 'I'll be with you in a second,' he said as he lead me into his home. 'Meanwhile, just gaze at the breasts. Feast your eyes on breasts and let them fill you with awe.'

So I spent a good half an hour examining his amazing memorabilia; movie posters, awards, framed reviews, even a wall full of mounted props from some of his films. Among the mementos I found especially fascinating were some wooden plaques mounted with three or four colour photographs, taken by Meyer, of several humongously breasted Amazons that have starred in his films. Beneath each set of photos was a brass plate inscribed with the woman's name, a date, and these words: 'IN COMMEMORATION OF THE MUTUAL EXCHANGE OF BODILY FLUIDS.' Then we sat down to talk . . .

How did you finance your first film The Immoral Mr. Teas?
My partners at that time and I contributed dollar for dollar . . . we both were making a pretty good amount of money every day shooting stills for television shows.

And you were a photographer for Playboy *at the time?*
Not ever a *Playboy* photographer. Like a lot of people, I managed to find a girl before some other guy found her, and rushed in there, and Hefner would OK her, and then we shot her. There've been a few staff *Playboy* people . . .

But it's mostly freelance?
Yeah, well if you have a girl that's it.

The birth of the 'nudie-cutie': The Immoral Mr. Teas *(1959) was the first film to feature nudity as its selling point, without the coyness of 'naturist' documentaries.*

The Very Breast of Russ Meyer

Where did you grow up?

I'm what you call a native son. Born in what we call Northern CA, which is really Mid-California, San Francisco/Oakland area. Lived in about 30 houses because we didn't have any bucks . . . then I got a job, and along came the wonderful war, which was the great experience at the time, I had a great time. Came back and had my sights clearly in place and went to work for an industrial filmmaker in San Francisco, which was a marvellous opportunity. It was very good that we couldn't get a job in Hollywood at that time. We were distraught, because we thought that we, as returning conquering heroes, should be given a shot at working in Hollywood. The only thing was there were a lot of other guys resuming who had worked in Hollywood before they went into the service. So being turned down, it was at the moment depressing, but when I went back to 'Frisco, with the aid of some people from Eastman, I was put in touch with a man named Gene Walker. He gave me a great shot, shooting industrial movies. My films are in a sense documentaries . . . I often have a narrator, exposition, minimal dialogue, people who are not professional actors, as a rule. Some are. So, here I am.

How long did you work for Gene Walker?

From late 1946 until 1951. Then I moved to Los Angeles with my wife Eve, where I started shooting a lot of stills for TV shows. And a lot of titty boom, which was the girls with the biggest tits I could find, which was my taste and still is. As we started making more money we started gallivanting around Europe a bit. Then along with Pete DeCenzie of the El Ray Burlesque in Oakland . . . he was one of the last of the really great entrepreneurs. He brought out people like Tempest Storm, Lili St. Cyr. In fact I did a film for him before I did *Teas* called *The French Peep Show* (1950). It featured Tempest Storm, and it was basically a burlesque show. Because I had become smitten for the moment by Miss Storm's giant tits, I undertook to take some shots of her and DeCenzie liked the idea. I didn't just set up the camera and make a 100 foot cut. So I made the film and presented it to him, and he turned it over to his hirelings and they promptly picked his teeth. He never really got anything out of it.

Will that ever come out on video?

It's been destroyed.

You didn't keep a copy?

I was never given a copy.

Was it a feature or a short?

No, no, full feature. And what I've since heard from a man whom I tried to put in touch with Pete's wife, who's hostile towards me, was that she said, 'I've destroyed all his stuff.'

So your first feature as a director doesn't even exist?

No, before that I did a film called *The Desperate Women* for Appleton and Newman.

Sam Newman worked with *The Perry Mason Show*, he was a script supervisor. Lou Appleton was a director, and through a friend I knew in the service, they approached me to do *The Desperate Women*. It had to do with the abortion racket, a very safe way to deal with sex. Showing it as a real crime, women being taken in by these terribly moustached slickers and then cast aside, after they've become pregnant. Then they're taken to an abortionist, who's generally a heavy drinker, with coke bottle lensed glasses, and the knife would slip and you'd hear a heart rending scream and the woman's body would be found in a ditch. Then some young pressman starts poking around and along with a young press woman they somehow manage to bring these people to task. And that was it. So *The Desperate Women* was just another one of those films that I shot. I don't know where it is; I've no idea if a print existed.

But it was released?
Released and released successfully.

Directed by you?
No, I was cameraman. Directed by Sam Appleton.

When you were in high school did you try to photograph some of your big-breasted classmates?
No, no I was very shy. There was a girl I lusted after who had giant tits named Polly. But no, noooo, I didn't get laid until I was twenty in France, thanks to Ernest Hemingway.

Tell me about that story.
We were trying to get into Paris, and we were ahead of our division, which was the French Division. And we encountered Hemingway, whose lieutenant, a Portuguese gentleman, suggested that Hemingway take the boys down to the local notchery. And he did. The place was closed but we got in, and we were placed in this humongous place for the evening, and I had a nice experience with a girl with giant tits because that was my taste even from much earlier years . . . I only lusted after women who had enormous tits! That was it, period. Soooo, I selected the biggest-titted girl there and we had a marvellous time. From then on, I've never bothered with small breasted women. I'd rather play cards.

Were you a cameraman during WWII?
Yes, I was a combat cameraman. I did things that were exciting, stuck my neck out, enjoyed it enormously, nothing that I will ever do in my life will begin to approach what I did in the war.

Were you ever wounded?
No, unscathed.

The Very Breast of Russ Meyer

Did you have to shoot any Germans?
No, but I shot at one once and missed him
. . . and he missed me. I was a cameraman,
I only carried side arms. Had I been
equipped to shoot the enemy and had a
chance to do so, I certainly would have
shot him, right in his tracks.

Did you have a happy family life?
Yes, my mother was a great lady, she was
just wonderful. I had a sister but my
father made himself absent from the
hacienda before I was born, I only saw
him once. I never missed him. He paid
for my support until I was 21, even
whilst, as the British would say, I was in
service. He was a policeman, and he
had to pay, they had him right by the
short hairs.

Staff Sergeant Russ Meyer, reporting for duty.
Meyer has remained close to his WWII buddies
throughout his life.

The sense of humour in your films is
pretty wild. What were some of your
influences to develop that tongue in cheek style?
My first influence was Al Capp. I would copy studiously his drawings, only I would
make the tits bigger, and the tits on his women were always pretty good-sized. I think
my first introduction to satire, which I prefer to call my stuff rather than humour, was
through Capp. It didn't really hit me as such at the time, but as time went on I began
to see that he was really dealing satirically with the country as a whole . . . politics,
religion and whatever have you . . . an amazing, remarkable man. I also developed an
enormous feeling for W. C. Fields. From the very early years I found him to be an
extremely amusing man. Unlike Chaplin or Keaton, Fields really represented the
essence of humour. Just as, for example, I enjoy Jonathon Winters. I really regret that
he's not doing more.

Did you ever see any of his early stand-up performances?
Yes, I saw him years ago opening for Thelonius Monk. He did a bit on the landing at
Tarawa, by himself, which was really super.

Any literary influences?
Well, I've read a lot. A lot of the early young men's books that are very well-suited to
what I do, I like Horatio Alger. Horatio Alger was certainly way before your time,

even before mine, but they had great titles like *Sink or Swim* or *Paddle Your Own Canoe*. And literally any of them could make a great Russ Meyer movie, just change the girl's chest measurements. The hero is always put upon, always beaten up and taken advantage of, stolen from. You could imagine any one of those things being turned into a Russ Meyer movie.

Uncertain Innocence Part One
by Kenneth Turan and Stephen F. Zito

The Nudie-Cutie was born in 1959, the year Russ Meyer, a one-time army combat cameraman and cheesecake photographer, raised $24,000 and made *The Immoral Mr. Teas*, the most important and notorious erotic film released in the United States until *I Am Curious (Yellow)* was put on the market by Grove Press in 1968. It is almost impossible to overestimate the importance of *Mr. Teas*. It set the formal and thematic standards for a new genre of narrative films that featured female nudity and poked gentle fun at the inept and sweaty participants in the game of love. *Mr. Teas*, which prompted a good deal of legal controversy and critical comment and returned about $1 million profit on its initial investment, was bankrolled on an even-dollar basis by Russ Meyer and Pete DeCenzie, the owner of the El Rey Theatre, an Oakland burlesque house. It was not the first time the two men had worked together, however, for Meyer had previously photographed *The French Peep Show*, a burlesque film featuring Tempest Storm, shot on the stage of the El Rey.

The Immoral Mr. Teas was largely improvised over a period of four days, and Meyer used what was at hand. He gave the starring role to an old comrade-in-arms and sometime comedian, Bill Teas, borrowed the office of a dentist acquaintance as the main set, and hired a number of beautiful models, including Marilyn Westly, Ann Peters, Dawn Dennelle, and Michele Roberts. It was directed and photographed in Eastmancolor by Russ Meyer, and the accordion music and sly, ironic narration for the 63-minute film were credited to Edward Lasko.

The plot of *The Immoral Mr. Teas* centres on a delivery man for a dental supply house who bicycles around town to deliver false teeth. This fellow, clad in pink coveralls and a straw boater, is an inveterate girl-watcher, ogling each and every girl who goes by, and a compulsive daydreamer, who mentally undresses some of the women. He goes to a dentist to have a tooth pulled and is given an anaesthetic. After he leaves the dentist, each woman he meets – receptionist, dental assistant, waitress – appears to him in the nude. On a weekend fishing trip he sees three nudes sporting in a field and stream. He also goes to a burlesque house and then to a beach where he watches a beautiful model being put through her erotic poses and paces by a professional photographer. Teas becomes resigned to his fate when he goes to see a female psychiatrist and sees her nude also.

The Immoral Mr. Teas created a scandal when it was released, partly because of the nudity and partly because it was a great financial success. The initial trade-paper notices on the film praised its quality, but one cautioned exhibitors, 'It packs more female nudity than ever before in any motion picture, including those devoted entirely to nudist camps and burlesque'. The same article also ran this estimate of the film: 'GOOD NUDITY NOVELTY FOR SPOTS THAT CAN SHOW IT.' But it was precisely by playing theatres that had never played sex-exploitation films before that *Mr. Teas* was to create a whole new market for sex films.

'There was an interesting vacuum there,' Meyer has said. 'The public was waiting for something new. I think they were becoming disenchanted with the so-called European sex films, like some of the early Lollobrigida pictures, in which there's a lot of promise but never any kind of real fulfilment . . . they would always cut to the curtain blowing and things of this nature. So there were a number of secondary art houses that were floundering and they were looking for product. It was this field that we were able to jump into. Once this goddamn picture caught on, it was booked all over the country in these art houses and the picture would just hang in there for a year and play incredibly.'

And the fact that *The Immoral Mr. Teas* played in theatres that had never before played erotic films made it the subject of a considerable amount of journalistic comment. When it played at the Monica Theatre in Los Angeles in January 1960, Charles Stinson wrote a short notice in the *Los Angeles Times* that stated, 'Last Friday evening the Peep Show finally moved across the tracks from Main Street, and to judge by the concourse of solid-looking citizens, presumably all aged eighteen or over, the film is going to be a GREAT success.' Stinson goes on to discuss the plot and dismisses the film as 'a montage of calendar art'. *Mr. Teas* later opened on Market Street in San Francisco, and after it had played an extended run there Paine Knickerbocker, the well-known critic for the *San Francisco Chronicle*, reviewed the film by noting, 'It is an innocent film, presenting its unclad beauties with unabashed delight. The commentary . . . is occasionally amusing and sly, the photography is excellent, and Teas, with his bug-eyes, his preoccupations and his beard, is a whimsical performer.' *The Immoral Mr. Teas* also caught the fancy of literary critic Leslie Fiedler, who wrote a long review for *Show* magazine, which said in part:

'In *Mr. Teas* there was not only no passion, but no contact, no flesh touching flesh, no consummation shown or suggested. For pornography the woman's angle of vision is necessary, but here were no women outside of Bill Teas's head; and Bill Teas was nobody's dreamed lover, only a dreamer, with his half-modest, half-comical beard, his sagging pectoral muscles, his little lump of a belly creased by baggy shorts or hidden by overalls. And Mr. Teas could touch no one – not in lust or love or in the press of movement along a street. Once in the film he lays his hand on flesh, the shoulder of an eight-year old girl working out with a hula hoop, and she beans him with a rock. Any really nubile, desirable female is doomed to disappear into the ladies room or the arms of some lover whose

Never again would sex appear so innocent. These three comely models
are being spied on by the passive voyeur Bill Teas.

face we never see – as unreal, finally, as the girl he embraces. Mr. Teas conducts his odd business and carries his frustrated dreams through a world of noncontact and noncommunication. As old restrictions crumble in our society, the naked flesh assumes its proper place among the possible subjects for movies, the place it has always held in the other, less public arts; but meanwhile, in the United States, we have been long corrupted by the pseudo arts of tease and titillation, conditioned to a version of the flesh more appropriate for peeking

than love or lust or admiration or even real disgust. Its makers have not attempted to surmount the difficulties which confront the American moviemaker who desires to make nakedness his theme; but they have, with absolute good humour, managed at once to bypass and to illuminate those difficulties. The end result is a kind of imperturbable comedy, with overtones of real pathos.'

The only real similarity between *The Immoral Mr. Teas* and the nudist-camp films was that both genres featured nudity. The nudity in *Mr. Teas*, however, occurs in an everyday context (at work, at home, and on the streets), and there is no attempt to rationalise nudity as a unique and beneficial life-style (as was done in the nudist films). The naked women in *Mr. Teas* are simply there to entertain the grind-house audiences, a fact that was played up in the advertising. The posters for the film included copy like: 'A RIBALD FILM CLASSIC . . . MADE IN HOLLYWOOD, THE PICTURE ITALIAN OR FRENCH MOVIE MAKERS WOULDN'T DARE TO MAKE.' They invited the audience to 'a peeping Tom's dream of ravishing beauty' and advised that the film was for 'unashamed adults only'. The nudity and notoriety of the film naturally made *Mr. Teas* subject to prior censorship and court cases across the nation. Meyer and DeCenzie won the court cases, but several censor boards, including the key one in

Meyer's second wife, the former Eve Turner, was a glamour model, seen here in Eve and the Handyman *(1960). She also produced most of her husband's 1960s output.*

New York state, cut the film before it could be released. (New York cut eleven minutes; Maryland banned it outright for several years.) A lot of people ultimately saw the film, however, and Meyer went on to become a millionaire and a filmmaker of repute whose collected works have been shown in a retrospective at Yale University.

The great success of *The Immoral Mr. Teas* altered the course of the sex-exploitation industry. In the following years what had been a cottage industry, supporting only the 40 Thieves, became a thriving business. Anyone with a movie camera and a few naked women could make a Nudie-Cutie and then make a few dollars selling it. It has been estimated, for example, that more than 150 imitations of *Mr. Teas* were made in the three years following its first release. Meyer himself made several of these – including *Eve and the Handyman, Erotica, Europe in the Raw, Wild Gals of the Naked West,* and *Heavenly Bodies.*

extracted from *Sinema: American Pornographic Films and the People Who Make Them*

The Variety Review

Nude comedy with touches of art appeal. Can do very well in art-house run.

The Immoral Mr. Teas is sort of a perverted *Mr. Hulot's Holiday*, saved from being entirely a burlesque film only by the reaction shots of Mr. Teas himself. There's nudity galore in the Los Angeles-made feature, and its female take-off artists should get the film high off the ground in special art house bookings. The Monica Theatre, where the picture is playing 'to unashamed adults only', reported its house record broken on opening night.

The allusion to *Mr. Hulot* is in form only, with Mr. Teas cavorting through life without a sound, backed by a whimsical musical score and taking an interested look at everything around him. He's actor W. Ellis (Bill) Teas and he rides a bicycle, carries a brown bag containing somebody's mouth and generally has a ball daydreaming about undressed females. There's only a slight story line, and Mr. Teas supposedly is 'common man' in a complex society, the comment apparently being that every man would like to get away from his work-a-day world to become a Peeping Tom.

The Very Breast of Russ Meyer

Russ Meyer wrote, directed and photographed the film and its physical values, particularly some artistic Eastmancolor lensing, are amazingly good. His direction doesn't seem overly important in the face of bare bosoms and bottoms, but he and actor Teas have come up with a rather interesting and amusing character. The film partially is narrated, and the patter, at the very least, is informative. For instance, the audience is given the date rubber was invented while watching a nude swing back and forth in a suspended rubber tyre. Edward Lasko's background music is properly arranged to maintain and heighten the mood. And the picture features the bodies of Marilyn Wesley, Ann Peters, Michele Roberts and Dawn Dinielle, who have all the necessary equipment for this sort of thing.

P. A. DeCenzie, said to be a San Francisco theatre owner, produced the PAD-RAM Enterprises picture. Depicting several days in Mr. Teas' life, the film runs 63 minutes. It would have come off far better as a subtle short subject depicting, say, one day in twenty minutes. But then, in that form it wouldn't have made much money, would it?

Eve and the Handyman

The Variety Review

Peep show cloaked in what is intended to be a satire.
Should do good biz in houses where sex is the big attraction.

Eve and the Handyman is roughly the cinematic equivalent of one of the more sophisticated pose magazines. It is a slick slice of sex suggestion, an anatomical peepathon accompanied by that double-entendre narration that is the hallmark of caption poets from *Dude* to *Nugget* to *Playboy*. More often than not, the intended satire sinks into double talk, vulgarity and low comedy, but the film is evidence that, given more reputable channels in which to direct his skill, producer-director-writer-photographer Russ Meyer (of *Mr. Teas* notoriety), who is responsible for this glorified hormone stimulant, might prove he is more than a mere flesh-in-the-pan impresario.

For its class, the picture is somewhat above average. It is superior in style and entertainment value to others of its ilk currently pulling big box office at theatres that cater to the bare-babe-ogling customer, so it ought to score at least equally as well along Filmdom's 'broad' way circuit.

Eve Meyer is the star attraction, undertaking a variety of roles, sole distinction among which amounts to the number and characteristic of garments in which she is frocked and/or unfrocked. Several other young ladies are intimately scrutinised, too. The degree of nudity in the film ranges from absolute zero (from an occasional aft vantage point) to form-fitting attire into which all forms fit admirably. Anthony-James Ryan is the handyman. Both he and Miss Meyer perform skilfully, considering the nature of their material.

Meyer has an affinity for extremely tight closeups. He will jam his lens right into someone's mouth for comic effect. Depending upon where he is jamming his lens, it is fairly effective. But Meyer would just as soon jam it into a ladies' toilet as he would into an eye. And some of his suggestive symbolism (notably a blast of explosives, sight gags and sound effects implying a sex act) appeals in the most arrested mentality way to the human animal's grosser sense of humour.

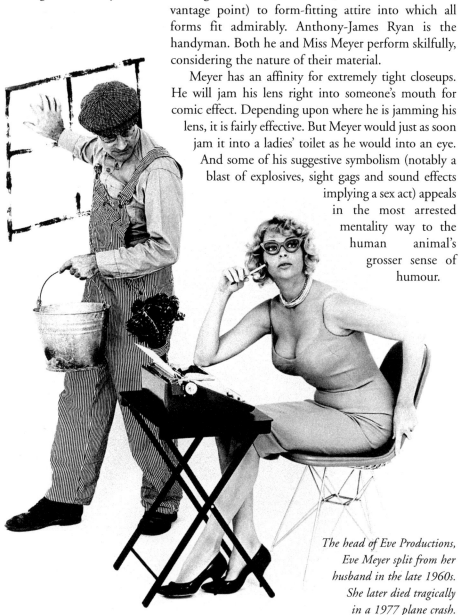

The head of Eve Productions, Eve Meyer split from her husband in the late 1960s. She later died tragically in a 1977 plane crash.

THE ROUGHIES

Uncertain Innocence
Part Two

by Kenneth Turan and Stephen F. Zito

After his great success with *The Immoral Mr. Teas*, [Russ Meyer's] subsequent films, such as *Eve and the Handyman* and *Erotica*, were only moderately successful. Finally, his *Wild Gals of the Naked West* fell on its face, probably because it had more belly laughs than buttocks.

What Meyer did then was produce *Lorna*, a strong melodrama in which sex, nudity, and violence were carefully integrated. It was his conscious intention to convince theatre bookers that *Lorna* was not just another sex-exploitation film, but an action picture with a lot more action than usual – sexual and otherwise. Meyer was once again successful and helped to create a vogue for Gothic dramas in which sex took second place to violence. As Meyer tells it, 'I said, now I must do something like the foreign films, only it will be Erskine Caldwell and it will be a morality play and we'll borrow heavily from the Bible and I'll find a girl with giant breasts.'

Meyer wrote the original story and acted as producer, director, photographer, and editor. Lorna Maitland, a sometime dancer with a sweet face and watermelon breasts, one of 134 women who answered Meyer's casting ad in *Variety*, won the starring role of Lorna, a voluptuous young woman who has been faithfully, unhappily married for a year to a naïve young man unable to satisfy her. Only when she is raped by an escaped convict does she first experience sexual satisfaction, and she brings her assailant back to the couple's run-down shack. The husband returns unexpectedly, and both the convict and Lorna are killed during the ensuing fight. The moral of this story is pointed out by a 'man of God', who appears now and then to give warnings and make dire predictions. There is little nudity in the film beyond a brief, startling exposure of Miss Maitland's remarkable anatomy, but this elemental revenge fable is crudely effective. As the press book for *Lorna* astutely states, it is 'a primitive work of art in which black is black and white is white and there is no shading or distortion. The characters in *Lorna* are simple; their lives reflect the basic emotions of man: love, lust, jealousy, fear and desire.'

The film did well at the box office, playing an extended run at the Rialto Theatre on Times Square, and was booked into theatres that had not previously been willing to play Meyer's Nudie-Cutie product. The trade press reviews were complimentary, and there has been a considerable amount of subsequent critical comment about *Lorna* as

The going gets rough. Crazed Hal Hopper will murder Lee Ballard, the wife of the preacher he has turned against his own adulterous spouse. From Mudhoney *(1964).*

The Very Breast of Russ Meyer

As with his wife Eve, Meyer featured Lorna Maitland in a movie that he named after her. In Lorna *(1964), she embodies fleshly temptation and biblical retribution.*

well, most of it favourable. *Lorna* was included in a retrospective of Russ Meyer's films held at Yale University in 1970, and it is still in spasmodic distribution in certain parts of the United States. Film historian Richard Schickel, who saw the film at Yale, has described *Lorna* as 'a film of preachment against hypocrisy, exhibiting no more skin than the plot absolutely requires . . . crudely vigorous in development.'

The great success of *Lorna* prompted Russ Meyer to make several more films in the same genre, including *Mudhoney* (also known as *Rope of Flesh*); *Motor Psycho*; *Faster, Pussycat! Kill! Kill!* (also known as *The Leather Girls and The Mankillers*); and *Common Law Cabin* (also known as *How Much Loving Does a Normal Couple Need?*). These films were shot primarily on location in black and white and in a severe cinematographic style; they have rough, coherent stories that feature murder, rape, beatings, whippings, hangings, arson, and fights; characters are motivated primarily by lust and hate; nudity is functional; and sexual motivation is realistically integrated into the plots. Meyer has spoken of the manner in which his films were shot: 'There's an excitement. It's a style, it moves very fast, they're not overly long. I like violence in films. I think it's highly entertaining.' The films are still rather crude and uncertain in intention, but Meyer's growing control over his narrative material, his consistency of vision, and his considerable technical skills make the hard-surfaced fables sometimes arousing and sometimes moving experiences. Professor and writer Fred Chappell, for example, has compared *Faster, Pussycat! Kill! Kill!* to the work of Thomas Kyd, the most bloody of Elizabethan dramatists. Writing of Meyer's work, Chappell cites its 'very odd, serious attempts, full of big, gloomy archetypes and Gothic puzzlements.'

extracted from *Sinema: American Pornographic Films and the People Who Make Them*

The Variety Review

Asort of sex morality play, *Lorna* was Russ Meyer's first serious effort after six nudie pix which started with *The Immoral Mr. Teas*. Still in slow playoff, the film has a weak script nearly overpowered with sexploitation angles which will relegate it, in general, to houses which feature such product. The pic had a successful, lengthy run at Times Square's Rialto, an exploitation house, earlier this year.

Meyer's story as scripted by James Griffith concerns Lorna Maitland as the buxom wife of James Rucker, a handsome young clod who each day joins Hal Hopper and Doc Scortt in commuting to work at a salt mine. (The latter is not the first Biblical overtone, since Griffith portrays a firebrand preacher-Greek chorus who greets the audience via a clever subjective camera intro with ominous foreboding of sin and payment therefore.)

Mark Bradley, escaped con and vicious killer, encounters Miss Maitland in the fields with predictable results, after which she takes him home for encores. Hubby's early return cues a climax wherein wife and fugitive die violently. Such quick moral retributions following leisurely sensual dalliance are not new, Cecil B. DeMille having derived much mileage from the same.

Miss Maitland has a sensual voice although vocal projection is her least asset. Bradley has rugged looks, a voice to match and a bigger future in films. His role requires expressions of fear, boredom, tenderness and amoral viciousness – he is up to them all.

Rucker acts poorly. Hopper and Scortt convince as the slobs who bait Rucker about his wife until subdued in an exciting brawl. Griffith is a two-time loser, having overacted a trite part which he himself wrote.

Meyer's direction is good, considering the talent and script, while his lensing and editing are excellent. Bob Grabeau sings Hopper's okay title tune, and the other canned track music was fine. Charles G. Schelling's sound, unlooped throughout, is excellent.

Russ Meyer vs. the Italian Masters:

A Discussion of Lorna with 'King Leer'
by David K. Frasier

*T*he heavy gothic melodrama in **Lorna** *is radically unlike your previous films in which you relied on humour and parody. Thematically, at least, it's very reminiscent of some European cinema. Why the transition? Was the public turning away from nudie films?*
Exactly. The last nudie film I made was *Heavenly Bodies!* (1963) and it barely got its nut back. I knew I had to come up with something different. That's when I started thinking 'What'll I do?' And I was influenced by the films of the Italian Masters . . . you know, *Bitter Rice* (1949), *Paisa* (1948), De Sica's things. That's it, I said, there's the angle. No colour. Do it in black and white, gritty. Shoot in circumstances similar to those in Italy.

So basically you took the European art film and put it in the sticks.
No, they weren't art films. They should be called foreign films. That 'art film' stuff, come on, is a misnomer. As in the case of *The Immoral Mr. Teas* (1959), I did it for greed. No other reason. I wanted success. I wanted recognition. No way was I going to make a film for the sake of critical acclaim. I had accepted that the main thrust was the almighty buck every time I mounted up. Every time. Nothing goes over as flat as a Dutchman's fart like an unsuccessful movie. How many asses are covering the seats is the answer.

I read in your book that when you were casting **Lorna** *you were not satisfied with the first choice you had for the title role.* (1)
She was the only choice. There is always only one choice. You never find two that are good, you know, except later in life when I found more girls.

But you weren't satisfied with your first Lorna.
I wasn't totally happy is what you're saying. I would have used her if I had to. Then when I was apprised of Lorna Maitland's pictures which my wife kept from me . . . she didn't want me to make the movie. Eve (2) did not want that movie made. She didn't like the idea of me making movies dealing with intercourse.

The nudies were okay with her because there was never any contact?
She didn't want me to get involved with other women, I guess, more than anything else. Whatever the reason, she didn't want it.

But you made it anyway. Who wrote it?
I wrote the treatment as I do with every film. I had the Man of God prophesying doom on Sodom and Gomorrah; the unfaithful wife driven to adultery by a husband who is an amateur lovemaker; two evil Jonahs as his 'friends'; and a powerful convict on the loose who satisfies her.

I noticed that in **Lorna** *there is heavy biblical symbolism. How aware were you of the possibility of being prosecuted by the authorities? Was the overt symbolism included as insurance against obscenity prosecution?*
No way. Put it in. Put everything you can in including the kitchen sink. I was never superabundant with story, so whatever I could put in the way of story I did. I was not looking for an escape valve. You see, I pushed everything to the edge. If you're pushing things to the edge you're not looking for built-in protection. For example, [Roger] Ebert thought that was the real reason in *Vixen* (1968) that I included 'socially redeeming' themes for safety. (3) A black guy . . . let's make him a draft-dodger. Where I made a mistake is that I didn't have another big sex scene right at the end of *Lorna*. We would've made twice as much money. It was just part of the story, that's all. There wasn't a particular reason why. You can't be that smart to say that I'm going to put all this in to keep from getting arrested. And at the same time you're putting in all you can and you get arrested. (4) They're not going to pay any attention to that. Some judge looks at it and says, '90 per cent of this is sex and ten per cent is narrative hokum.'

Getting back to Lorna Maitland, the photos of her were initially given to Eve.
She [Lorna Maitland] had an agent named Clancy Grass, III. She was a stripper. At the time we didn't know she was pregnant. Tits were so big. He brought some polaroids, gave them to Eve, but of course she didn't give them to me. The day I was leaving to shoot she said, 'I gotta show it to you.' She knew I wasn't happy and I was using our money and she knew right then and there that I was certainly going to use Lorna Maitland. (5) So it was only through Eve's professionalism that the project squeaked through. So, I immediately changed my mind and we paid off the other girl. My associate at the time, James Griffith, said, 'Oh, that's terrible, you agreed to cast her.' I said, 'Fuck. Shut up. I live with this film. It's my ass. You think I care about principles? I care about the film. Don't give me any of this shit. Pay her off. Give her a thousand bucks, say goodbye, and tell her Meyer says he's sorry.'

So your cast is set and you're ready to shoot. What location did you choose?
I filmed up in middle California in the Slough area, Sacramento River. I picked that purposely because it represented the closest thing I could find short of Louisiana with its terrible vipers and I knew I couldn't get anybody to get in there with a water moccasin. There were no water moccasins up in the Delta area, so I had the kind of gritty landscape that I always wanted.

The Very Breast of Russ Meyer

'Too much for one man': Meyer claimed the buxotic Lorna's ample breasts were partly due to her falling pregnant shortly before filming.

When you used black and white film stock, did you do it because you wanted the grittiness you observed in the films of the Italian Masters?
No, I wanted to go colour 35mm and I couldn't afford it. If I could've had colour 35mm I would have taken it. Again, I'm exploding another myth. If I had the money I'd have shot it in colour. To fuck with the grit. I said, okay I'll do it in black and white. Did I shoot in black and white for the purpose of grittiness and to emulate the Italian Masters? Horseshit. I didn't have the money to do it in colour. Alright? You see, these are the honest things you should be told. Unmasked again! (6)

It has been widely written, though, that you were a fan of the Italian films, their sexual candour, their gritty, earthy quality.
The only gritty thing I liked about them was Gina Lollobrigida, not Sophia Loren.

What about Silvana Mangano in Bitter Rice?
No, she didn't have big enough tits. I was not a fan of hers, only of Lollobrigida. Lollobrigida was constantly bending over, her tits swaying. Forget all the rest. Silvana

Mangano wore bad laundry. Sure she wore real tight clothes and stuff, but she didn't have a body that I'd really thrash around over, you know. You see, when you talk about the Italian Masters you talk about, 'If they can get away with it, why can't I?' I didn't hold them in reverence, in awe or anything. So what? Most of them, I didn't care for their movies. Antonioni's thing, *Zabriskie Point* (1970): crap! You know, one of the best reviews given to my *Cherry, Harry & Raquel* (1969) was '*Zabriskie Point* in gym socks.'

Well, even if Silvana Mangano was not an influence on Lorna, there is the oft-told story of the first time you saw Lorna Maitland nude in the bedroom scene in which she got up and walked to the window.

No, no that's not right. It started with a daylight scene. These two scenes I shot without crew because I didn't want the leading lady being rattled by facing a crowd. And Lorna kind of had my number . . . she did a number on my head. She had a feeling that she wasn't going to be pushed around. I'd never seen her naked. So I just set the camera up in the room with the help of Bud Kues, an old army buddy . . . in daylight, not at night, not going to the window or anything like that. I explained what I wanted; the waking hour. I shot it from one angle. I told her, 'I want you to be disturbed. You had a bad experience with your husband. He'd been lightning quick. You had no satisfaction. You don't have anything to say and I want to read it on your face.' But I wanted to say, 'Read it on your big tits.' I said, 'Alright now, the camera's set. What I want you to do is disrobe.' I'd never seen her naked. I said, 'I'll go out. When you're ready, call.' I came in by myself, left Bud outside. Did a camera test and said, 'Alright, roll 'em.' She did it marvellously. She laid there, got mad in her own way, then threw back the covers very carefully, got up, still with her big tits away from me. From the side I could see the confirmation of those dreadnaughts. Even when she bent forward to put on some sandals the configuration of those pregnant tits did not change one iota. It turned out that her nipple hit a kneecap. And all I said to myself through the finder was 'Boxoffice'. That was it . . . no shadows or nights in the window. Everything that came later was with the full crew of five. By that time it was okay, cool. Another myth shot down.

How many weeks did Lorna take to film?
Two weeks. The crew was like five guys.

How long to edit?
I can't say. A long time. Editing always takes a long time. After I edited it picture-wise, I had to call in a sound editorto do synchronisation of the dialogue. Jim Nelson was his name. I was editing it when the news came in that Kennedy was assassinated. Remember it clearly.

The Very Breast of Russ Meyer

On a film like Lorna, *how many prints do you have made for distribution?*
Too hard to remember all that. Can't remember, not too hard, just can't, but I guess *Lorna* might have had 100 prints. By today's standards that's a pittance, but great for an independent. That was because we had the money. We were making lots of money.

Where did it premiere?
I think it played for the first time in Boston at Ben Sach's Capri Theatre which was going to be demolished. A guy by the name of Ellis Gordon conned him into leaving it open one more week to let us play. It played there for six months. A big hit. And then we opened elsewhere. The first screening for industry people was in the Monica Theatre. This guy Albert Zugsmith (7) and his son-in-law, George Costello, saw it. That's how I got the job to do *Fanny Hill* (1964). (8) The first private screening for non-industry people was at Hugh Hefner's mansion in Chicago under terrible conditions. It had the medieval vaulted hall with hard walls and terrible echoes. A lot of people that saw it . . . blase bunnies, bombed-out poets . . . sat there saying, 'Like, oh yes. I see . . .'

American Gothic, Meyer-style: in this moonshine party scene, abusive husband Hal Hopper enjoys the atention of mute prostitue Rena Horten (left). From Mudhoney.

They call Lorna *your second breakthrough movie, the first being* The Immoral Mr. Teas . . .
I call it that, not 'they'.

I guess others have adopted it. Was this the first time in these movies that sex and violence were so consciously linked?
Go back to *Road to Ruin* [1928; remade in 1934]. (9) The story's always the same way. The girl gives herself to the dashing young man and gets pregnant. He won't marry her and 'boo hoo hoo' she's forced to go to the drunken abortionist. The knife slips. They take her and throw her in the gutter. This is exactly what I did on a grander scale. Maybe *Lorna* is just a small film, but it's the same thing DeMille's been doing. Cut the guy's head off and throw him to the lions. The only thing new I brought was big tits. My films wouldn't have survived without the big tits no matter what anyone says. Even for the greatest fan, tits are the thing, the anchor post.

Is everything else hitched to that?
Sure, that was the trademark. That was it.

But beyond that, the films are well made.
Sure they are well made, but so what? So what? Tits are my trademark and it'll always be that. Sure the films are well made. *Blacksnake!* [1973] is extremely well made. Zero. I'd have had a great picture if I'd been able to have used the big Roman Anita Ekberg type babe who overdosed prior to filming. I could've had her galloping in the surf, making love to somebody and so on. But I couldn't with this thin little girl who was built like a plow handle. (10)

Seen in the context of the push that The Immoral Mr. Teas *made towards the lessening of censorship restrictions on what could be shown, wasn't* Lorna *the inevitable next step?*
Well, after *Teas* a lot of embarrassing bummers were made by people just jumping on the bandwagon. (11) True, it permitted the filmmakers a chance of doing a film with a lot of nudity simply because of *Teas*'s breakthrough. All it takes is one hit and *Teas* happened to be that one. The thing is as I've said, had the prosecutors, and there are no censors – the only censors are the members of the ratings board with their R, G, and blah blah blah – remained quiet the whole sex thing would've more or less just kind of gone away. But they weren't quiet. They kept stirring it up, then it was self-defeating in a sense because so many imitations of *Teas* were made that the public just grew tired of seeing the same old thing. I know I imitated myself five times. (12) So when you bring up *Lorna*, the innovations just happened to be the result of my craving for recognition, desire of money, and to make something of myself. I just hit upon a scheme to do a heavy, heavy melodrama. I made *Lorna* to get a lot of asses on the seats. It was not, as

so many people have written, an earnest desire to really lay waste to all this hypocrisy. I like that hypocrisy. It's very good. It makes people go to theatres and see films. It's good to have people like those in Cincinnati get after you. (13) They don't realise that the secret of any so-called pornographer's success rests on their behaviour. It's the do-gooders who create all kinds of interest and publicity in this field. Whether I'm a pornographer or not, that's beside the point. I've always said that I'm a high class pornographer. I make films for one reason, and that is to make money. They're made well, I like the idea of the recognition, but the basic reason is how many asses can you get on the seats in the theatres. That's the fault, in my opinion, of the so-called cult films. People make an experimental motion picture . . . if they'd only just look at themselves straight in the eye and say, 'Really, why am I doing this? Is there some reason I'm doing this?' The best reason in the world is greed. Plain and simple. That's the basis of Hollywood, greed.

But once you hit upon a formula and you know that you're going to make money and have a following, isn't there still the drive and the desire to do the project as best you can?
I take exception to that. You don't know. Each time it's a gamble. I made a gamble with *Mudhoney* (1964) and failed. (14) I thought I had the whole answer. *Mudhoney* was not a success and that followed *Lorna*. They compared it to *Lorna*. It wasn't as hot as *Lorna*, the tits weren't as big. Lorna Maitland's tits didn't look as great in *Mudhoney*. Most people didn't realise that she was pregnant when I shot *Lorna*. So *Mudhoney* was terribly disappointing. You just don't know each time. I don't know . . . I thought I knew, but each time I made a movie I went in holding my left nut. The only reason I made *Mudhoney* was that I was in love with a girl named Rena Horten. (15) That's plain and simple. I should have not made the film, but you do these things. But later on it's looked upon as this and that. But in Russia they rejected it totally. (16) They didn't want to see or hear about the Depression. They'd had enough of it. They wanted stuff like the bathtub stomp in *Supervixens* (1975). So I've just been lucky, really lucky. *Motor Psycho!* (1965), a good box-office draw, was followed strangely enough by *Faster, Pussycat, Kill! Kill!* (1966). It was successful, *Pussycat!* was not. *Pussycat!* was a big failure. People complained because I didn't show Tura Satana's naked tits. They discovered that movie later, unlike *Beyond the Valley of the Dolls* (1970) which they discovered immediately. It took five years for them to discover *Pussycat!*. So every film I ever did was not bulwarked by the fact that I knew what I was doing. No way. I just made money on one, lost it on another, made more on yet another, lost it once again. By the time we got around to *Mondo Topless* (1966) we were in dreadful shape. (17) We barely had enough money to produce a film that only cost $12,000. But it was such a success that I just jumped on the gravy train and embraced the topless craze. See, here I leaped onto something and took advantage of it. You might have confidence in the distributors that you trust and so forth, but when they get back to you and say, 'Hey, what happened? It wasn't hot enough. The

tits weren't big enough,' then, boy, you've got an empty feeling.

What was the feedback from the distributors on **Lorna?** *Did they love it or were they afraid to show it?*
They were all afraid of it and that's the wonderful thing. When someone is afraid to show it or concerned about prosecution, then you know you've got something.

So the distributors told you they couldn't show this, it's too hot.
No, there weren't that many distributors. There were three, that's all. That's all there were. Meyersdorf in Dallas, he'd have done anything, but the guy who really kicked off the film's success was Ellis Gordon. He knew of one theatre that he thought he could get it into which was ready to close. Ben Sach's theatre in Boston. Sach's theatre was ready for the wrecking ball. Gordon talked him into it and it played for six months. It opened up all of the East Coast.

Were there some sections of the country that it didn't play because of a lack of distribution?
We didn't have any difficulty in Ohio, strangely enough, because we had sold the picture to Lou Shurer who represented the Art Theatre Guild with the good help of a guy named Abbot Schwartz in Minneapolis. We had some help from Wasserman, the critic in San Francisco. He always had fun with my films. Business in LA wasn't bad. Margaret Harford gave it a great plug . . . helped it along. (18) Again, the Art Theatre Guild had bought the picture nation-wide, so they were very helpful in that area. But then *Lorna* started to acquire new distributors as more people became aware of what I was doing. That was beneficial. So Eve and I were just very bold, very gallant, very lucky. We just kept going, but they weren't all successes.

In production you announced that Lorna Maitland was 'Hollywood's answer to foreign sexpots'. Was this a conscious attempt to compare this film to the films coming from Europe?
Those films from Europe were over with. They were through. They didn't have the amount of nudity or the sexual byplay that *Lorna* had. *Lorna* was a lot franker than what Europe had done. Europe just gave me an idea. It was not an opportunity for me to break through because of what they had done. They had produced films that were, at their time, important and worthwhile. *Lorna* made them all look like amateurs.

1. Meyer's self-published two volume autobiography, *A Clean Breast: The Life and Loves of Russ Meyer*, is tentatively set for publication in early to mid-1991.
2. Eve Meyer, the filmmaker's second wife and chief photographic subject throughout the 1950s and early 1960s. Meyer photographed her for the centrefold of the June, 1955 issue of *Playboy* as well as for numerous other male-oriented magazines. Featured in Meyer's second nudie, *Eve and the*

The Very Breast of Russ Meyer

Handyman (1960), she became associate producer for *Lorna* in 1964 and a co-owner with Meyer of the company named for her, Eve Productions, Inc.

3. *Chicago Sun Times* critic Roger Ebert has long been an articulate champion of Meyer's work and has collaborated with the director on three films: *Beyond the Valley of the Dolls* (20th Century-Fox, 1970 – screenplay); *Up!* (RM Films International, Inc., 1976 – Ebert co-credited for original story under pseudonym 'Reinhold Timme'); and *Beneath the Valley of the Ultravixens* (RM Films International, Inc., 1979 – Ebert co-credited for screenplay under pseudonym 'R. Hyde').

4. *Lorna* was prosecuted for obscenity in at least three states: Maryland (1964-65); Lebanon, Pennsylvania (December, 1964); and Pensacola, Florida (1966 and 1968).

5. As discussed in note 2, Eve Meyer served as associate producer on *Lorna* and, with husband Russ, co-managed the company Eve Productions Inc. from its first release, *Eve and the Handyman* (1960), through its final release in 1969, *Cherry, Harry & Raquel*.

6. Meyer's decision to shoot *Lorna* in 35mm black and white rather than the 16mm colour of his earlier nudie period eliminated the need for a laboratory blow-up into the more theatrical 35mm format. Referred to by the filmmaker as his 'cinema noir' period, simply because he could not afford colour film, Meyer's 35mm black and white work includes *Lorna* (1964), *Mudhoney* (1964), *Motor Psycho!* (1965), and *Faster, Pussycat, Kill! Kill!* (1966). Meyer's denial, however, that the Italian Masters were an influence on him in Lorna is contradicted by numerous statements he has made in the past best summarised in an excellent piece done on him by William L. Kahrl entitled 'Peep show becomes fine art: the transmogrification of Russ Meyer', *World's Fair*, 2(4):1-6, Fall 1982. Meyer tells Kahrl, 'When I made *Lorna* I was just as serious as hell. I was influenced by the Italian directors who were making serious films about Silvana Mangano in a rice paddy wearing tight shorts. I thought I'd do the same sort of thing and throw in a little bit of my own kind of biblical morality – Lot's wife, Sodom and Gomorrah, all that kind of stuff . . . I simply wanted to make a very heavy, straightforward melodrama that turned me on.' (pp. 3-4).

7. Although having produced such films as *Written on the Wind* (1957) and Orson Welles' *Touch of Evil* (1958), producer-director Albert Zugsmith is best known for a string of exploitation epics produced in the fifties and sixties which include, among numerous others, *High School Confidential* (1958 – producer), *College Confidential* (1960 – producer-director), and *The Private Lives of Adam and Eve* (1960 – co-directed with Mickey Rooney).

8. *Fanny Hill: Memoirs of a Woman of Pleasure*, produced by Zugsmith, was a co-production of the Famous Players Corporation and West Berlin's CCC Filmkunst GMBH.

9. Meyer uses this early example of a typical exploitation film to make the point that these types of 'road show' productions (which often played to segregated audiences of men and women) followed a strict morality play-type formula: the 'sin' is shown in graphic detail for most of the film with the sinner severely punished in the closing minutes of the final reel. Though the plot of *Road to Ruin* does not follow exactly the scenario outlined by Meyer, it is illustrative of the exploitation genre in particular, and, Meyer believes, motion pictures in general.

10. The drug overdose of the statuesque Roman actress, originally set to play the lead in this R-rated historical melodrama filmed in Barbados, forced Meyer to hurriedly recast British actress Anouska Hempel in her role. Though a competent actress, the diminutive Hempel was not a heroine cast in the traditional Meyer mould. The box-office failure of *Blacksnake!* prompted Meyer to decide never to let acting ability take precedence over anatomical considerations in future. Instead, he would rely upon his skill as an editor to compensate for any acting deficiencies in the cast.

11. Meyer is credited with having created the 'nudie-cuties' genre in 1959 with his landmark film *The Immoral Mr. Teas*. The film's phenomenal financial success, eventually grossing over $1.5

million on a $24,000 investment, spawned an estimated 150 technically inferior imitators in the three years following its release. Notable among these productions are David Friedman's *The Adventures of Lucky Pierre* (1961) and Bob Cresse's *Once Upon a Knight* (1961).

12. *Eve and the Handyman* (1960), *Erotica* (1961), *Wild Gals of the Naked West* (1962), *Europe in the Raw* (1963), and *Heavenly Bodies* (1963).

13. *Vixen* was successfully prosecuted for obscenity in Cincinnati based on a citizen's complaint filed by Charles H Keating, Jr., founder of Citizens for Decent Literature, in September, 1969. After several appeals, the Ohio State Supreme Court upheld the lower court's opinion in a 5-2 decision and ruled in July, 1971 that scenes in *Vixen* which seemingly depicted 'purported acts of sexual intercourse' could not be shown in Cincinnati. In April 1984 a planned showing of the film by the University of Cincinnati Film Society was cancelled after the Hamilton County Prosecutor's office declared the ban on *Vixen* to be yet in effect. On September 18, 1990, a California state grand jury indicted Lincoln Savings & Loan Association former owner Charles H. Keating, Jr. on 42 counts of criminal fraud.

14. Considered by Roger Ebert to be 'Meyer's overlooked masterpiece', this surprisingly complex tale of 'poor white trash' living and loving amid the tobacco-road squalor of Depression-era Missouri received only a lukewarm box office reception. Meyer attributed this to the unsophisticated sexploitation audience more traditionally interested in flesh than Freud.

15. Meyer had met Rena Horten, real name Renate Hutte, while in Germany directing *Fanny Hill* for Albert Zugsmith in 1964. Though Horten had only a minuscule part as a prostitute in the film, Meyer was so impressed by her that he brought her to America to co-star with Lorna Maitland in *Mudhoney*. Nor did he let her heavy Teutonic accent clash with the mood of a gothic drama set in the Midwest . . . he cast her as a decorative mute!

16. In July, 1989 Meyer was invited to the Sixteenth International Moscow Film Festival to participate in the 'Sex in American Cinema' series co-sponsored by the American-Soviet Film Initiative, the San Francisco Film Society, and the USSR Filmmakers Association. Of the three Meyer films screened at the festival, the campy *Beyond the Valley of the Dolls* (1970) and the cartoonish *Supervixens* (1975) were enthusiastically received, while the dramatic *Mudhoney* failed to hold its Soviet audience.

17. A curious 'documentary' on the swinging topless scene which features several buxom strippers dancing to fast music and commenting on their bodies. The film also includes footage from Meyer's earlier nudie, *Europe in the Raw* (1963), as well as Lorna Maitland's screen test for *Lorna*.

18. In a September 18, 1964 review in the *Los Angeles Times*, critic Margaret Harford called *Lorna* 'an unintentional caricature . . . of the adult art film' and Meyer a 'Tennessee Truffaut'.

Fanny Hill: Memoirs of a Woman of Pleasure

The Variety Review

Hollywood has frequently taken the rap for a good many scurrilous accusations and attacks it has not deserved. As a commercial industry involved in the presentation of an artistic, but mass appeal, communications product, there are those areas of production that sometimes fall victim to the so-called high-minded, purist reactions and end up with an unwarranted slap in the face. Not so with Albert Zugsmith's production of *Fanny Hill*. This picture deserves every slap it may get – and more. It is an insult to the integrity and sensibility of the Hollywood motion picture industry, a setback for the business.

John Cleland's eighteenth century book, on which the title and obvious exploitation elements of the picture are based, was banned for 200 years, until recently. The book, while a vivid descriptive account of sexual pleasures, has a bawdy, lusty and lively point of view. Had Zugsmith filmed it with taste and with proper facilities, it might have made a special and probably successful film. What he has done instead is taken the first chapter, filled it with ridiculous, smutty, cheap bedroom activity in the manner of a low class nudie and then tried to save the day by cutting to the end. Fanny herself loses her virginity and marries her true love in the end, which apparently makes all the vulgar tomfoolery in between proper.

Ads for the picture call it 'a female *Tom Jones*'. Would that it had the same bawdy style done with the same believable mood and artistic quality. There will probably be plenty of interest on the part of the public response to such ads, but in the end these insult the public. No self-respecting exhibitor of prominence should bow to such cheap exploitation and no respectable house should dupe its patrons into seeing the picture under this veil. It is doubtful if most major dailies will accept its advertising. Money might be made on the first round, but the loss of community respect multiplied over the nation must be detrimental to the film industry.

Aside from the slipshod manner in which the film is made, a chief fault is in Robert Hill's academic screenplay and Russ Meyer's dull direction. The dialogue is as low as can be found and the storyline is just old fashioned, thin and uninteresting.

The production has a couple of clever laughs, like the shop sign for the piemaker, M. Sennett. And there are some deliciously motley character people throughout, like a silent bit by Ellen Velero and a bit by Zugsmith himself as the Grand Duke.

Miriam Hopkins, so fine an actress in the past in many first class films, is woefully disgraced by inadequate material and ludicrous situations as the madame, who notes, 'It isn't much, but we call it a house.' Letitia Roman is pretty as Fanny and Ulli Lommel, who looks emaciated without his clothes, does have a few moments of interest as Fanny's suitor. Walter Giller has an evil sensitivity as one lusty patron and Karin Evans could be fine as a grumbling maid if the role were well written. Others are generally inadequate throughout.

To comment on the film's design, it was badly dubbed with no background or normal room sounds, leaving it with a dull aural thud. Editing is sloppy and there seems little attempt at matching the photography. Scenes look like day and night at the same time. The picture runs much like a documentary, with a good deal of narration throughout and a busy series of lithographs aimed at the plates of a book as the film takes its way through the ordeals of Fanny, the country lass who never once found out about the house she thought was a home.

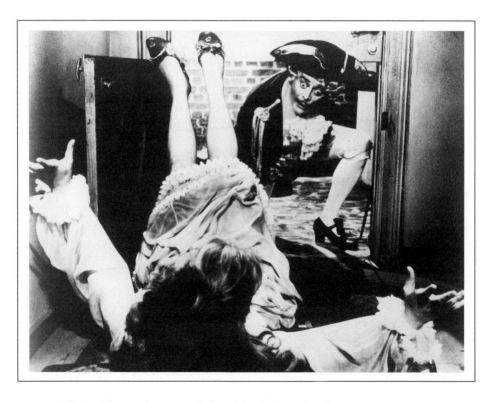

Fanny Hill *(1964), an adaptation of John Cleland's classic bawdy novel, is more attributable to exploitation producer Albert Zugsmith than to director Meyer.*

The Very Breast of Russ Meyer

Rope of Flesh (aka Mudhoney)

The Variety Review

*R*ope of Flesh concerns the mental decay of a jealous depression-era sharecropper, and its effects on his family and town. Some good acting by unknowns and lesser names enhance a script which is the strongest of three produced and directed by Russ Meyer since exiting the strict nudie sphere. Sexploitation elements exist, but in such a way that near-complete removal would still yield an acceptable and absorbing entry in the general adult market. When California-bound John Furlong arrives at the Missouri farm of Stu Lancaster after a prison stretch, his employment cues the declining sanity of Hal Hopper, wife-beating husband of Lancaster's niece Antoinette Cristiani. The latter projects very well as the loyal wife who takes all the punishment even after falling in love with Furlong in a tastefully-handled affair. Hopper is very good as the cheating, frustrated hubby who is variously taunting, remorseful, scheming, brutal and submissive. Top thesp honours go to Lancaster, the stolid landowner who wills his property to Furlong instead of Hopper, knowledge of which sends the latter into a final crazed spree of murder and barn-burning.

Interjected at intervals are Lorna Maitland and Rena Horten of the local bordello shanty run by toothless Princess Livingston whose derisive cackles soon wear thin. The babes are lookers, natch, and Miss Horten does well in her role as a deaf mute.

Frank Bolger is the film's Elmer Gantry, whose fire and brimstone talk is tinged with curiosity until Hopper corrupts him with a trip to the sporting pad. He helps Hopper turn the town against the latter's wife and lover until his own wife, Lee Ballard, is strangled by the unglued husband, then becomes the fanatic leader of a lynch mob over which sheriff Nick Wolcuff has no control.

The unusual climax finds a town full of embarrassed lynchers afraid to look at one another, Miss Horten shocked into speech, and an upbeat note for the young couple. Raymond Friday Locke and William E. Sprague scripted a Locke story which has some strong dramatic angles and salty dialogue which is not out of place.

George Costello and Meyer allocated the $60,000 negative cost to good advantage. The latter's direction is excellent. Walter Schenk's camera is crisp. Editing and sound by Charles G. Schelling is also excellent, particularly the recording achieved sans looping.

*The hellfire-and-brimstone preacher, played by Frank Bolger, with Antoinette Cristiani
as the parishioner's wife he morally condemns. From* Mudhoney.

Motor Psycho!
by Kim Newman

Made in 1965, *Motor Psycho!* predates the popular Hells' Angels cycle of exploitation movies by a good few years in its story of a wandering trio of scuzzbag bikers who come to a bad end in the desert. The plot is an elaborate pun on the word 'vet', as a crazed veterinarian sets out to seek revenge on the crazed Vietnam veteran who has 'assaulted' his wife. Into this conflict wanders a provocative Creole wench whose dress keeps getting torn but remains miraculously decent. It's another absurd spoof melodrama, with the grim violence continually undercut by ridiculous comedy – the hero fixes a bullet wound in the heroine's head by sticking on a band aid, and one thug pauses in the middle of trashing a terrorised victim's house in

Alex Rocco battles it out with Meyer regular Haji, her breasts bared, in Motor Psycho! *(1965).*
This 'roughie' displays Meyer's love of violence as entertainment.

order to make a long distance phone call to his devoted mother. Because it is locked into the traditions of macho violence and vengeance prevalent in low budget action/exploitation, the film is less interesting than the later, similar, peculiarly subversive *Faster Pussycat, Kill, Kill!* but its jazzy kinetic idiocy is compelling in a way few non-cartoon movies are.

Faster Pussycat, Unpleasant Film
by James Powers

*F*aster, Pussycat! Kill! Kill! is the unimaginative, meaningless title of a sordid sex film, exploiting perversion, violence and murder. It probably will be a big item in the grimy grind houses along 42nd street in New York, and other such exhibition haunts. Other exhibitors should be warned away. Russ Meyer produced it with his wife, Eve, and directed it and edited it himself.

Jack Moran's screenplay is about three prostitutes, at least two of whom are lesbians, who go whirling about the southwest desert country looking for excitement. They find it when they encounter a young man and his girl, brutally murder the man and kidnap the girl. Their next port of cal is an isolated ranch occupied by a senile, crippled old man and his two sons, one mentally retarded. The remainder of the plot concerns the efforts of the three women to squeeze a hoard of cash they believe the old man is hiding out of him or his sons.

Meyer has displayed in the past a talent for film-making, a knowledge of what can be done with film and a facility for doing it. Unfortunately, he seems to have no judgement whatever about what to do with this talent. Either that, or he is deliberately debasing it and his audiences with the most superficial, sensational presentation of the vicious, the depraved and the mentally ill.

Faster, Pussycat! is in the class with the bare bosom 'nudies', but far worse than those simple-minded cheapies. This is a sick picture for sick people.

'While violence cloaks itself in a plethora of disguises, its favourite mantle remains sex' - from the narration to Faster Pussycat, Kill! Kill! *(1966).*

Russ Meyer: Master

by John Waters

Russ Meyer is the Eisenstein of sex films. He is single-handedly responsible for more hard-ons in movie audiences than any other director, despite the fact that he has refused ever to make a hard-core feature. Married couples have flocked to his films for twenty years because they know Russ delivers and feel that the erotic images he is so famous for give them fodder for fantasies and actually add a little zing to their dull sex lives. Even without the credits, a Russ Meyer film is instantly recognisable – top-notch production values, split-second editing, low-angle shots leering up at almost deformed, big-busted, domineering, sex-starved heroines, and plot lines so ludicrous that all you can do is laugh along with the director. Russ Meyer makes films about sex and violence and you can tell he is proud of his work. He writes, produces, directs, films, and edits his own productions, and they all make money. Russ Meyer has never made a bad film.

Faster, Pussycat! Kill! Kill! (Russ's tenth film) is, beyond a doubt, the best movie ever made. It is possibly better than any film that will be made in the future. I first saw the film in 1966 at a local drive-in after being attracted to the radio ad that blared, 'It will leave a taste of evil in your mouth!' At the time, I was totally unfamiliar with Russ Meyer's work, but after seeing *Faster, Pussycat* he became my lifelong idol. I went back to the drive-in every night of the run, even if I had to go alone, just so I could watch the picture over and over while I had the chance. (I always respected people I saw alone in the drive-in for their unabashed devotion to films.) I wrote Russ gushing fan letters, which he politely answered. I got a job as a film reviewer in a local underground paper for the sole purpose of raving about the film. If there is such a thing as a film being a bad influence on youth, here was the perfect example. Russ's nasty 'pussycats' became a role model for all the characters in my productions – especially Divine. The one big difference was that Divine was a man and his big set of knockers was nothing but a pile of old wash rags.

For the past fifteen years I've driven hundreds of miles to catch the film whenever it's revived. I've rented the film and forced friends and members of my crews to watch it in hushed silence. When my own films started to catch on, I made sure I gushed about *Faster, Pussycat* in every interview. When the Bleecker Street Cinema in New York showed *Multiple Maniacs* at midnight, they chose *Faster, Pussycat* as the alternate late-night attraction, and I was wild with excitement. Today when *Faster* is screened at the Roxie theatre in San Francisco, the ads read, 'John Waters' all-time favourite movie,' and I couldn't be prouder.

Faster, Pussycat, Kill! Kill! is a violent gothic melodrama built around three bisexual psychotic go-go girls: Varla, Billie, and Rosie. The film opens with an offscreen narrator lecturing the audience about the possibility of running into violent women ('One could be your secretary, your next door neighbour') and suddenly cuts to the three stars wildly watusi-dancing in a bar as dirty old lechers cheer them on ('Go, baby. Go! Go! Go! Go!'). As the credits begin, we hear a group called the Bostweeds sing the title song 'Faster Pussycat', and we see Varla, Billie, and Rosie cruising around the desert in their three separate Porsches, looking for trouble. The leader of the gang, Varla (Tura Satana) is one of the best villains in screen history. Dressed in a low-cut, skintight, one-piece jumpsuit, and black leather boots and gloves, she gives new meaning to the word butch. Her girl friend Rosie (Haji) is a mean Mexican with a weakness for switchblades who emphasises her many moments of disgust by spitting or picking her teeth with whatever is handy. Billie (Lori Williams) is the femme of the group, the main things on her mind being sex and alcohol. In her white shortshorts, halter top, and knee-high patent-leather go-go boots, Billie is forever breaking into torrid go-go steps whenever trouble arises.

As the 'pussycats' skinny-dip, a young all-American Joe (Ray Barbow) in Bermuda shorts and his bikinied girl friend (Susan Bernard) pull up in their MG and try to make friends. Varla immediately turns nasty and challenges him to a drag race. When she sees his car is faster, she cuts across the makeshift track and forces him to a near crash. He hops out of his car to yelp, but Varla gives him a swift karate chop in the neck and, in one mindboggling shot, grabs both his arms, yanks them behind him, and breaks his back. The girl friend faints from shock and the pussycats give her knockout pills, tie her up, and take her as a hostage.

At a gas station they hear about an old crippled man (Stuart Lancaster) who is rumoured to have a large insurance settlement in cash hidden on his broken-down ranch, where he lives with his two sons: the Vegetable (Dennis Busch), a mentally retarded muscle man; and Kirk (Paul Trinka), a normal, hotblooded ranch hand. Horny for loot, the three sex bombs and their hostage feign car trouble and ask the old man if they can camp out on his ranch until their car is fixed. Sceptical, but panting at the sight of the girls, he agrees.

In hopes of finding the money, the pussycats immediately go to work and try to seduce the sons. Billie soon finds the Vegetable is impotent, but Varla has more luck with Kirk in a hayloft. 'My cup runneth over,' she moans, but, alas, she still can't get him to reveal where the stash is hidden. Rosie just stands around picking her teeth and spitting. Billie gets fed up and tries to 'split' ('See you girls in church' is her exit line), but Rosie hurls a switchblade into her back. The old cripple and the Vegetable see the murder and try to flee, but Varla and Rosie track them in their sports car ('Get in and don't miss'), and floor it, squashing the cripple and sending his wheelchair flying through the air, spilling out all the cash, which was hidden under the seat. The Vegetable retrieves the knife from Billie's back and stabs Rosie in the stomach. Varla goes nuts at the sight of her dead girl friend and tries to grind the Vegetable up against a wall with her car, but he is so strong he manages to hold off the horsepower of the Porsche. Kirk, the good-guy son, realises the truth about the moral character of Varla and escapes with the hostage. Varla takes chase in a truck she steals and a climactic karate fight takes place in the desert between the hero and the deadly superwoman,

The Very Breast of Russ Meyer

leaving Varla dead and bleeding and serving as future food for desert vultures. Kirk and the hostage run off, presumably in hopes of a calmer life.

After *Faster, Pussycat* I made every effort to catch up with the earlier work of this great director. I was amazed that each of his films was as fabulous as the next – *Wild Gals of the Naked West, Mudhoney, Lorna, Motor Psycho* – they were all classics. When Russ moved on to make his more modern sex-scorchers, such as *Good Morning . . . and Goodbye!* and *Vixen*, the box-office take set records and the big studios were forced to sit up and take notice and hire him. The result was the funniest film ever made, *Beyond the Valley of the Dolls* (written by Pulitzer prize-winning critic Roger Ebert), and I think that in 1999 this film will still be shown and enjoyed in much the same way as *Golddiggers of 1933* is today.

After nearly twenty years of being the top fan of *Faster, Pussycat*, I tried to locate the star, Tura Satana, to find out what her life is like today and how she felt her involvment in such a masterpiece. I finally got her telephone number in Los Angeles and decided to give her a call. A little girl answered the phone and when I asked for Tura, I was startled to hear the child say, 'Hold on,' and yell, 'Mommy.' After so many years of fantasising about the real life of the meanest pussycat of all, it was a shock to realise that Tura Satana was, after all, just an actress. Our interview was short but sweet. Tura explained that today she is working as a nurse and runs a doctor's office. Noticing my surprise at her career switch, she laughed and added, 'My patients don't give me any trouble, though.' She claims that Tura Satana is her real name, and I try to imagine the buxom beauty in a nurse's outfit with a little badge saying 'Nurse Satana'. She used to be a popular burlesque star and reminisces, 'It kept me in good shape.' She got the part in *Pussycat* because her agent suggested her to Russ, feeling she was 'built right for the part', with the added attraction of 'knowing karate'. Tura has never seen any of Russ's films except 'the one I'm in' and shrugs that the film 'neither helped nor hurt my career.' She was also in *Irma La Douce, Who's Been Sleeping in My Bed?, Astro Zombies*, and *The Doll Squad*.

Tura seems to have fond memories of *Pussycat* and its other two cinematic sisters in crime, but didn't seem to care for the actress who played her victim. 'She was a typical Hollywood brat. She was never on time for anything. I'd get so mad at her that I'd turn away and smash a railroad tie with a karate chop.' Her leading man evoked even harsher memories – 'Ha! Those love scenes were real acting. The guy was a health-food nut and had bad breath!'

Miss Satana's opinion of cult stardom might give pause to any aspiring actress of today – 'When the film came out, everybody who saw it wanted to punch me. I got lots of letters from guys who wanted me to beat the crap out of them.'

Meeting Russ Meyer is exactly like being in a Russ Meyer film. The fantasies he creates

The incomparable Tura Satana as Varla – the kitten with the sharpest claws, and post-feminist icon.

The Very Breast of Russ Meyer

for his audience are obviously his own in real life. When I first met him in 1974 in Rotterdam, he politely excused himself with, 'I have to go back to the hotel and have sex now, John.' When I called him many years later to interview him for this book, he asked if I minded that his new girl friend, Kitten Natividad (star of his newest film, *Beneath the Valley of the Ultravixens*), would be present. 'You'll like her,' he deadpanned, 'she has big tits.' After the interview Kitten, Russ, a photographer, and I went to eat at Musso and Frank's Grill in Hollywood, and I was thrilled to see that Russ drives the same kind of four-wheel-drive vehicle that his male stars drive in his films. Kitten, a soft-spoken knockout version of every heterosexual man's masturbatory fantasies, who also happens to hold the title of Miss Nude Cosmopolitan, waited outside the vehicle, unable to step up into the seat because her pants were too tight. Russ, always the gentleman, seemed used to this predicament, grabbed her by the back of the legs above the knee, and lifted her straight up until she managed to get in the door as she squealed, 'Ohhhhhh, Russ!' As soon as we entered the restaurant, Kitten gave out nude photos of herself to the waiters, and the maitre d' treated Russ as if he were Cecil B. DeMille. During dinner, Kitten loved to try to shock me and would casually toss in bon mots such as 'I love it when Russ gets hard, because he's such a creative genius.' 'Pass the salt, please,' I'd stammer, excited beyond words at being with the ultimate of old-time Hollywood couples. At last, we had a chance to talk:

Russ, lately your films are being shown in museums and other classy institutions. How do you react to those who still call your films 'trash'? Does it offend you?
Yes, it offends me. Then I decide I'm going to go along with it. I admit to all the things they'd prefer I didn't – it takes all the sting away. I exploit women, I'm a dirty old man, I take advantage, I make my living from this and I do it with zeal and gusto. I am a pornographer, but a class pornographer.

Your film Faster, Pussycat *is my all-time favourite. I've been obsessed by it for years. How much did it cost to make?*
About $61,000. I couldn't afford colour at the time. *Motor Psycho*, which preceded *Pussycat*, was really the catalyst. I had made a picture with three tough guys and then I made one with three tough girls.

Pussycat *has a lot of lesbian overtones. Were they supposed to be obvious dykes?*
I didn't really know that much about so-called dykes. A lot of people who are inclined that way like the film very much. I had an aversion to wanting to know too much about that because it wasn't really Boy Scout, macho-male. Tura, as far as I know, is very much unlike that in real life.

Who wrote the film?
Jack Moran. He was the child-star prodigy in the *Flash Gordon* serial. He was in *The*

Best Years of Our Lives. He made a lot of pictures and I ran into him through an Army friend. Moran tried to do a little writing and it was brought to my attention. First he did some narration for a picture of mine called *Heavenly Bodies.* Then he wrote *Pussycat* and then *Good Morning . . . and Goodbye!.* Lovely guy, we really got along famously.

How did you meet Tura Satana?
Through Haji. I had used Haji in *Motor Psycho* and she brought Tura to me. Haji had just had her nose fixed. They both were strippers.

How about Lori Williams? She was great in it.
She was a showgirl from Vegas, I recall. Then she married a wealthy, well-established businessman in a small town in Pennsylvania.

I've been looking for the record 'Faster, Pussycat' by the Bostweeds all my life. Did it ever come out?
No. They were a group up in Oakland, California. You know how sometimes a group will sit in a bar and they'll never go any further? That was them.
extracted from *Shock Value*

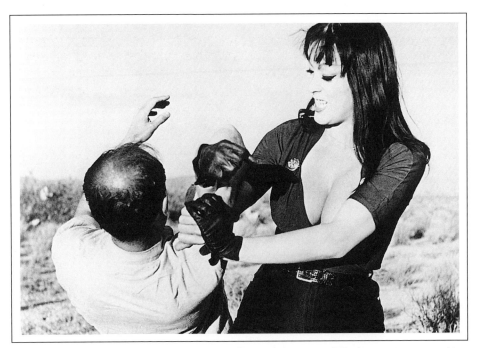

'This is a sick picture for sick people' – The Hollywood Reporter. *'The best movie ever made'* – John Waters. Faster Pussycat *'s feminine violence now has cult status.*

THE
SEXPLOITATIONERS

Mondo Topless

by Jimmy McDonough

The insistent sound of a telegraph's dit-dit-dit. Shots of a street sign labelled 'Twin Peaks', houses and apartment buildings jumbled row upon row on hillish terrain, crowded by masses of telephone poles and wires. 'This is San Francisco Calling!' blares the hyped-up voice of producer-director-cameraman-editor-narrator Russ Meyer. Guitars jangle as title credits flash over quick dissolves of the Golden Gate Bridge seen from different angles. Cut to a close-up of a car radio. A blonde woman – extremely large, well-built, with a mannish face and huge red lips – wearing nothing but bikini briefs bops wildly at the wheel of a fast car. Her name is Babette Bardot. The Voice of Meyer bellows above shrieking guitars.

'San Francisco, the pearl of the Pacific, has long been recognised as an impressive and significant contributor to the American scene . . . situated on precipitous peaks and poised on the tip of a peninsula, San Francisco thrusts itself into the bosom of the Pacific . . .'
A stream of oddly angled buildings, street signs, trolley cars, and sped-up, cartoonish crowd shots (showing the only men in the movie – John Q. Public passersby and one poor sap trying to *push* a cable car into action). Babette keeps driving. The images fly by at a jackhammer pace. The Voice of Meyer continues its antagonistic travelogue.

'Quaint Fisherman's Wharf, the mass purveyor of cracked Dungenese crab and garish souvenirs fabricated in Japan and Yugoslavia, hawked by screaming minions . . . San Francisco's arts colony is dominated by the arrogant and imposing Coit Tower, thrusting its bulk majestically to the sky, the Broadway Tunnel offering a yawning orifice through which to enter fabled North Beach . . .'

Babette keeps driving. 'San Francisco! A spumoni-like hodge-podge of wild architecture, harbouring wonderful old-world restaurants and emporiums of pleasure, exploding dusk to dawn with the way-out craze of . . . THE TOPLESS!' A rapid-fire montage of garish neon signs for strip joints, adult movies, drive-thru banks . . . 'Mondo Topless captures the basic quintessence of the movement . . . with movement, way-out movement!'

We see an explosion of women, topless, mostly naked, women with gargantuan assets, overpowering, surreal women, constantly in motion – Sin Lenee, a frenetic blonde in black panties and pink beads, dances wildly in a farmhouse window, a portable radio hangs by a nail outside . . . Pat Barringer, another blonde in a pink go-go outfit and long white gloves, shimmies in front of another radio in the middle of the desert . . . Darlene Gray, a skinny dishwater blonde in bangs and pigtails whose gigantic breasts make up 23 of her 112 pounds, rolls in a muddy pond, a small transistor perched nearby . . .

'FANTASTIC women, FANTASTIC dances, featuring the world's loveliest buxotics . . . You've only DREAMED there were women like this until now, but they're REAL . . .

'You've only dreamed there were women like this until now. But they're real – unbelievably real!' – Mondo Topless (1966).

The Very Breast of Russ Meyer

UNBELIEVABLY REAL!!!'

The movie whips back and forth between dancers, the segments joined by whiplash pans and manic chord changes (BOING!) or a honk on the sax. Conversational bon-bons by the dancers rise and fall through the din: 'I can't find a bathing suit to fit me. You gotta have one custom-made.' 'I find I am alluring to a man – with or without clothes. And I try to be. This is my main purpose in life.' 'I want at least four or five more children.' 'Even if it *does* excite them, this is *good*.' 'People who say, "Honey, that's all foam rubber," I say believe what you want. I don't care.'

The montage moves on: fragments of female anatomy . . . bursts of close-ups detailing fishnet hose, diamond earrings, open red lips, black plastic belts. There are naked women playing spangled guitars, helping mules up hills, bouncing red balls on sticks, scuba diving in swimming pools, climbing electrical towers and doing the split, frugging madly beside oncoming trains. Tape decks and radios are everywhere: on the beach, sitting in trees, carried through the woods by topless women in blue hip-huggers.

Nature girl: the larger-than-life Babette Bardot in Common Law Cabin *(1967), the first of a series of colour versions of Meyer's rural melodramas.*

How is this movie to be taken? An intense magnification of a completely negative sexual mythology? Or only a frenetic drone, an unrelenting meditation on nothingness best put into words by Pat Barringer, the dancer on the electrical tower: 'All that you're doing is a *dance* – it has no meaning whatsoever . . .' As the last shot goes by – an unbelievable composition of Donna X's rear end shaking out of a tight red dress (with a cut-out bottom) next to a large, white reel-to-reel tape deck – the Voice of Meyer says cryptically over the yakkety-sax: 'Mondo Topless *measures up to more than a gang of great gals, it makes it MOVE.'*

Uncertain Innocence Part Three
by Kenneth Turan and Stephen F. Zito

The films produced by Russ Meyer in these key years were *Common Law Cabin* (also known as *How Much Loving Does a Normal Couple Need?* and *Conjugal Cabin*); *Good Morning and Goodbye*; *Finders Keepers, Lovers Weepers*; *Vixen*; and *Cherry, Harry & Raquel*. *Common Law Cabin* and *Good Morning and Goodbye*, further entries in the Meyer school of backwoods melodrama, are less violent and bizarre than the Roughies like *Lorna* that Meyer had made in previous years. *Good Morning and Goodbye* was well cast (including Capri, Haji, and Karen Ciral), and the direction and cinematography were up to professional standards. Its only weakness was the endless bickering among the various characters – farmer, farmer's wife, farmer's daughter, construction-worker lover of wife, daughter's boyfriend, and sorceress.

Good Morning and Goodbye was followed by *Finders Keepers, Lovers Weepers*, a gangster melodrama in the Don Siegel tradition of rough, realistic, understated melodrama about two small-time hoods who plan and almost pull off an after-hours robbery of a bar. It is the first film in which it becomes absolutely clear that Meyer is less interested in exposed nipples and hardbreathing sex scenes than he is in the exploration of the erotic tensions that compel people to commit rape and adultery. Its rough, endemic violence is the logical result of too many angry people thrown together in a narrow dramatic space. The limited number of sets and the small casts of Meyer's films were a necessity because of the low budgets with which he worked at the time, but he nevertheless used the claustrophobic spaces to advantage. Meyer's sophisticated use of timing and staging to create and sustain dramatic tension is perhaps most evident, however, in *Vixen*, which starred Erica Gavin and is concerned with incest, miscegenation, lesbianism, wife-swapping, draft-dodging, sexual dysfunction, nude bathing, hijacking, and the victory of democracy over communism. There is little overt violence, but once again Meyer exhibits his fascination with eroticism, large breasts, and the hostility and tensions between people on sexual, political, and racial grounds. 'What is significant today that we can put in to give it a thread of a story?' Meyer recalls asking his partner, Jim Ryan. 'The hijacking thing, the Cuba bit, the black man running away to Canada. We'll get some real redneck broad who hates Negroes and get that confrontation going, and we'll have her make it with all sorts of people.' The movie did enough business – $7.5 million gross – to get Meyer a contract with Twentieth Century-Fox for *Beyond the Valley of the Dolls*.

extracted from *Sinema: American Pornographic Films and the People Who Make Them*

Russ Meyer 1967!
by Moose McGill

1967 looked like being a lean year for Russ Meyer. His triple whammer of *Lorna* (1964), *Mudhoney* (1965) and *Motor Psycho* (1965) had failed to take in big bucks at the box office and his follow up *Faster Pussycat Kill! Kill!* (1966) was hardly doing much better. It would be a few years before critics would dust them off and refer to them as his Gothic Melodramas.

The Immoral Mr. Teas (1959) had been a runaway success but the next Meyer film to really pull in a heavy profit was the zest-filled *Mondo Topless* (1966). Russ, always a shrewd businessman, realised that he needed a successful follow up to keep the coffers full. *Mondo Topless* was a colour filled quickie which documented the *Topless* craze, a fad which was sweeping through the U.S.A like a high powered tornado. Meyer captured the frenzy and the 'way out wild movement' in this swinging tribute to 'unrestrained female anatomy'. *Topless* also featured his current companion Babette Bardot, a gal whose attributes totally defied gravity. She is seen in the opening scenes driving a car topless through the streets of San Francisco . . . truly an unbelievable sight! It's hardly surprising that his next venture should feature her fairly indescribable talents.

Meyer aimed his next couple of features at the drive-in market, as it was here that he would be assured of a profit. This meant that nipples and nudity would have to be kept to a minimum – in the drive-in titillation and suggestion were the name of the game, especially during the early Sixties. Violence was OK but nudity was always cut out by drive-in owners and was considered Taboo.

Russ was the master of suggestion, so working within these constraints was no problem. After all, he had cut his teeth in glamour photography where suggestion was the name of the game. Earlier features like *Lorna* featured lipsmacking dollops of nudity but were unfortunately commercial failures . . . the climate was not yet right for large doses of nipples. For his next couple of films Meyer decked his female stars out in all sorts of body hugging clothes, deep cut bikinis and revealing dresses. The clothes could barely contain their ample curves and their breasts seemed to overflow onto the screen . . . this fitted perfectly with their drives and needs which were also larger than life.

In 1967 Russ Meyer made two films: *Common Law Cabin* (or *How Much Loving Does a Normal Couple Need?*) and *Good Morning and Goodbye* (released in Britain as *The Lust Seekers*). They are two of his least talked about and critically discussed films. Both are typically Russ Meyer, in short overflowing with all the things we've come to know and love from his productions. Sumptuous colour, sizzling one-liners and characters who live for fighting and loving. Like all his films they feature 'cantilevered women with watermelon breasts' (the type that only Russ Meyer seems able to find) and one-dimensional men saddled with sexual problems.

In *Good Morning and Goodbye* it's an impotent husband while *Common Law Cabin* features a father with a Freudian hang-up about his daughter – she looks too much like his dead wife. In all the Russ Meyer films it's the interaction between the sexes that's important. The male-female thing is never sexually hunky-dory and this is what must be resolved in the course of the film. In *Good Morning and Goodbye* the impotent Burt (Stuart Lancaster) helps create a voracious unsatisfied wife (Alaina Capri) and in *Common Law Cabin* the overprotective father (John E. Moran) causes unease and tension in the family unit. The underlying thesis in all of Meyer's movies is that misdirected sexual energy leads to all sorts of problems . . . a healthy society is a humping society.

Russ is a lusty chap and his films reflect this outlook on life. Sex in his films is natural and unstoppable – problems arise between men and women when this energy is blocked, diminished or diverted. Meyer Men need Meyer Women and there's an easy companionship when they're really getting it together. *Common Law Cabin* and *Good Morning and Goodbye* are prime examples of this philosophy in action – allusions to Nature and Sex abound in both of these films.

In many ways nature has always been central to his films. He always chooses a secluded, rugged and beautifully sunlit location for his stories. And his photography thrives on the vividness, punch and brightness that only a truly sunbaked area can provide. This approach goes way back to his days as a glamour photographer when he favoured outdoor and offbeat locations. There's something about a beautiful woman, ragged rocks and washed up driftwood that's guaranteed to get the pulse pounding. Who knows why, perhaps it's the idea of unfettered carnality – anyway, it's definitely more appealing than the usual hemmed-in shots of half-nude girls taken on a tacky indoor set.

The Very Breast of Russ Meyer

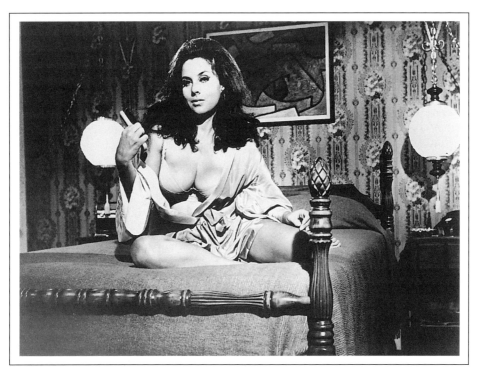

Alaina Capri as Angel: 'the luscious cushion of evil . . . perched on the throne of immorality.'
From Good Morning . . . and Goodbye! *(1967).*

Nature permeates every Meyer film, not just in the photography and the underlying sexual imagery but in the very production itself. Russ likes to drag his small, tight-knit cast and crew off to some rugged spot miles away from anywhere (it helps keep production costs way on down). This means that the cast have nothing to distract them, they must devote all their energies to the production at hand. Sex is strictly Verboten on the Meyer set – he likes to encourage that certain lusty spark or frisson between his crew and the male and female cast. He hopes this little current of excitement, magic, will be generated on screen and somehow his films will have captured some of the odour of S-E-X.

Meyer likes the physicality and arduousness of shooting miles away from anywhere. It's back to basics in more ways than one . . . In fact the whole thing is kind of like a lusty boot camp with women! His cast and crew are always small, closely knit . . . everyone gets involved, feeding ideas and doing different jobs on the production. Meyer usually works with a seven-man crew and many of his technicians are non-union. This means they have no qualms about mucking in and doing all sorts of jobs at a fairly cheap rate.

Common Law Cabin is a prime example of how small and incestuous Meyer's production crews are. The technical crew of Jack Lucas, Richard Brummer and George Costello worked on many of Meyer's earlier epics. John Furlong – the man who does many of the voices in Meyer's films (radio voices and voice-overs, etc.) also played the impotent Dr. Ross. Jack E. Moran – who wrote the screenplay for *Cabin, Faster Pussycat Kill! Kill!* and *Good Morning and Goodbye* – also played the main role of Dewey Hoople, the fairly hung-up papa.

While Meyer liked to surround himself with technicians he was familiar with, he also liked to vary the cast, especially the female lead, after each film. In the sexploitation film business this made perfectly good sense. *Common Law Cabin* and *Good Morning and Goodbye* each had three female leads – which gave the audience plenty to look at. Alaina Capri starred in both films. She was a Catholic schoolgirl from Los Angeles who had ambitions to be an actress . . . unfortunately, she disappeared after *Good Morning and Goodbye*. In *Common Law Cabin* she played the testy but vulnerable Sheila, but she really came into her own as Angel, the hot-blooded, sex-craving wife in *Good Morning and Goodbye*. In this one she slung lines with the best of them, droning out killer comments in a nasal twang – *yowww! Common Law Cabin*, easily the weakest of the two features, is basically the story of a bunch of losers who end up in some godforsaken dump in Colorado. The whole thing lacks any kind of consistent logic . . . but there are enough good bits to keep it steaming along quite nicely. In *Cabin* the main attraction is definitely Babette Bardot, a woman who the word pneumatic barely describes. She sports some of the most wildly cut dresses ever made, and when she hits the screen wearing one of those creations the only response possible is slackjawed amazement. B.B. delivers her lines in a crazy faltering French accent which is deliriously daft. Like most Meyer women she is larger than life and thinks nothing of diving off a mountain top into the lake below while holding lighted torches in her hands!! The film is also peppered with fairly lame jokes about her cooking.

Most critics describe Meyer's characters as cartoonesque or one dimensional – this applies to some of them, others are imbued with a vitality and energy far beyond what is normal. Babette's wild amazon bit is clearly way beyond the norm. It's wild, it's primitive and it's excessive. It reeks of overabundance and fertility. As Barney Rickard, the satyric cop, remarks, 'You couldn't kill that broad with an axe!' To her husband she's 'too much woman, all of the time.' Clearly, the characters in any Meyer film are merely the channels through which natural drives and energies flow . . . if they appear to be one-dimensional it's because these are the most important things in the Meyer world. Meyer Men and Women are meant to be happy and horny together.

This emphasis on Nature, drives and energies beyond our control comes out in Russ's films in many ways. In *Common Law Cabin*, when Rickard is crunched like a watermelon by Cracker's boat it's as if the spirit of the dead sailor influences the speedboat to put an end to the evil copper.

Good Morning and Goodbye is practically a homage to Nature, fertility and unrepressed carnality. After all, it opens with some unnamed nymph running carefree and unfettered through some luscious undergrowth . . . the viewer's imagination begins to run riot while the voice-over asks, rather pruriently, 'How would you define Nymphomania, Irregular Union, Deflower, Wenching, Voyeurism, Strumpet, Hedonist? How would you define Doxy, Scabrous, Promiscuity, Poulet, Ribaldry, Debauchery, Adulterer?'

When we first see Angel (Alaina Capri) she is bathing in a leafy pool. It is clear that this 'monument to unholy carnality', this 'luscious cushion of evil' enjoys splashing around nude and uninhibited. A few minutes later, Haji emerges from another calm pool. She is a wood nymph or spirit, a 'mistress of the lost art'. Later on she rekindles the impotent Burt's flagging fire . . . she does this through weird rituals and suggestive dancing. The sight of Haji dancing around in skimpy costumes made of deerskin, flowers, leaves and feathers would be enough to restore anyone's potency. Yep, it's another slab of primitive exotica served up as only Russ Meyer can.

If all this talk of Nature, Sex and primitive shenanigans sounds a mite overblown or heavy handed, don't despair – it's all there in *Cabin* and *Goodbye* but it's done in such a glorious, irreverent and fun-filled manner that you can't help but laugh. Self deprecation and self mockery have always been among Meyer's strong points, especially in his early films. *Goodbye* and *Cabin* are well worth seeing as they were made before he started to parody himself . . . the tongue was still firmly in his cheek and not up his ass.

The sheer verve and fun of these films makes them classic sexploitation. The snappy screenplays by John E. Moran plus the colour-filled photography and editing by Meyer guarantee a racy slab of entertainment. *Good Morning and Goodbye* is easily the more interesting of the two films (*Cabin* was slung together in a matter of weeks) . . . It's jam-packed with all sorts of gaudy American iconography: flashy cars, revealing clothes and clipped but hip lingo. As usual, Meyer piles on all sorts of unusual camera angles and wildly sassy music to produce something with his own unique trademarks. Like any Meyer film it's jam-packed with energy, his shots are short, original and dynamic. Action is everything, his characters let rip with piercing one-liners and move in freewheeling motion . . . it's this sort of brassy dynamism that gives almost any Meyer film its charm.

Looking at them now, it's obvious that these films are very much products of their own time – what is wonderful about them is just how much suggestion Meyer can wring out of each shot. Each film is packed with loads of mammoth gals in various stages of undress . . . they are always putting clothes on or taking them off. The soundtrack is, as usual, glorious. Sleazy strip-type muzak seems to pour out from behind the wallpaper every time someone makes a physical or verbal suggestion. Working within the constraints of the time, he managed to achieve an incredible amount of titillation and humour. If you don't believe this, check out *I, a Woman* – the Swedish/Danish co-production which influenced *Good Morning and Goodbye*. While the Euro-flick is po-faced, serious and downbeat, *Goodbye* is a fun-filled slice of pure Americana. No one else but Russ could or would show a close-up of his leading actress

(Alaina Capri – *Good Morning and Goodbye*) putting her bra on and produce such a wide mixture of emotions . . . Shock, Titillation and Humour. It's a salute to Russ Meyer that he can produce films with a large number of moments like these.

Finders Keepers, Lovers Weepers
by Vincent Canby

Is Russ Meyer archaic? The question is as frightening to contemplate as the possibility that Prince Rainier and Grace Kelley may one day have their own neutron bomb. The rapidly changing patterns of sexual behaviour in conventional films are making decently intended, soft-core pornographic films increasingly difficult to achieve with any amount of success. These addled intimations of mortality passed through my mind yesterday afternoon at the theatre where Meyer's newest film, *Finders Keepers, Lovers Weepers*, opened to a large and docile audience . . . Meyer deserves, I think, his considerable, mostly underground reputation as a directorial talent who stoops without condescension. Although I find his fantasies basically unpleasant – they are almost exclusively concerned with insatiable ladies and the men they wear out – they are made with some cinematic complexity (lots of different camera setups in any one scene) and a minimum of mock piety. You'll never hear a Meyer heroine ask herself: 'Why, oh why must I give in to this shameless desire?' Her needs are chemical, and no amount of psychological or economic aid will answer them . . . To be successful as soft-core pornography, movies like Meyer's require a certain innocence on the part of the audience. Meyer's sole preoccupation with extraordinarily well-developed female breasts, usually photographed from a low angle and while they're in some sort of motion, is no longer particularly erotic. Nor do grunting love scenes, photographed from the waist up, suggest much more than difficult physical labour. The virtues of *Finders, Keepers* are a lack of moral pretension (his characters have only one thing on their minds) and a sort of low humour that, during one scene, has the camera cutting away from the lovers to show a series of collisions between out-of-control stock cars . . . The cast is, as usual, comparatively small but extremely healthy, the most noteworthy performer being Jan Sinclair, a large, ageless blonde who plays an Amish girl turned enthusiastically to prostitution. She is a dreadful actress but sounds, perhaps intentionally, like Mae West. Paul Lockwood is the young man who owns the go-go club and Anne Chapman plays his unsatisfied wife. From the neck down she looks very much like Miss Sinclair and it may be they work out in the same gym . . . Meyer, I understand, has temporarily abandoned the genre that made him rich and is currently preparing the sequel to Jacqueline Susann's *Valley of the Dolls* for 20th Century-Fox. Now, perhaps. he'll make a really erotic movie.

The Variety Review

Russ Meyer's latest film is another of his technically polished sexplicit dramas, this time free of (non-erotic) physical violence and brutality, and hyped with some awkwardly developed draft-dodging and patriotism angles. 'Vixen' is a girl who can't say no, and she proves it every seven minutes, including some detailed

Auto-eroticism: Anne Chapman and Gordon Wescourt get it on underwater, in a scene intercut with Finders Keepers, Lovers Weepers *(1968).*

dalliances with two strangers, her brother, his Negro buddy and, for change of pace, with another gal. She finds time for her husband too. Very good box-office prospects are likely in those male-oriented situations where Meyer's product has proven itself.

There is a frankness to Meyer's sex scenes, in that they are unabashed in their frequent amorality, motivated without hypocrisy, and executed with dispatch. No tortured rationalising here (Meyer's budgets – still $70,000 – couldn't afford it anyway!), nor any sophisticated gloss-over. His people simply meet, rut a bit, then move along. 'Untouched' in touching. Often the sequences are hilarious in their unbelievability. It's important to note that most patrons simply take the pix for what they are.

Erica Gavin is featured in the title role, and, besides the ample visual aspect, carries off the dramatic moments to okay effect. Garth Pillsbury is her square husband, Jon Evans her motorcycle hood brother, Peter Carpenter the passing Mountie with whom she passes the first few minutes. Robert Aiken and Vincene Wallace play a couple guesting at the British Columbia ranch setting, and Vixen has them both.

The ultimate course of the plot turns on Harrison Page, a Negro who ankled the US to avoid the draft. The final sequence introduces Michael O'Donnell as a communist, who plans to force Pillsbury to fly him to Cuba. The plane hijacking serves as a confrontation between the white establishment and the communist establishment.

At fadeout, Page decides to return to the US, on the grounds that it is, as far as attitudes towards Negroes are concerned, 'the lesser of two evils'. Not a bad resolution and the other dialogue is occasionally sharp. Robert Rudelson is given the script credit. It is amusing, however, that Vixen becomes the defender of Western civilisation.

Meyer's accomplished camera work, and the overall excellent production polish, is a regular feature of his films. Stories have been getting better, in their fashion, and, reacting to the current wave of down-playing violence, this pic has none.

Meyer also reacted immediately to the new Production Code four-ply rating system: within hours of disclosure, his ads for films in release bore the X label.

From Vixen to Vindication

by Dannis Peary

Several years ago Erica Gavin gave a truly zestful, highly-spirited performance as the most aggressive female of them all, *Vixen*. In a little over 70 minutes, she performed adultery, incest, a lesbian act, was raped, shouted countless racist clichés, and did a dance with a fish. And through all this, she almost made it to stardom. But as we all know only *Vixen*'s director, Russ Meyer, was welcomed into the industry's mainstream. After an all-too brief stint in Meyer's *Beyond the Valley of the Dolls*, Erica Gavin virtually disappeared from the spotlight while appearing in such non-classics as *Captain Milkshake*, *The Godmother*, and *The Rebel Jesus*. She emerged once more with a talented performance in Jonathan Demme's *Caged Heat*, doubtless the best and least offensive of the many sexploitation films to date. I met Erica Gavin at an autograph session for that film, and, though a bit apprehensive, she agreed to this, her first interview, which was done in January of 1975.

It can be said that Vixen *was the* Deep Throat *of its day. Both were low-budget films that initially grossed over $6 million. Both films showcased a sexually aggressive female lead, and both were financially assisted by well-publicised court cases. Each film catered to couples and played in 'legitimate' theatres. In many ways the two films were similar except that* Deep Throat*'s star Linda Lovelace became an instant 'superstar' while you drifted off into obscurity. Why didn't you become a star?*

It's true that *Vixen* was a major breakthrough for sex films seeking a mass audience but, except for in places like Chicago, San Francisco, and Atlanta, many of the people who saw *Vixen* came and went hiding their faces and wearing a hat or sunglasses. No one but Russ Meyer cultists talked about the film, whereas everybody in America seemed to be openly into the *Deep Throat* craze. The lines for it were incredible, with men and women without the disguises. Consequently Linda Lovelace became a household name. You must also remember that the title was *Russ Meyer's Vixen*. And, of course, Russ went on to a contract with 20th.

But why did Meyer go upward while you went nowhere?

That's what was weird, and I don't really know why. He was around years and years, but nobody had really noticed him until *Vixen*. And I really think – if he reads this, he's going to freak – that the only reason that *Vixen* made it was because of me.

Why haven't any of the women that Meyer has starred gone on to anything more creditable?

I don't think anybody wants the image he projects his women to be. Everybody really thinks that you are who you play in a film. Even now when I go on interviews, people think that was me, the real me, in *Vixen*, that I wasn't acting but just playing myself, and that's as far as my talent goes. It's frustrating. I've thought of taking my *Vixen* picture out of my portfolio. Certain commercial companies wouldn't hire me. They check out the people they put in their commercials very carefully, because they don't want to run the risk of somebody in Ohio saying, 'I'm not going to buy Viva Paper Towels because that slut Erica Gavin, who did that movie *Vixen* and played a nymphomaniac, is doing the advertising on TV.'

How did you get involved with Vixen?

I got my 'film break' from a very inexpensive ad in a *Variety* that I just happened to be thumbing through. Though I hadn't seen any of Meyer's films, I knew of him from Haji, a really interesting lady who had played the spooky, space-like wood nymph in Meyer's *Finders Keepers, Lovers Weepers*. She told me that he was nice and great to work with. The person I saw first was George Costello, who was fabulous, a great worker who did everything for Meyer. He read me through the parts and actually cast the movie. When I first met Meyer, he said to me, 'In all my films I've used big-breasted girls. This time I want to try something different. I want to use a girl that has a good figure but could be the girl down the street, a girl who can be related to by men and women.'

Despite her later reservations about Vixen *(1968), Erica Gavin went on to appear in* Beyond the Valley of the Dolls *and a skinflick entitled* Erika's Hot Summer.

The Very Breast of Russ Meyer

Yeah, but the reviews mentioned your acting only after they had discussed your chest . . .

I suppose so – 'The lusty, busty va-va-voom girl' – or whatever. Maybe he was just rationalising at the time why he wasn't going to use a girl with three cup sizes larger than me. I don't know. Anyway, I looked about the same as I do now, except that I weighed twenty pounds more then, and my hair was a bit longer. For the picture I pulled back some of my hair and wore a heavy fall. Meyer loved those eyebrows that I painted on. They curved upward and made me look evil and menacing. It started out as a mistake, but he had me keep doing it. My eyebrows change throughout the film. An important characteristic I incorporated into *Vixen* was a look with one eyebrow raised that she used anytime she was about to come on to somebody.

At nineteen, you went off into the wilderness to do a sex film . . .

I didn't know where I got off the plane but I took a Greyhound bus for a few hours until I came to Miranda, a little town near the Oregon border. Then I was driven about ten miles down this dirt road to an isolated cabin owned by a friend of Meyer's. In the seven weeks that I was on location, I was allowed to leave that spot, the cabin, twice. The entire cast was restricted, but I was the only one there the whole time. I had my own room in the cabin which I shared with Vincene Wallace while she was up there. Russ, George, and the assistant cameraman, Jamie Ryan, had their own rooms. I think everybody else camped out in tents. It was an incredible experience. Even though it was hard work, I loved it because I learned so much – much more than I could have learned in years doing major studio bit parts. I slated my own scenes. I did my own makeup. At times I was a script girl, I marked down the footage shot, I did continuity, I did hair, I did cooking. I learned an incredible amount that people in the business don't realise I know, including how to shoot fast like they must do on television productions. Just from doing *Vixen*, I learned everything there is to making a low-budget film.

Whose idea was it to have you dance with the fish?

It wasn't mine. It was horrible. Russ wrote the script in a matter of hours in a laundromat. Later, a lot was improvised. I held the fish and thought of all the different things I could do with it. I took it and put it down my shirt. Russ started the camera and didn't say anything, so I knew everything was all right. I just went on using my imagination. One thing Russ wanted me to do was to put it in my mouth. And that was just the worst. This fish smelled like a fish, and it was a fish, it was a dead fish! It wasn't a play fish or a rubber fish; it was a real fish! I just went, 'Are you kidding me? You want me to put this in my mouth?' And I did it but I remember I put my tongue way back so it wouldn't even touch the inner part of my mouth. That was horrible. But it was fun. It was different. The whole thing about *Vixen* was that I didn't question anything; I just did it. I was young and totally uninhibited. I didn't see dailies, which was good. If I had, I would have said, 'Oh, no! Why?' and changed my whole performance. Today, though

I still don't see dailies, I tend to be more guarded in the things I do.

Let me tell you about the lesbian scene. It was almost impossible for me to do, and Russ almost blew it. Everything else required of me in the script had been really fun and easy, but this was the one scene I was really nervous about. I sort of tried to put it out of my mind and hoped we'd forget about doing it. Russ saved it for one of the last scenes to shoot. Finally, on the day we were going to do it, Russ verbalised the scene to me and explained the positions Vincene and I were supposed to get into. I freaked and said, 'Oh, no, no, no, no, no!' Then he told me a story about how a lesbian told him how lesbians get it on. It was so full of shit. I'm sure it was one of his deep fantasies.

Anyway, we did four or five takes, and I froze each time and started to take on the passive role with Vincene. Russ started screaming that I was ruining the most important scene in the movie, which made me even more nervous. He wasn't handling it right at all. Finally, he sent me to my room.

Costello came in to talk to me. When Russ could no longer communicate with you, Costello could. He had been an actor himself and was much more sensitive and softer than Meyer. He suggested that I draw from my experiences to change the situation that was happening (the lesbian scene) into something else. It was a simple bit of acting advice that Russ could never give. It totally enlightened me. At Costello's suggestion I changed my breathing pattern. That brought out a freaked-out thing in my brain, and I became detached from the situation. I knew that I had the key, so I went back out and said that I was ready to do the scene. As soon as I said my first line, Russ cut the rehearsal and rolled the cameras. I did it so well that he didn't have me do the position thing. All we did was kiss while I was on top of her, body to body. It just flowed, and I think he was afraid to cut it because he didn't want to lose anything. It was about 106 degrees and really humid, and all the sweat on me was real, which added to the whole atmosphere. Russ was down on the floor pounding it and yelling, 'Great! Great!' It took only twenty minutes. Afterwards, Russ was so happy with me. He hugged and kissed me. Then he called a lunch break, because I suspect he had been turned on.

Would you have preferred a woman to have directed the lesbian scene?
Yes. The thing that freaked me out in the beginning was all the rough and crude positioning Meyer wanted. I think a woman would have handled it with more sensitivity than Meyer is capable of. I believe relationships between two women are very easy, a lot easier than male-female relationships. That's because women have much in common and are sensitive to each other's needs. Psychologically, Meyer knows how to handle his actresses. He'll put a trip on your head, and you'll work your ass off for him even when he's yelling at you or putting you down, which I think is the only way he goes about getting good performances. But Meyer cannot handle the sensitivity required to make scenes like mine with Vincene work.

If you were to direct Vixen, _how would it be different?_

The Very Breast of Russ Meyer

I wouldn't do it, and I can't see any other woman wanting to either. *Vixen* really is a put-down of women. It says that all that women want is sex, that they're never satisfied, and they'll go anywhere to find it. It shows that women have no loyalty, no sensitivity in sexual relationships. Although I didn't direct the film, I believe that I directed my own character. To Meyer the whole thing was sex, and I was a sex object just going from one sexual experience to the next. That was Meyer's whole concept of *Vixen*. I tried myself to give her something more. I tried to do each scene a little bit differently, with a different feeling. I tried to show that my husband was something special to me and that everyone else was just part of a maze of people. I don't know if any of this came across, but I tried.

To promote **Vixen**, *you went on the television talk show* Chicago. *Another guest was Betty Friedan. What happened?*
Friedan gave me so much trouble. I didn't get to say ten words. She just went on lecturing about how I allowed myself to be exploited. One side of me was thinking, 'Hey, I totally agree with everything you're saying!' But if I had said, 'You're right, lady, and I'm not going to fight you. I really did blow it for women. I really disgraced women. You're right! You're right! You're right!' – the show would have been nothing. I was there on promotion for *Vixen* and I wanted Russ Meyer to like me after the interview – I wanted to be liked – so I said that I didn't feel I had been exploited and that I enjoyed making the film, and that was it. Friedan took it from there. Give me Gloria Steinem anyday.

Although you still aren't fond of Betty Friedan personally, you would now say . . .
. . . that I was exploited and I feel that females were exploited in *Vixen*. Now that I know, I've changed a lot. That was eight years ago. A lot has happened in America since then. Then the feminist movement was very small; now it's really coming along.

I think that some woman really fucked Russ up. He doesn't like women. He does but he doesn't. I think that somewhere along the line someone hurt him drastically because he portrays women as freaks. They're plastic. It's sort of sad how he sees women: that there's no way they'll ever be loyal to him.

Are you still happy that you did **Vixen**?
I'm really glad that I did *Vixen*, and I'm not ashamed of it. In *Vixen* I never fucked anyone really, not that that's okaying it for me – or maybe that is what it's doing in my head. But I don't really need to okay it. At the time I had a lot of fun. I dug it. I've done further-out things than I did in *Vixen* in my own personal life, but that's private. And I did like her character a lot in that she had no guilt over anything she did. I know *Vixen* made it for me and that without it I wouldn't be in the business. And I'm even grateful to Meyer for giving me my first acting break.

*Vixen's lesbian scene, with Vincene Wallace on the bottom, made Erica Gavin uncomfortable.
Meyer's skill as an editor turned her nervousness into erotic passion.*

You got fan mail after Vixen . . .

I remember the first letter I got. I couldn't believe it. A fan letter! I must have gotten
300 or more letters after *Vixen*. A lot of them were from servicemen, a lot from
couples, some from women, some from husbands and their wives. Some were totally
illiterate. I got mostly 'I-liked-your-performance' letters and ones that asked for my
picture. So, at my own expense, I had a whole bunch of pictures printed up and
answered every letter personally. I really had fun. The thing about *Vixen* was that there
was something for everyone in there. Women, I think, either identified with me on the
level of their fantasy desires to be aggressive and make lots of people or because they
were gay or bi. I got a lot of mail from the South where the film was really popular.
This mail wasn't pro-racist, as you might expect since *Vixen* was a racist, but just pro-
me. I like to think that they liked me – just liked me – but I don't know. Maybe they
liked me sexually or had some deviate weird kind of lust for me. I hope people went
beyond just the sexual thing and saw more to me than that. I think certain aspects of
my character came out. It's that old Raquel Welch syndrome, I guess, that you want to
be something other than what made you what you are.

The Very Breast of Russ Meyer

What was your relationship with Meyer after **Vixen***?*

We weren't on very good terms. Russ is really hard on people, and he had done a lot of yelling at me during the last days of filming *Vixen*. After *Vixen* he was very disillusioned with me because I had lost a lot of weight and I refused to paint my eyebrows like they were in *Vixen*. Still, he gave me a part in *Beyond the Valley of the Dolls*, which made me very happy. One of the main reasons he gave me the role was because he knew from *Vixen* that I could do a lesbian scene. Ironically, despite having me on thousands of feet of film, he had me do a screen test.

The three leads in **BVD** *were given to* **Playboy** *centrefolds who had no real acting experience. Did you resent being bypassed by Meyer?*

Yeah. I resented it, inwardly. I never expressed it outwardly at all. Russ gave me the script and said, 'There are a couple of parts that you could do.' Both of them were involved in the lesbian scene. I wanted the other part that Cynthia Myers was given, but I was more or less willing to take anything. It was a major film, and they were going to be paying me scale for ten weeks. I thought it was going to be a really big film, and it was another chance to be seen on the silver screen. And at the time my part was much bigger. Looking back, I could kill Russ for cutting out so much. People don't remember me in the film until I remind them of the girl in the end who gets the gun in the mouth and gets her head blown up and has blood shoot out of her eyes, nose and mouth. That they remember.

Was Meyer less difficult to work with at 20th?

I preferred working with him on *BVD*, because with the studio I felt more protected. I didn't feel alone. People were really nice to me. Whereas, on *Vixen*, he had such control over everybody that if he was mad at me, everybody else was afraid to talk to me. After the first few weeks of shooting, there were some hassles on *Vixen*. He got angry with me and wouldn't sit at the same table and eat dinner with me. He'd take his food into the other room. It got really crazy, and I felt isolated a lot.

Meyer seemed unhappy at 20th because he didn't have the control he wanted. He didn't have you overnight on some location in nowheresville, and he couldn't really scream and do his whole number on you in front of 200 people.

Who were the other women who appeared in Meyer's films?

Topless dancers, strippers, cocktail waitresses, models. I didn't get to know many of them. As I said, I knew Haji, who is a really incredible person. She's really smart and sharp, and knows a lot about life and is very street-wise. She's been through many hassles herself and has a child. You ask her where she's from and she says, 'Plato.' I really can't speak for the other women. I'm sure that some of them get off at being filmed and having the camera there and having the whole thing centering around them. That is a big thing for me too and added to my performance in *Vixen*. I do know Edy Williams because I shared trailers with her on *BVD*. I know that Russ made a lot of promises to her about starring her in *Foxy*, which has since been retitled *Super-Vixen*.

If Meyer offered you Super-Vixen, would you take it?

No. He wouldn't offer it to me either. If he had offered it to me right after *Vixen*, I probably would have done it. After seeing the film, I don't know. After the reviews came back and the money started rolling in, I started to see that there was more to me than that. Now, I don't want to do any more independently-made Russ Meyer sex films.

What do you think of Russ Meyer as a filmmaker?

He knows how to make a low-budget film quickly. He's a good editor, I think. He's not a director, he's a cameraman. He's great at shooting that slick look, having colours very good, the light very bright, with no muted tones and everything looking sharp. As a director, I don't think he really knows what he's doing when he does it. He doesn't set out to make campy films. To him they're all serious, but they come out that way. The reviews come out saying, 'It's great, beautiful camp!' and he goes along with them, 'Yes, it's all camp. It's all a big joke.' That's bullshit! He's just still back in the Sixties.

For balance, do you have any personal compliments to give Meyer?

I don't want to say only bad things about him. Let me think . . . I know . . . One thing good about Russ is that he never once came onto me sexually. Also, at the beginning before we were fighting and he had become very defensive about me, I could go to him like a father figure and tell him my problems. All he wanted from me was a good job and to have *Vixen* be the only thing on my mind. *Vixen* was the only thing on his mind.

Cherry, Harry & Raquel

The Film Bulletin Review

Russ Meyer's latest independent production (his last before helming Fox's big-budget *Beyond the Valley of the Dolls*) continues his string of exuberant 'healthy' sexploitation entries, this one bolstered by instances of real directorial merit and a cast which seems to genuinely enjoy its work. Massive doses of sex and nudity plus a few scenes of hysterical violence are crowded into the wisely brief running time and help

The Very Breast of Russ Meyer

Cherry, Harry & Raquel

...just contemplate the possibilities!

Cherry (Linda Ashton) and Raquel (Larissa Ely) embrace in Cherry, Harry & Raquel *(1969).*
By the late Sixties, girl-on-girl softcore was a Meyer staple.

make *Cherry, Harry & Raquel* ('Contemplate the possibilities,' suggest the ads) one of Meyer's best efforts, guaranteeing it will duplicate or better the great sex-market grosses of his previous films. The Eve Productions release also marks Meyer's first use of complete male and female frontal nudity, an added talk-about factor which the director has long been on record as deploring, and obviously a sign of the times. The acting is as overstated as the thin script by Tom Wolfe and Meyer calls for, and Meyer's photography, much of it on desert locations in Arizona, is of high quality. It begins with a 'pity the poor pot-heads' narration exposing the evils of marijuana which would sound like a put-on were Meyer's anti-drug stance less well-known. From his hospital bed, venal, dying criminal Franklin H. Bolger, who masterminds a narcotics running operation across the Mexican border, orders the killing of the Apache, a mysterious Indian whose importation activities have angered the Syndicate – and about the only character who doesn't get one of the girls. Carnal-minded county deputy sherrif Charles Napier (Harry), a toothsome, granite-jawed type who looks like he stepped directly from the pages of a *Sgt. Fury* comic book, has the assignment. Bolger is often resourcefully ministered to in his bed by Harry's nurse girlfriend Linda Ashton (Cherry) as well as by blonde Larissa Ely (Raquel), the lover of Mexican-American Syndicate tool Bert Santos. Harry and Raquel make it in the back seat of an old car, Harry and Cherry make it in a sand dune, Harry and Raquel make it in Santos' bed, Raquel half-makes it with Bolger before realising he's been killed by the Apache, ad infinitum. There is a really fine scene in which the Apache drives his jeep in ever-closer circles around the doomed Santos, pinioned in his Chevrolet, in a modern version of the traditional attacking-the-wagon-train gambit. All this is interwoven with cut-ins, pregnant with meaning, of a mystic, incredibly buxom, thoroughly naked 'Soul Girl' running around the desert in an Indian headdress clutching at phallic rock formations, and seen in various surrealistic poses such as pouring milk all over herself. These amusing but confusing elements mesh into one final obfuscation at the climax: Harry and the Apache shoot each other to bits, *Wild Bunch* style, intercut with Cherry and Raquel making love to each other while high on pot, as we hear typewriter sounds and cut to Harry asking if anyone will believe the book Raquel is writing. To quote from the pressbook: 'Is it just a novel? Is Raquel's brother her lover as we see in the opening scenes? Can anyone explain the interweaving throughout the plot of the unbelievably endowed "Soul-Girl"?' Probably not even Meyer, who is seen briefly standing waist-deep in a swimming pool. More purple prose follows the usual montage of steamy highlights from the film, including unused takes, enabling Meyer to squeeze the last drop from the budget. The narration babbles on in a pretentious pseudo-metaphysical style which *must* be a put on about 'Soul' being 'the captain of your ship' and 'a constant equation', and ends up by concluding that, after all, 'Everything is relative.'

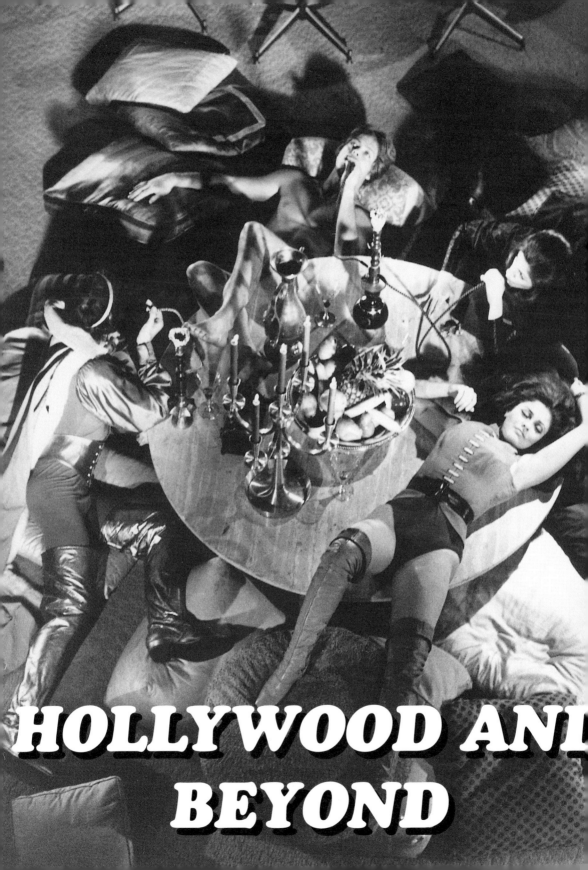

HOLLYWOOD AND BEYOND

Beyond the Valley of the Dolls

by Nick Yanni

The ads say that this picture goes way, way beyond the *Valley of the Dolls*. This time, the ads are modest. Much more than just an overblown Russ Meyer 'nudie' film, *Beyond the Valley of the Dolls* is one of the biggest put-ons ever released. It's wickedly entertaining, grossly exaggerated, and terribly camp. Although the picture has an X rating from the MPAA, it could very well have gotten away with an R rating. The X appears more an acquiescence to Meyer's reputation, since the film's sex scenes are more often than not imagined rather than graphic, by today's standards. There are, nevertheless, extended lesbian scenes, but these are rather mild. The scenes of homosexuality between two men are clearly intended as a joke, especially with 'Stranger in Paradise' as a musical background. And the more conventional sex scenes are obvious satire, with no visible frontal nudity other than beaucoup bared bosoms, for which Meyer's films are generally known.

What makes *Beyond the Valley of the Dolls* torrid is the final mass-murder sequence, the most brutally violent of its kind ever: a head is lopped off and then carried around; a gun is forced into a girl's mouth and fired, as blood spurts out and her head explodes; a German Nazi-type servant is repeatedly stabbed to death with a sword and drowned in the surf. This is all topped off by a grotesque finale in which a homosexual character and party-giver named Z-Man, in drag as 'Superwoman', reveals himself as a woman, as the berserk climax leaves very little to the imagination, to the accompaniment of the 20th musical logo.

Meyer has exaggerated absolutely everything in this picture: the perversity, the melodrama, the action, the sex, the music, the sets . . . The performers, many of whom have appeared in previous Meyer films, never act – they simply stand around cruising each other while mounting dialogue which is, incidentally, loaded with some of the most hilarious one-liners screen writer Roger Ebert could manage to squeeze into 109 minutes. Yet, the language, although incredibly nitty-gritty at times, never really offends. It's shockingly silly. That's all.

For those who are not familiar with Meyer's style of film-making, the first few minutes of this film may take a bit of adjusting to. His manner, different from any

'This is my happening and it's freaking me out!' Clockwise from left: John LaZar, Michael Blodgett, Erica Gavin and Cynthia Myers in Beyond the Valley of the Dolls *(1970).*

other major film-maker in the country, hurtles into action at breakneck speed, quickly cutting from scene to scene eclectically, without any discernable narrative intention. Yet, Meyer's seeming sledgehammer approach is fascinating. It's refreshing to see an unpretentious film which, although it does not take itself seriously, entertains. The old cliché, 'it has to be seen to be believed' applies here.

The story is paper-thin and has to do with a bosomy all-girl, hard-rock trio's exploits through the Hollywood jungle of Disneyland perversions: pot, pill-popping, bed-hopping, attempted suicides, abortion, et al, all strung together by some niftily co-ordinated cinematographic effects as the group, known as the 'Carrie Nations', sings its way through sin with a torrid tempo. The girls are played by Dolly Read, Cynthia Myers and Marcia McBroom. The group, in between grossly overdone parties at Z-Man's, outrageously played by John La Zar, meet and become involved with various 'types' such as gigolo Lance Rock, played by Michael Blodgett, lesbian Erica Gavin, star of *Vixen*, sex-queen Edy Williams, the new Mrs Russ Meyer in real life, who likes to 'do it' in the Rolls-Royce in the picture, and many more whose faces are familiar to Meyer buffs.

In the end, Meyer's film is a surprising lot of fun, despite the gore. We are treated

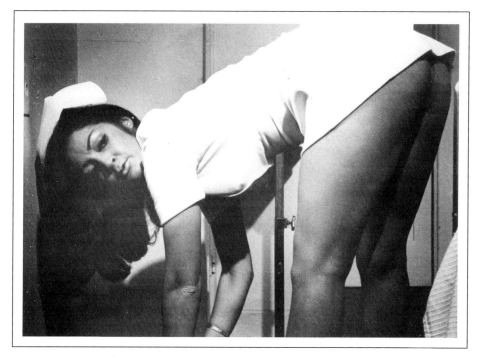

Cherry (Linda Ashton) in Cherry, Harry & Raquel. *Her short-cut nurse's uniform is another classic male fantasy, as much teasing as revealing.*

to a one-line moralising synopsis of each character's 'failings of life' at the picture's end, the audacity of which makes the film worth sitting through. Meyer even provides an epilogue, a triple-marriage, happily-ever-after ending. Commercially, the picture's prospects appear boundless, since not only will the Meyer buffs and lovers of camp want to see it, but also those who are curious as to what all the fuss is about. Considering the film's roughshod pace and incredibly soap-operaish plot, it may do much to burst the current sex-violence wave in films by simply revealing it all for what little it really is.

Russ Meyer: King of the Nudies

by Roger Ebert

The first time I saw Russ Meyer at work, he was filming an underwater scene in his own swimming pool. He has since moved into a much larger house with a much larger swimming pool, but this would have been in early 1969 when he was living a few blocks down from Sunset Strip in a four-room house with a pool that literally occupied the entire backyard. You walked out onto the back porch and dived in.

Meyer was a millionaire at the time, *Vixen* having opened the previous autumn, but he had settled into this bachelor lair with little thought of luxury. The front bedroom was for storage – sound effects, outtakes, racks of prints of his earlier films. There was a bedroom, a kitchen, and the pool. Meyer lived here for a couple of years with his late cat, Chester, and it was out of these digs that he made *Good Morning and Goodbye, Common Law Cabin, Finders Keepers, Lovers Weepers, Vixen* and *Cherry, Harry & Raquel.*

The personal nature of his films has been much written about, and everybody who is interested knows that the Meyer independent productions were shot in the wilderness with casts that frequently outnumbered (or doubled for) crews. *Cherry,* with a budget of around $90,000, was Meyer's most expensive independent film. You know this, and yet when you watch Meyer at work the intensely personal nature of his involvement is surprising all the same. If there was an auteur working in American commercial filmmaking during the Sixties – a man totally in control of every aspect of his work – that had to be Meyer. It isn't so much that he operated his own camera as that he also carried it.

The Very Breast of Russ Meyer

The underwater scene was intended for *Cherry*, and appears near the end of the film when the two nurses are revolving in the swivel chair. Meyer was concerned at this period about private censorship pressures (mostly from the Citizens for Decent Literature) in some of the Midwestern and Southern states that represent his best markets. He wanted the lesbian scene in the swivel chair, but he wanted to take the edge off it somehow. *Vixen* had contained a celebrated lesbian scene, but even there the position of the two girls was face-to-face (a technical detail much questioned by some critics) because of the censorship situation. For *Cherry*, Meyer hit upon the idea of diluting the lesbian encounter by intercutting the two nurses with subjective underwater shots of two girls embracing: 'We'll get the effect of subliminal pearl-diving,' he explained. 'We won't have to show it.'

The two actresses in *Cherry* had completed their commitments some time ago, and drifted away to wherever it is that Meyer stars go (he rarely uses actresses more than once, although he has a male stock company). So Meyer hired two different actresses to portray the symbolic underwater nurses. One of them, Uschi, can also be seen in *Cherry* as the symbolic figure named 'Soul' who appears from time to time in Indian head-dress, playing a saxophone, or leaping through wheat fields. The other actress Meyer hired was black. The original nurses had both been white, but this discrepancy did not concern Meyer. 'It's part of the symbolism,' he explained.

Is he serious when he talks about his symbolism? Almost never. One of his chief delights on his independent productions were the spoken narrations he used for prologues, epilogues, and the underlining of the morals of stories. He usually composes these right after breakfast in less than half an hour, and they are designed to sound portentous and universally significant while, in fact, having little logical meaning at all. I was working on the screenplay for *Beyond the Valley of the Dolls* while Meyer was in post-production on *Cherry*, and I was awakened at six one morning by a telephone call: Meyer wanted to read me the epilogue he had just written, and found it so amusing that he could hardly get it out between gasps of laughter. Audiences reacted to it in the same way, and yet (of course) its anti-marijuana message is part of the film's socially-redeeming content.

But I digress. On the evening of the underwater scene in question, Meyer and an old Army buddy named Fred were the entire crew. An underwater light had been placed in the shallow end of the pool, the girls were treading water in the middle, and the camera was at the deep end. Meyer's idea was to backlight the girls in order to get explicit silhouettes without excessive nude detail. The shooting strategy was simplicity itself. Meyer had an Ariflex in an underwater mount. When the actresses were ready he took a deep breath and went under. Fred stood on his shoulders and called out, 'Action, girls.' The girls went under, Meyer shot until he ran out of breath, tapped Fred on the ankle, Fred let him up, and Meyer gasped 'Cut' with a big grin. 'You don't see Preminger doing this,' he said.

All of the Russ Meyer independent films were shot in this direct and informal way, without large crews or costs, and their remarkably high technical quality is due mostly to Meyer's training, experience, and compulsive perfectionism. He was a combat newsreel photographer in the Second World War (some of the Signal Corps footage of Patton in the movie *Patton* is his). After the war, he failed, like most of the service cinematographers, to find a job inside the Hollywood union system. He moved to San Francisco, shot many industrial films, gained a reputation during the Fifties as a leading pin-up photographer, did about half a dozen of *Playboy*'s earlier Playmates, and shot an obscure mid-Fifties burlesque film in which Tempest Storm had a plaster-of-paris cast of her bust made, for insurance reasons and to offset the publicity generated by Evelyn (Treasure Chest) West.

The first actual Russ Meyer film was, of course, *The Immoral Mr. Teas*, shot in 1959 at a cost of $24,000 and largely improvised during a four-day shooting schedule. *Teas* was partly bankrolled by a San Francisco burlesque theatre owner, and was the first authentic American nudie. Meyer's assignment was to imitate the popular nudist-camp films imported from Europe. Their inevitable strong point was a volleyball game made somewhat awkward by the necessity for the male actors to keep their backs to the camera. The nudist-camp movies were one of the most pathetic and least significant of the Fifties sub-genres, and were of interest largely because of the actors' difficulties in manipulating bath towels and standing in shrubbery. Their bookings were typically limited to burlesque theaters (as audience chasers) and marginal hardtop operations.

The notion of directing the ultimate nude volleyball game did not much appeal to Meyer. He felt that the success of *Playboy* had prepared the American market for an unabashed, high-quality skin flick. The occupation of his lead character and a great many of his interior locations were suggested when his dentist agreed to let his office be used on a weekend ('The chair was well-lighted,' Meyer explained). And so Mr. Teas, played by a Meyer Army buddy named Bill Teas, came into life as a bicycle delivery-man for false teeth. The rest of the movie was more or less made up as they went along, Meyer recalls, and the voice-over narration was added later.

The premise of *The Immoral Mr. Teas* is simple: Teas is a harassed city man, cut off from the solace of nature and burdened by the pressures of modern life. He can find no rest, alas, because he has been cursed by a peculiar ability to undress girls mentally. At the most unsettling times (in a soda fountain, in a dentist's office) women suddenly appear nude. What's worse, Teas cannot even control his strange power, it seems to have been invested naturally in him, and doesn't require the magic sunglasses or secret elixirs employed in such *Teas* imitations as *Bachelor Tom Peeping*.

As plots go, *Teas* was not terrifically subtle. It is essentially a silent comedy with counterpoint narration. But the movie's jolly irony overcame any feeling of embarrassment or self-consciousness on the part of audiences who were, for the most part, seeing a nude woman on the screen for the first time. *Teas* caused a moderate sensation on its release in late 1959, and would probably have caused a greater one if more

The Very Breast of Russ Meyer

theatres had been available for skin-flick bookings at the time. It played for nearly a year in some college towns. *Teas* was the genesis for the years of increased screen nudity that were to follow; *The Wall Street Journal* claimed in an article that it inspired 150 imitations within a year, or more films than the genre had produced in the previous five decades.

Almost all of these films (the most successful early nudies also included *Bachelor Tom Peeping, Goldilocks and the Three Bares, Not Tonite, Henry*, and Meyer's own *Eve and the Handyman*) have dropped out of release and are not even available for film society rental. It is hard to say how they would look today; Meyer tends to be of the opinion that his pre-synch-sound films have dated, and he doesn't include them in retrospectives such as the one held at Yale. My own memory of *Teas* is that it worked because of its good-natured humour, not its sex, and that it would survive well. There is certainly a place for it in the current cultural renaissance of the Fifties. The other film from this period that deserves attention is Meyer's *Naked Gals of the Golden West*, an ambitious attempt at comedy and satire. It is one of Meyer's personal favourites, but did badly at the box-office because, he now believes, he paid too much attention to the humour and not enough to the sex, and was over-cautious in assigning pasties to his actresses.

All of Meyer's independent productions (with the exceptions of *Eroticon, Mondo Topless* and *Europe in the Raw* – significantly, among his less-successful titles) were to follow in the direction of *Teas* and present characters who had a problem and existed within a narrative situation. This is one of the reasons, I think, why his films found such large audiences and made so much money; the sex occurred in context (whether farcical or dramatic) and was never just trundled on screen.

This was such a novelty in the genre, and yet so easily perceived, that it's astonishing so few of Meyer's competitors seem to have noticed it. One of

EROTICA

the most distracting enemies of film eroticism is a lack of context. This is particularly true of the new generation of erotic movies – the gynaecological specials, or Frisco beaver flicks – which often reduce themselves to a survey of disembodied sexual apparatus. While there is apparently a novelty for some audiences in taking a voyage up the vaginal track with gun and camera, the general falling-off of business in the hard-core houses is not surprising.

Meyer has generally avoided full frontal nudity in his films, not because of prudishness, but because he feels that complete explicitness is an enemy of erotic fantasy. He has also avoided, for the most part, films in which nudity for its own sake is the only subject matter. All of his most successful films have placed strongly-defined characters in a particular situation, however elementary. And so his films are structured narratives, and the sexual activities in them involve characters with personalities and motives. True eroticism is therefore more possible, Meyer believes, because eroticism is caused by interplay between the imagination and a specific fictional situation – and is not inspired by essentially documentary records of genitalia.

Meyer's independent productions fall into three categories which are more-or-less chronological, with some overlapping. There were the early voyeuristic comedies, always in colour and with voice-over; the middle period of black-and-white, synch-sound Gothic-sadomasochistic melodramas; and the last five colour, synch-sound sexual dramas. All three categories were inspired to a large degree by Meyer's reading of the marketplace, and in each case he moved into the new area of filmmaking ahead of his contemporaries. Thus each of his three largest-grossing independent films was the first of its type. *Teas* was the first uninhibited American nudie; *Lorna* was the first fully-scripted sex-violence-and-nudity movie to attempt to escape the limited booking situation of the skin-flick genre; and *Vixen* was the first American skin-flick intended to appeal to women as well as men, and aimed at bookings in respectable first-run situations.

Because market considerations dictated his themes as much as, or probably more than, Meyer's personal sexual interests, it is a little tricky to attempt to psychoanalyse Meyer on the basis of his films. This is true despite his own willingness to imply that his films are his fantasies. During a panel discussion at the Meyer retrospective at Yale, he was accused by a feminist of being a breast-fetishist. His response was to grin and wag his eyebrows. In discussing the lesbian scene in *Vixen*, he has claimed that the rhythmic camera movement, barely perceptible during the photography of the scene, records his own personal response to it. 'I won't do a sex scene unless it personally turns me on,' he said in a 1969 interview about *Vixen*. 'I get involved in a scene, and I'm down on the floor looking through the viewfinder, shouting instructions to my actors, to my crew, and don't bother me then. We can discuss it tomorrow, but don't hassle me now.'

Early Sixties kitsch and tits like torpedoes in Erotica *(aka* Eroticon, *1961). Meyer's style of eroticism is more dependent on the allure of suggestion than full-frontal nudity.*

The Very Breast of Russ Meyer

This is part of his image, and it is no doubt true that some of the sexual situations in Meyer films mirror his own fantasies. But he is not the primitive or untutored artist he sometimes likes to appear to be; his method of work on a picture is all business, he is a consummate technical craftsman, he is obsessed by budgets and schedules, and his actors do not remember how 'turned on' a scene was, but how many times it was re-shot. In a genre overrun by sleazo cheapies, he was the best technician and the only artist.

He was also, perhaps, one of the canniest psychologists. His films found such large audiences because he understood, instinctively or not, why men go to skin-flicks. His imitators noticed his use of actresses with unusually large breasts, and either tried to out-cast him or derided him, depending on their own taste and preferences. But the big boobs were symptomatic of an overall psychological orientation in Meyer's skin-flicks. The girls were overdeveloped not because Meyer was a breast-fetishist (although he says he is) but because he wanted them to seem like pornographic fantasies in the flesh. His female characters were often caricatures, broadly drawn, and their common denominator was insatiable sexual hunger.

The typical non-Meyer erotic film of the decade usually featured a male lead as the dominant character. (An exception was the stylish Radley Metzger, whose leads were women and, as often as not, lesbians.) He was a satyr with no capacity for exhaustion, and he rutted his way through his co-stars whether they were willing or not. In Meyer's films, however, the women were often the dominant characters, initiating the action and (more often than not) getting too little of it. This was a fantasy more suited to skin-flick audiences, who perhaps felt uncomfortable identifying with male characters who would employ coercion or rape, if necessary. The fantasy came to the audience; it did not require identification with aggression.

Meyer's male characters fell into a limited number of categories. At first (memorably in *Teas*) they were voyeurs, primarily because in the very early days of the American skin-flick it was legally not prudent to show physical contact. In Meyer's middle period, the men tended to be impotent (the husband in *Lorna*) or aggressors (the convict-rapist in the same film). In his later colour films, the men tended to level out somewhat into the delighted partners of such nymphets as *Vixen*. Another character who often crops up is the middle-aged, hard-as-nails woman-hater. Hal Hopper played such a character in *Lorna* and *Mudhoney*, and Franklin Bolger plays him as the bedridden lecher in *Cherry*. The good guys generally got the girls in the end, and poetic justice was an obsession during the last five or ten minutes of most of Meyer's melodramas.

This mix of a variety of men and a single kind of (insatiable) superwoman gave Meyer's films the possibility of a variety of sexual situations, and there was apparently at least one that suited most members of his audience. It is hard to say. The patrons of skin-flicks have many and various reasons for patronising them, but they mostly share one common circumstance: they are without an alternative means of sexual fantasy or release at the moment. They join together in the democracy of the darkened theatre, the middle-aged husbands, the servicemen, the tourists, the horny high-school kids.

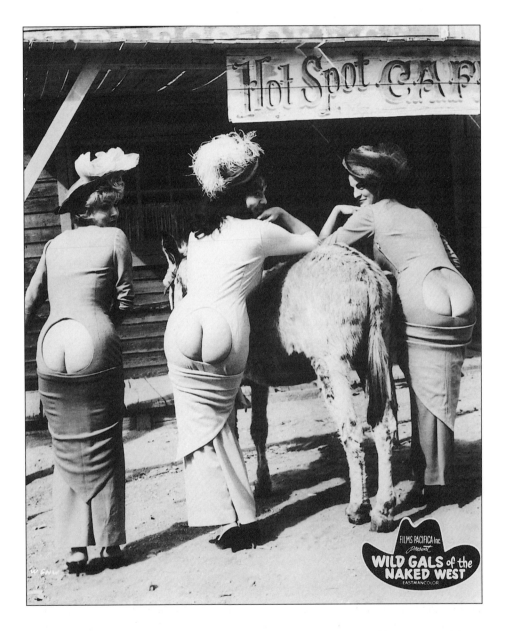

Peek-a-boo. Wild Gals of the Naked West *(aka* Naked Gals of the Golden West, *1962) is more comedy than erotica – almost suggestive of a softcore Benny Hill.*

The Very Breast of Russ Meyer

The audience is almost always all-male, and its members are careful to avert their eyes from one another and choose seats as far as possible from the nearest neighbour. Some of them come to masturbate (Meyer cheerfully calls them 'the one-armed viewers'), but most do not. They sit in silence as complete as it is depressing.

There is a difference, however, in the way a skin-flick audience reacts to a Meyer picture. I noticed it as an undergraduate attending *The Immoral Mr. Teas*, and I have seen it consistently during my latter days as a film critic. Meyer audiences enjoy themselves more obviously; they laugh. It is such a good thing to hear laughter during a skin-flick. Meyer's films never imply, or inspire, the sense of secretiveness or shame present in so many examples of the genre. They are good-hearted, for the most part, and the action scenes are as liberating and exhilarating as the work of a Siegel or Leone. What sometimes comes across most strongly in a Meyer film is a burly, barracks-room heartiness, a gusto. What came to be most impressive about Russ Meyer's work, as the Sixties wore on, was that audiences came to see them for other than specifically sexual reasons. Meyer apparently realised this at about the time he made *Lorna*, and perhaps a survey of his independent productions will help to show this development.

After *Teas*, which Leslie Fiedler praised in a celebrated review in *Show* magazine, there was *Eve and the Handyman*, starring his wife and business partner, Eve Meyer. (They have since divorced, but maintain a friendly business relationship; Eve was the associate producer on Meyer's two 20th Century-Fox productions, and they are currently co-producing *Blacksnake!*.) The male lead was once again a shy voyeur, portrayed by another of the large supply of Meyer's old army buddies, James Ryan. One of the most interesting scenes in the movie has Eve dancing in a low-cut dress while playing a pinball machine: the rhythm and cutting suggest sexual intercourse, and the scene has a nice balance between eroticism and humour. A frequent Meyer turnabout theme – the desirable woman who is rejected by the undesirable man – turns up in *Eve* in a hitchhiking scene. Unable to get a lift, Eve takes off one garment after another, still with no success.

At some point in this early period – the dates are difficult to determine because his films were not always released in the order they were made – came *Eroticon*, advertised as 'the footage the producers of *Mr. Teas* had to leave on the cutting-room floor'. Most of the movie was new, actually, and some of it is semi-documentary footage showing 'America's leading adult filmmaker' hard at work. *Naked Gals of the Golden West* came soon afterward, but was not successful for some of the reasons already noted. It contains scenes satirising several famous moments in Western classics (and ten years later Meyer was to return to *Duel in the Sun* for the final shoot-out in *Cherry*).

Naked Gals helped convince Meyer that the traditional skin-flick had outlived its useful life at the box office, and that his field was crowded with competitors. With *Lorna* (1964) he attempted to open up a new market. He wanted to make a well-acted and scripted melodrama with a strong action plot to support the necessary nudity; theatre bookers were supposed to recognise it as a 'real' movie and not a nudie, and enough of them did that *Lorna* eventually became Meyer's fourth most profitable independent production. He used a budget of around $60,000, or nearly three times his previous high, and there was a crude vitality in the production that made it work.

Lorna's plot, summarised, sounds like a morality play, and so were the plots of the next three Meyer productions: *Mudhoney, Faster Pussycat, Kill! Kill!* and *Motor Psycho!*. This group of four black and white pictures forms a quartet apart from the rest of Meyer's work, and exhibits (Fred Chappell wrote in *Man and the Movies*) 'very odd "serious attempts" full of big, gloomy archetypes and Gothic puzzlements.' Chappell even described *Pussycat* as a 'blood brother' to Kyd's *The Spanish Tragedy*, which is perhaps going a bit far to make a point. Meyer himself refers to *Lorna* and *Mudhoney* as his John Steinbeck period, when he went out into the woods and filmed stark (but semi-tongue-in-cheek) melodramas about demented hillbillies, religious fanatics, over-sexed baby dolls, violent woodsmen and obscene grandmothers.

Lorna has been widely seen, and is still in release as part of a Russ Meyer Film Festival package. But *Mudhoney* is Meyer's neglected masterpiece: his most interesting, most ambitious, most complex and longest independent production. He describes it as a case of over-achievement; it was not necessary, or perhaps even wise, he believes, to expend so much energy on a movie that had so few directly exploitable elements. Nevertheless, it won an enthusiastic response at the Yale retrospective, and one critic described it as looking like a recently rediscovered Thirties Gothic drama in the visual style of King Vidor.

Mudhoney's plot is impossible to synopsise in a limited space (Meyer's plots are either capable of being described in a sentence or impossible to describe at all). But it has to do with a fanatic preacher, a terrorised town that turns to mob violence, and a backwoods family that is apparently deficient in all genes not related directly to chest development. The visual style is unlike Meyer's other work: he opens with a protracted shot of feet walking through the village, and closes with a terrifically effective point-of-view shot of a body toppling into an open grave; in between, there is more mood, more languorous camera movement, and less quick-cutting than we expect from Meyer.

There are three films from this general period that fall outside the categories we've established. They are *Fanny Hill, Europe in the Raw* and *Mondo Topless*. Albert Zugsmith, the independent producer of exploitation pictures, hired Meyer to direct *Fanny Hill* in Berlin. It was Meyer's first experience with a film produced by someone else, and he remembers it unhappily. He found Zugsmith difficult to work with, the German backers of the film unreliable, and the shooting conditions all but impossible. I haven't seen *Fanny Hill*, but Meyer agrees with the general consensus that it isn't representative of his work.

'The only thing that got me through at all,' he recalls, 'was working with Miriam Hopkins, who was our star. The two of us pulled that picture through somehow. I told her once that it was remarkable how much she knew about making a picture, and she reminded me that, after all, she had once been married to Fritz Lang.'

The Very Breast of Russ Meyer

While he was in Europe, Meyer made an independent production; *Europe in the Raw* is of interest primarily because of the way he filmed it. He concealed a 16mm camera in a suitcase and got footage in the red-light districts of Paris, Amsterdam and elsewhere. The trailers for this film explained the shooting method and displayed the concealed equipment, but I recall thinking at the time that the footage must have been conventional and the 'hidden camera' was a fake gimmick. Meyer assures me, however, that he did indeed use a suitcase camera, that it was unhandy and difficult to use, and that he would not recommend making a film in that way again.

Mondo Topless is in some ways quite an interesting film, especially for the light it sheds on Meyer's attitude to his big-busted actresses. It was a colour nudie made to cash in on the San Francisco topless boom, and has nothing in common with the black and white Gothics he was making at the same time. It opens with a voice-over documentary about the topless industry. The cutting is quick, and we see a montage of neon signs, stage performers, topless waitresses, and so on. But Meyer is of course not interested in shooting a movie from the orchestra pit. Almost all of the rest of his footage involves topless dancers in incongruous situations. The stripper Babette Bardot, for example, is seen topless while driving a convertible through the city. Another performer, the

Jack Moran and Alaina Capri in Common Law Cabin. *Co-screenwriter Moran's soap opera plot basically served as support for the female breasts.*

remarkably-endowed model who uses the name Candy Morrison, does a go-go dance in the desert (and in doing so gains a certain immortality as undoubtedly the most voluptuous actress Meyer has ever used in a film). Meyer also has topless girls halfway up oil rigs, on top of Cadillacs in the desert, and dancing next to a railroad track (this last includes a nicely-timed zoom reaction shot of a passing diesel engineer).

The film's real interest is in its soundtrack, which consists of tape-recorded interviews with the dancers. They talk about the hazards and advantages of having large bosoms. There seems to be something subtly sadistic going on here; Meyer is simultaneously photographing the girls because of their dimensions, and recording them as they complain about their problems ('I have to have my bras custom-made'). This sets up a kind of psychological Mobius strip, and the encounter between the visuals and the words in *Mondo Topless* creates the kind of documentary tension Larry Rivers was going for in *Tits*.

After these three films and the Gothic quartet, Meyer turned to the more direct colour melodramas of his most recent independent period – the films that finally won him a general reputation. Some of his best work can be found in the films of 1967 through 1970, although the dramatic intensity of the Gothic movies is often missing. With the exception of the man-versus-machine desert scene and the final shoot-out in *Cherry*, there is nothing in Meyer's last five films to match the sustained action direction of *Faster Pussycat*. There is one montage of images in *Pussycat* – a woman in a Volvo is attempting to crush the muscular hero against a barn – that is classical in its urgency and impact. The heroines of *Pussycat* and *Motor Psycho!* were dominant, castrating and sadomasochistic, and both of these films contain very little nudity. They were intended for the action-exploitation market, especially in the South.

With *Common Law Cabin, Good Morning . . . and Goodbye!, Finders Keepers, Lovers Weepers, Vixen* and *Cherry*, however, Meyer returned to heroines that were mostly complaisant; there seems to be some kind of mellowing process going on in these films. Meyer does occasionally use a scene of symbolic castration (the hero having the hair on his chest shaved off in *Finders Keepers*, as a prelude to sexual intercourse), but he dilutes his effects with humour. (The same scene ends with intercutting between the bed and a stock-car demolition derby, and then the heroine announces that she wants to go to the symphony: 'Erich Leinsdorf is conducting Maxim Gorky's *Prelude in D Major*.')

Neither *Common Law Cabin* (briefly titled, in some situations, *How Much Loving Does a Normal Couple Need?*) nor *Good Morning . . . and Goodbye!* represent Meyer's best later work. The plots are too diffuse to maintain dramatic tension, the acting is indifferent, and there is an uncharacteristic amount of aimless dialogue. In retrospect, however, these films can be seen as Meyer's gradual disengagement from plot. The Gothic quartet was heavily plotted, sometimes (as with *Mudhoney*) dripping with such a wealth of complication and detail that they seemed baroque. *Cabin* and *Good Morning*, on the other hand, were essentially soap operas whipped up to display voluptuous actresses, and their plots were not only superfluous but distracting. Meyer seems to have realised this, and with his final three independent productions he makes an almost surrealistic use of plot. Plot is *there*, but somehow just offstage, or buried, or set aside for the moment. He uses the conventions of movie genre fiction – dialogue cliches, music that points, character stereotypes – to give us the impression that a genre story is unfolding. But then he doesn't bother to unfold it. He sort of slips around it, but so deftly that we have the uncanny impression it's all there anyway.

This directorial sleight-of-hand can be most clearly seen in *Cherry, Harry & Raquel*. It is not generally known, I believe, that Meyer edited this film under a rather considerable handicap: the De Luxe colour lab inadvertently destroyed a fourth of his footage. So occupied was De Luxe in rushing through the print of *Hello Dolly!* that the error was not discovered until after Meyer had returned from his desert location and disbanded his cast and crew.

The cost of re-shooting the missing footage was prohibitive, and so Meyer took what seems to me a brave and inventive course. He hired the actress Uschi to *symbolise* some of the missing scenes. When footage was missing, Meyer simply cut to Uschi

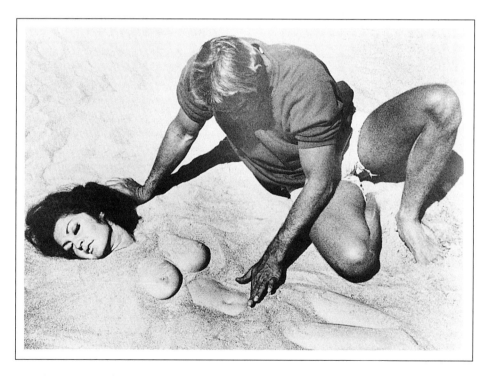

Irredeemable Sheriff Harry Sledge digs Cherry (Linda Ashton) from the sand, in Cherry, Harry & Raquel *(1969).*

doing something that substituted for the lost action or replaced it. He also shot a great many other brief takes of Uschi (who nowhere appears in the story proper) in order to give the film a consistent texture. The result is that audiences don't even realise anything is missing; a close analysis might reveal some cavernous gaps in the plot, and it is a little hard to figure out exactly how (or if) all the characters know each other, but Meyer's subjective scenes are so inventive and his editing so confident that he simply sweeps the audience right along with him. *Cherry, Harry & Raquel* is possibly the only narrative film ever made without a narrative.

Vixen is another film that suggests plot without labouring it. Its story situation is pure simplicity: Vixen and her husband, a wilderness guide, live in the 'bush country' of the Canadian northwest. Rooming with them, for the time being, are Vixen's brother and a black American draft-evader who's a friend of his. An American couple come to spend the weekend, a red-bearded Scottish communist happens down the road, and most of these characters interact sexually and/or politically with each other for about an hour.

At the end of that time, the communist and the black (who has been instantly radicalised by Vixen's racism and the Scottish communist's recitation of several pseudo-political ravings no doubt concocted by Meyer in a fit of hilarity before breakfast that morning) attempt to force Vixen and her husband to fly them to Cuba. The movie ends with a ten-minute sequence in the air, during which the characters discuss communism, Cuban Marxism, Vietnam, draft evasion, civil rights and airplane hijacking. This is the socially-redeeming content, of course, and it is just possible that Meyer stuck it all in at the end in order to (a) avoid interrupting his main storyline, and (b) chase the audience. It's certainly true that the word got around during *Vixen*'s year-long Chicago run: When everybody gets on the airplane, Meyer audiences told each other, it's OK to go.

The word also got around about *Vixen before* the movie opening in Chicago, and there was the unprecedented phenomenon of a dozen or so patrons every night who bought tickets simply to see the *Vixen* trailer. *Vixen*'s astonishing success may have been because it was the first skin-flick to really break into the quality first-run markets; it was the first booking of its kind in many engagements. It may also have appealed because it was good-natured, for the most part, and celebrated the typical Meyer gusto and lack of inhibition. Meyer himself thinks it may have made it because it was the first skin-flick designed for couples to attend on dates.

None of these factors by themselves seem to account for the movie's $6,000,000-plus gross, however. My own notion is that *Vixen* is the quintessential Russ Meyer film (not the best – *Mudhoney* and *Beyond the Valley of the Dolls* rank ahead of it). The opening sequence clearly establishes the movie's ground: Vixen, wearing a bikini, is pursued through the Canadian Northwest bush country by an unclad man. He pins her to a tree. She struggles . . . to undo her bikini. They make love. Afterwards, she gazes up dreamily at him, and the reverse shot shows him putting on his Royal Canadian Mounted Police uniform. Meyer's ability to keep his movies light and

The Very Breast of Russ Meyer

farcical took the edge off the sex for people seeing their first skin-flick. By the time he made *Vixen*, Meyer had developed a directing style so open, direct and good-humoured that it dominated his material. He was willing to use dialogue so ridiculous ('We decided to stop doing this when we were twelve,' Vixen's brother protests as she seduces him in a shower), situations so obviously tongue-in-cheek, characters so incredibly stereotyped and larger than life, that even his most torrid scenes usually managed to get outside themselves. *Vixen* was not only a good skin-flick, but a merciless satire on the whole genre. It catalogued the basic variations in skin-flick plots, and ticked them off one by one.

Of all the sex scenes in *Vixen*, the only one with genuine erotic impact is the lesbian encounter between Vixen (Erica Gavin) and the wife of the visiting fisherman (Vincene Wallace). And this one works, I believe, because Meyer wanted it to. He doesn't cut into it with asides or embellishments. He stays with the characters. His editing rhythm is deliberately sensuous. And his direction of the actresses (Erica Gavin remembered in an interview several months later) was 'exhaustive'. The scene was talked over, run through, rehearsed and finally shot so many times, she recalled, that the thin edge of exhaustion began to look like the thin edge of passion.

That was apparently Meyer's strategy; his actresses, who were not experienced movie professionals and who felt some personal awkwardness about a lesbian scene, naturally tended to be inhibited. The repetition of the scene eventually wore through their reserve until their primary concern was simply to get the scene over with, somehow, as soon as possible. And this essentially grim determination was created, photographed and edited by Meyer to result in what looks like a totally authentic erotic scene. There is no doubting Erica Gavin's wild magnetism as an untrained but natural actress, and her personality as Vixen was central to the movie's working, but Meyer's effects are almost always brought about through great effort. His willingness (in an *Argosy* interview about *Vixen*, for example) to make it all sound like a good time up in the hills is primarily for public-relations purposes.

Perhaps the most brilliant scene in *Vixen*, cinematically, is the dance Vixen does before the campfire for the benefit of the visiting husband. The scene is comically counterpointed with her own husband's pipe-smoking complacency (his characterisation is one of the funniest things in the movie), but there is no doubting her own erotic intentions. She fondles, of all things, a freshly-caught fish, finally dropping it down the front of her dress and then leaning forward so that it slides out and creates one of the most inexplicably erotic shots in all of Meyer's films. Inexplicable, because – with apologies to the Marx Brothers – why a fish?

Meyer's ability to find subjective metaphors for his scenes of eroticism and violence is one of the most distinctive characteristics of his cinema. The desert chase scene in *Cherry, Harry & Raquel* is transformed, for example, when Meyer uses camera placement music and montage to transform his wounded Mexican into a matador, and a jeep into a vengeful bull. He also has fun with his cutaways (a wild sexual encounter is likely to be translated into a stock-car demolition derby); his literal cuts among scenes (in *Cherry*, there is three-way cutting between sexual entry, a gynaecologist's vaginal examination, and a tyre tool plunging into an auto jack); and his musical puns (Z-Man's homosexual advance on an unwilling partner in *Beyond the Valley of the Dolls* is scored with 'Stranger in Paradise').

Meyer doesn't mind being obvious with these devices and, indeed, his cheerful willingness to go for an outrageous effect is one of the things that makes his movies endearing. His cuts to subjective substitutes for the same action are so literal, so direct, so basic, that they recall a kind of filmmaking not seen in the commercial cinema since the Twenties. Some of his effects are so old-fashioned that in his hands they seem positively experimental, and audiences react to them with a delight that has nothing to do with the erotic impulse of the movie.

Many critics have wondered in print, however, whether Meyer really knows he's being funny. This might seem like an incredible question to be asked by anyone who has seen his films: his sense of humour is so clearly up front. But the question does get asked. One of the New York reviews of *Beyond the Valley of the Dolls*, for example, found it full of stereotypes and clichés: The critic apparently was unwilling to believe that each stereotype and cliché had been put into the movie lovingly, by hand. My own contacts with Meyer over a period when he was casting, preparing, shooting and editing three films, left me with the impression that very little gets into one of his films by accident. He is a surprisingly enthusiastic film buff, has seen almost every American sound feature of importance, was a still photographer on location for such directors as George Stevens, and has – I keep getting back to this – an instinctively satirical sense of the ridiculous that comes from something of the same Fifties sensibility that produced Bob and Ray, Lenny Bruce, Stan Freberg and *Mad* magazine.

This became apparent to me when we began work on the original screenplay for *Beyond the Valley of the Dolls* (which will hereafter be abbreviated to *BVD*, and which I intend to discuss in terms of my memories and experiences – leaving it to others to evaluate it critically). At the time Meyer was approached by 20th Century-Fox about the project, it consisted mostly of the title, which had been purchased by Fox for a possible sequel at the time Jacqueline Susann sold them her *Valley of the Dolls*. Miss Susann had worked from time to time with several writers on a series of potential *BVD* scripts, but none of them had succeeded in pleasing the Fox management. The only pre-Meyer *BVD* script I saw was a melodrama set in New York and involving the office politics and sexual intrigues of a group of people in the magazine and fashion photography industries.

Meyer was brought in on a highly speculative deal. He was given a suite of offices, a sum of money, and six weeks to produce an acceptable treatment for a movie to be called *Beyond the Valley of the Dolls*. No specific subject matter or characters were specified. It was originally intended, however, that, the movie be in some way a sequel, and Fox had Barbara Parkins under contract to portray her original *Valley of the Dolls* character, Anne Welles.

The Very Breast of Russ Meyer

Singer Kelly (Dolly Read) with gigolo Lance (Michael Blodgett): 'He never gave of himself,' says BVD's narrator. 'Those who only take must be prepared to pay the highest price of all.'

Even in the original treatment, however, Meyer, suggested that another actress be used instead of Barbara Parkins, whose salary would have stretched the movie's $900,000 budget. Meyer's plan was to pay close to Equity minimum and use the savings to buy extra shooting days. As it happened, a lawsuit by Jacqueline Susann made it necessary to drop all of the names of her original characters from the screenplay; 'Anne Welles' became 'Susan Lake' and, in the process, *BVD* added a line to its advertising pointing out that it was 'NOT a sequel – there has never been anything like it before.'

At the time we began work on our screenplay, however, we were under the impression it would be a sequel. This explains certain residual characters in *BVD* who do not seem organic to the story. We were not much concerned with Miss Susann's original novel or film, however. Neither of us ever read the novel, although I attempted to at one time. We did screen Mark Robson's film version of *Valley of the Dolls* before starting to write, and this gave us the notion of making *BVD* as a parody. We would take the basic situation (three young and talented girls come to Hollywood, find love and success, and then are brought low by booze, drugs and pride), and attempt to exaggerate it wildly. We would include some of the sensational elements of the original story – homosexuality, crippling diseases, characters based on 'real' people, events out of recent headlines – but, again, with flat-out exaggeration. I originally saw the movie as a total parody; Meyer, with his characteristic unwillingness to stop at the merely total, saw it as a total parody *and* a total sex-and-violence trip. At one point we described our project to Fox executive David Brown as 'the first exploitation-horror-camp-musical', and that wasn't far off.

Working with Meyer, I found, was simplicity itself: I only had to devote nine hours a day, seven days a week, to the actual writing. The evenings could be spent in story conferences and discussions about the style of the film. Meyer had determined to give Fox not a treatment, but an actual screenplay at the end of the six weeks.

We devised the plot more or less in collaboration by creating characters and then working out situations to cover the range of exploitable content we wanted in the film. Meyer wanted the film to appeal, in some way, to almost anyone who was under 30 and went to the movies. There had to be music, mod clothes, black characters, violence, romantic love, soap opera situations, behind-the-scenes intrigue, fantastic sets, lesbians, orgies, drugs and (eventually) an ending that tied everything together.

In the event, it was hard to keep so many characters floating all the time, and the first hour of *BVD* moves somewhat slowly through all the set-ups of character and story. But we did manage to tie everything together at the end, with a quadruple murder and a triple wedding that effectively punished all the bad guys and rewarded all the good ones. We knew we would have the murder-orgy (we were working before the Tate case was solved, and it was one of the exploitable elements we wanted to use), but we didn't know how we would follow it. Meyer wanted to end the movie with a happy ending to end all happy endings. Inspiration came one night during dinner: Harris, the paraplegic rock-group manager, would be jostled during the final shoot-out, and his wheelchair overturned. As the violence subsided, we would cut to a close-up of his toe moving. And then we'd pull the old 'I can walk again!' routine and cut to a parody Easter Seal commercial of Harris and his original girlfriend, Kelly, walking through a meadow. A triple wedding would come as an epilogue. This was so totally impossible, ridiculous and obvious that we saw it as pure gold inspiration and used it. There's a scene near the end where Kelly assists Harris, on crutches, to cross a log across a little stream. There was some talk of having him fall into the water, but Meyer felt this would sabotage the emotional uplift of the scene and its function as visual satire. He also saw the epilogue as a parody of old Justice-of-the-Peace wedding scenes, and shot and scored it in a frothy Forties style.

The Very Breast of Russ Meyer

The movie itself seemed to take shape quickly after we had our basic premise, which was that nothing could be too outlandish, obvious, stereotyped, clichéd, gaudy or extreme. We needed a heavy, of course, and created one in the person of Ronnie 'Z-Man' Barzell, the Teen-Age Tycoon of Rock (a character that was meant to *seem* to be based on one of the young rock music producers, although neither Meyer nor myself had ever met one – a neat touch, we thought, after all the guessing-games about Susann's characters). Z-Man began his career as a boy, and it only occurred to us to make him a secret transvestite as we were writing the orgy scene. We had done the lesbian encounter between the two girls, and symmetry seemed to dictate a homosexual encounter between Z-Man and the movie's other heavy, Lance Rocke. Meyer was of the opinion that the American mass audience was not ready for an erotic homosexual scene played straight, and we had already written the Z-Man/ Lance bedroom scene as it now exists when it occurred to us, off-hand actually, to reveal Z-Man as a character who had been female the whole time. This kind of triple-twist (girl plays male homosexual) would have audiences coming out of the theatre, Meyer said, 'totally confused'. He greeted this possibility (as he had greeted the notion of making Harris walk again) with an immensely satisfied chortle.

The basic thrust behind *BVD*, Meyer said more than once, was to leave the audience wondering what had hit it. The movie had to be outrageous; a total put-on; and *still* work as melodrama. Individual scenes were conceived on two levels, usually at the dramatic level, and then at the level of whatever inside joke was to be conveyed. Sometimes this dualism works quite effectively, I think, as when (a) Harris is discovered on the catwalks of a TV studio, prepared to commit suicide on live time, and (b) the camera movement quotes Welles' famous opera-house shot in *Citizen Kane*. (The shooting script called for the camera to duplicate Welles' effect exactly, but we couldn't do this without spending extra money. We did not know at the time that the middle section of Welles' shot was, in fact, a miniature. We wouldn't have had the money for the miniature either, however, and so a zoom was used.) Another dual scene involves the surgeon, Dr Scholl, advising the grief-stricken friends that Harris may not walk again. This scene was written and scored as soap opera, as was the chess game scene between Kelly and Harris.

The movie's transitional montages, intended to symbolise Z-Man's growing influence with the rock trio and Harris's personal disintegration, were conceived as a kind of throwback to Forties and Fifties musical biographies. We didn't use *Variety* headlines only because we had already used a series of roadside signs superimposed on a map to indicate a journey; we wanted our visual fun to be as eclectic as possible. The movie originally began with a symbolic bedside and coffin-side scene between Kelly and her mother (who had been disowned by her family years before for marrying an Irish-American Catholic, and who only now told Kelly about her rich Aunt Susan and the family inheritance). This scene was cut, and about 90 per cent of the scene in Aunt Susan's photography studio (where she first meets Kelly) was also cut: Meyer felt they moved too slowly, although it disappointed him to cut a fashion photography sequence designed as a parody of *Blow-Up*.

The supporting characters in the movie were intended as a glossary of Hollywood character and name types. 'Porter Hall', the shyster lawyer, was Meyer's contribution, and a bow in the direction of the late character actor. 'Randy Black', heavyweight champion of the world, probably needs no identification. 'Ashley St. Ives', the superstar of sex movies, has a splendidly Hollywood name, but I liked her better when she was 'Ashley Famous'. Unfortunately, the Fox front office wasn't sympathetic to our reference to Ted Ashley of Warner Brothers and his former agency.

Our actual writing fell into a pattern fairly easily. We talked out the characters and the plot, making notes on yellow legal pads and then I wrote the scenes and Meyer embellished them with technical notes and indications of his visual strategy. The final screenplay was not a polished shooting script, however, because Meyer's intention was to work in his usual manner and develop scenes shot-by-shot on the sets. This was a particular challenge at Fox, where he was supporting a large overhead and daily shooting costs and couldn't afford the perfectionism of his independent productions.

He was able to gain shooting time not only by economising on actors' salaries, but by using existing Fox sets and props where possible, and bringing in associates from his independent days (including composer Stu Phillips) to work at less than Fox's ordinary

Lesbian lovers Roxanne (Erica Gavin) and Casey (Cynthia Myers). 'Theirs was not an evil relationship,' warns BVD's moralising narrator, 'but evil did come because of it.'

expense. Z-Man's ornate bedroom was mostly gotten together from old Fox props for historical swashbucklers. The elaborate living room of the Z-Man manor was actually a set for *Myra Breckenridge*, but can be seen only briefly in one shot in *Myra*.

Meyer's personal opinion was that *BVD* was really about Harris, the bedraggled manager who passes through impotence and paralysis and lives again to walk through the valley of the dolls. I was never really sure whether the movie had a focus on one character; in writing it, it felt more like a juggling act, and the problem was to keep all the characters alive. It's possible that there were too many characters, but I don't think so. The profusion of cast members gave the movie a nice chaotic feeling, and there are times when I believe *BVD* is the only movie that actually duplicates on the screen the insanely crowded feeling of the Jack Davis cartoon ads for comedies like *It's a Mad, Mad, Mad, Mad World*.

It was also slightly easier to keep the characters in mind because each one was drawn as a caricature and then typecast. Meyer was able to heighten this effect by directing all the actors in an absolutely straight style. This was his intention from the outset: to write a parody and direct it deadpan. If he succeeded, he said, there should never be a moment in the movie when any actor seems to understand the humour of his dialogue or situation. This was even true in a scene of deliberately extreme exaggeration (later cut from the screenplay for reasons of length) in which Casey, the latent lesbian, is pursued around an office by the lecherous 'Marvin Fruchtman', head of 'Bellevue Studios'. Some of the acting in *BVD* was criticised as inept and amateurish, but in fact the movie must have been terribly difficult for the actors, who were given (deliberately) impossible lines and asked to read them as realistically as they could.

The movie was also linked with *Myra Breckenridge*, attacked for its violence, and seen as the harbinger of various alarming trends. It seemed to me that *Myra Breckenridge* was a chicken-hearted movie, timid about its own vulgarity, while *BVD* was saved by Meyer's gusto. In writing *BVD*, I tried to keep a classic like *The Producers* in mind. It was impossible, I thought, to handle bad taste in good taste, but possible for a movie (as Mel Brooks once put it) to 'rise below vulgarity'.

Beyond the Valley of the Dolls was Meyer's highest-grossing film, taking in an estimated $9 million world-wide (*Myra* grossed $3 million on a cost of $4 million). But Meyer's next production at Fox, *The Seven Minutes*, was his first commercial failure. This should probably not be surprising; the project itself was unsuited to Meyer's strongest points, which are eroticism, action and parody in about equal doses. *The Seven Minutes* was intended as a serious consideration of pornography and censorship and, alas, that is the way Meyer approached it. He got serious about the theme. He had been harassed for years by various amateur and professional vigilantes, and intended *The Seven Minutes* as his statement against censorship.

The result, whatever it was, was not a Russ Meyer film in the classical vein. There were some nice touches, like making the US Senator from California into a woman played by Yvonne De Carlo. There were a few flashes of Meyer humour, like a self-important character speaking on a car telephone that turns out to be in a Volkswagen.

Erica Gavin (left) comes on to Cynthia Myers in BVD. *As in* Cherry, Harry & Raquel, *marijuana's sensualising effect is a plot device to introduce a lesbian scene.*

But Meyer's main thrust seemed to be to bring *The Seven Minutes* to the screen more or less faithfully and seriously, and I think that was a mistake. The courtroom scenes and philosophical discussions clashed with the melodrama (as they also do in the Irving Wallace novel), and the result was a film that should probably not have been made at all, and certainly not by Russ Meyer.

By this time, however, Meyer was occasionally being seen as an *auteur* whose gifts consisted of something quite apart from the dynamic, sexy, funny personal style his admirers cherish. An earnest critic for the UCLA *Daily Bruin* perceived that *The Seven Minutes* was shot entirely from stationary camera positions (except for one pan which kept a car in mid-screen, and thus had as its purpose a stationary composition), and described Meyer as the stylistic heir of Eisenstein.

I don't think that says it. He is an original, who developed his own style during a decade of independent productions he totally controlled. He has a direct, vital, literal approach to his material, and the ability to make the same scene fully effective in two different ways for two different audiences. Unlike many contemporary directors, he doesn't seem to have been directly influenced by anyone – his approach to a scene is a visceral and intellectual expression of his personality. He is considering doing a movie titled *Beyond Beyond* – a locale that, if you stop to think about it, his best films have always occupied.

The Very Breast of Russ Meyer

Interview with Russ Meyer and Edy Williams

by Maureen Koch

Near dusk on a Hollywood evening, I drove my car to rendezvous with director Russ Meyer and his actress wife, Edy Williams. I laughed to myself as I thought over the last few weeks since I'd seen his latest frolic, *The Seven Minutes*, and what I'd gone through to finally have an interview. Jet Fore, the publicist at 20th Century Fox, thought the idea was a gas and arranged for me to meet Russ and his wife one evening at their home in Mulholland Drive. But a last minute call from Jet advised me (rather tongue-in-cheekly) that the Meyers were having some routine marital problems and could they please postpone their interview a week? They'd be happy to see me after they'd returned from New York, where they were due for a screening of Russ's *Beyond the Valley of the Dolls* at the Museum of Modern Art. I called Jet the following week, whose you-may-not-believe-this response was that Meyer was hospitalised with a hernia. Of course I believed it. My phonecall to Russ the week after found him safely convalescing in his swimming pool, and tickled with the idea of having dinner that night at the Luau, a Beverly Hills spot that he thought would be a great atmosphere for an interview. And why not?

I arrived late, but spotted the couple immediately at a table near the front. Edy sipped a pink and gargantuan tropical concoction which partially obscured her delightful frontality. Russ, rising to shake to my hand, said he'd thought I had decided not to come (though I can't imagine what could have kept me away). He looked alert and athletic, and totally recovered. By way of introduction, I gave him a current issue of *Inter/View*. He quickly noted the Andy Warhol logo.

Edy: He fell asleep in *Trash*.
Russ: I'll be honest with you, I don't care for Warhol much.

He flipped through the magazine, which happened to be the special *Death in Venice* issue, making scattered comments.

Inter/View *liked* Death in Venice. *But critics don't matter so much.*
Russ: But it does, you know, they're important. Their opinions really do affect a picture like *Death in Venice*. But a picture for the hoi polloi . . . they could chop it to hell and it

King Leer holds court with the female leads of Beyond the Valley of the Dolls – *with his then wife, Edy Williams, who took the role of porn actress Ashley St Ives, at the forefront.*

wouldn't mean a damn thing. Those films can attract huge audiences just on publicity; or, in the case of *Beyond the Valley of the Dolls*, the association with a name like Jacqueline Susann. That was a very successful film despite its X rating. I hope to appeal the rating so that more people will be able to see it. With an R rating it could make another $5 million! You see, at that time the MPAA rating system had just gone into effect, and I don't think the studio realised how serious the implication of an X would be. 20th Century ended up with a kind of stigma, having released *Dolls* and another X-rated feature, *Myra Breckenridge*, almost back-to-back. But Edy and I have been on the road with both *Dolls* and *The Seven Minutes*, and I think she'll agree it's been a good experience for us.

It must be interesting to watch the audience's reactions to your films.
Russ: Sure. The two of us used to go to the drive-ins where *Dolls* played, walking around and watching people. If they're interested in what's on the screen, and aren't diverted by conversation or whatever else they're doing, then you know you've got something! Think of the film as having a socially redeeming function . . . it's keeping

them from worse evils.

What happened at the museum screening in New York?
Russ: We answered questions after the films. But they weren't the wise questions we usually get from, say, college audiences, who want to know how many chicks you make it with at the casting sessions. The museum crowd were real fans! They followed us right out to the cab. Many have seen the film several times. They feel it's a classic of its kind . . .

I haven't seen it, though I've heard it's terribly frightening.
Russ: This time around the violent scenes even shocked me, though during shooting we laughed about it. As a whole, it's a tremendous put-on, a highly exaggerated picture. But the individual scenes are the strong points. I'm interested in horror films now; I think that's what people want. Take the success of *Willard*. Those audiences didn't go to see Borgnine.
Edy: They went to see the rats. They were the stars.

Who wrote the script for **Dolls***?*
Russ: Roger Ebert. He's a film critic for the *Chicago Sun-Times*. We became friends during my earlier films, which he refers to as 'Gothic'. I think the best film I've ever made was *Dolls*, without any question. It's my genre . . . a lot of fast action. *The Seven Minutes* is in many ways a better picture, but it's Irving Wallace you know, a lot of talk. I'm not putting it down, but I guess just coming from the museum I can't help but be affected by the reaction. I'm sure it affected Edy, too.
Edy: They like it because I rape a guy in the back seat of a Rolls.
Russ: But it was done with charm and humour. It wasn't some coarse, porno thing.

I understand you've had a lot of trouble with **Vixen** *in the courts.*
Edy: This past week the Ohio Supreme Court decision came through. After spending hundreds of thousands of dollars, we lost. They said the film is obscene, and can't be shown.
Russ: Now we have to go to the Federal Supreme Court. What they've judged in Ohio is that they have the right to request any producer to remove a sequence that they may feel to be indecent, no matter what the context of the film is. They'll let me release *Vixen* if I eliminate all of the sexually explicit scenes.
Edy: Then there'll be nothing left of it.

Do you feel that censorship should be done away with completely?
Russ: I'd like to see censorship by a small minority done away with. They're dictating what the majority should see. Morals are a very personal thing, and one person's outrage shouldn't be allowed to raise such a furore.

Our society is becoming so liberated that I think eventually there'll be no market left

Meyer goes to Hollywood: the sexploitation auteur directs Erica Gavin in Beyond the Valley of
the Dolls, *simultaneously his most expensive and most successful film.*

for pornography.
Russ: If a couple are sexually adjusted, they don't need it. The people that go to see
these films may go the first time out of curiosity, but as a routine thing it really only
attracts people who are terribly deprived.
Edy: You mean horny.

Have you seen many of your husband's films?
Edy: Some of them. *Vixen* is my favourite, it's completely different from the others,
in which women are always sex objects. Vixen is the aggressor, the playgirl having all
those men whenever she wanted. All women like that picture.
Russ: In *Vixen*, I set out to make a picture that would be a kind of sexual steeplechase
. . . everyone that came along, she nailed. But it was never sordid. And the outcome
was always happy, and light. The films I made in those days never dwelt long on the
story, you know. The point was to never let the story get in the way of the film. A lot
of people complain that *The Seven Minutes* has too much dialogue.
Edy: They complain if there's too much sex, and they complain if there's not enough!
Do you think you could make a film with no sex in it?

The Very Breast of Russ Meyer

Russ: Sure. My next two films are horror stories, they hardly have any sex in them. Although there is one sequence in which a girl has an affair with Donovan's Brain. It's just a woman alone, being made love to by the sand and the wind, and the vibrations from the brain of a man who's not there. That interests me. But two people in bed . . . I've photographed it in so many different ways . . . different angles . . . Edy, what do you think of that idea, something new? The other stuff is in the past, I want to do other things now.
Edy: What do you mean, in the past? Sex is the most interesting thing there is! You can't leave all that behind.
Russ: Not entirely, but I can't let it be my only motivation.
Edy: I think sex motivates everything . . . industry . . .
Russ: I believe sex films per se have had it. I don't mean to say I'd never use it again, but I don't think you can base a film today on sex and have a success. The young people ridicule it, put it down. I'd rather make an outrageous film; perhaps with sexual overtones.

Would you make a completely straight, serious film?
Russ: I don't think so.

I saw The Seven Minutes *with another couple, and we got into a great argument over it. We thought it was hilarious, and very satirical, and they thought it was a perfectly serious film made by a person with a very warped mind.*
Russ: . . . a serious film made by a . . . That's interesting, I'd like to hear more about that . . . I think my films can be taken on two levels; as parodies, or as being completely straight . . . I guess they're both at various times. But to me, *The Seven Minutes* represents sophisticated soap.

Some of the dramatic scenes reminded me of old Dragnet *episodes. Really funny.*
Russ: But how else could you play it? It could have been very dull, otherwise.

What do you think of The Seven Minutes?
Edy: I like the way Russ can make a subject extra glossy, and glamorous, but I wanted less talk and more action, even if the book didn't call for it. I think he did it that way just to please some people, and not in the way he would have if it were a Russ Meyer production.

Do you think he's trying to change his style?
Edy: I think he was catering to the critics, not wanting them to put him down the way they did for *Dolls*. I think the public really digs the Russ Meyer style.

Do you think he wants to change his image?
Edy: Definitely. He wants to be accepted, but I believe that what he will finally be accepted for is staying himself. The establishment puts down things that challenge it,

but will respect it if it's finally successful. There are plenty of sex films around that no one goes to. Russ's style really delights and amuses audiences . . . it's a wild, comic-strip type action that entertains everyone.

Russ: I'd like to do a Western, a story about the Pony Express, one man riding 1200 miles through all kinds of peril, just to deliver a few pieces of mail. And the story would involve the people affected by that mail, say, six people who were to receive letters, or money, or whatever, and the mail's arrival a day late would seriously affect all of their lives. You know . . . destroy a corrupt politician, save a love affair, and so on. A story of fate. Different from the usual Western. It's hard to know what will make a film successful. *Willard*, for example, excited a lot of people for scenes that really threw them. And that's what I have to achieve in my next two projects . . . one of them called *Choice Cuts*, and the other, *Eleven.* They're exciting, fast-moving, highly exaggerated properties. Just mind-blowing. I think I'm pretty confident now about what the public wants to see . . .

And judging by Russ Meyer's successes, he always has been. The three of us had a gay dinner, talking loudly over the strings of Hawaiian music and surrounding conversations. Mr. Meyer signed the cheque, and the waiter graciously asked him and his glamorous wife for their autographs, and thanked them profusely. As we rose to leave the table, I noticed Mrs Meyer's bolero and hot pants, shimmering white satin in the dark, smoky room. Sheer coincidence would have Wayne Maunder, the male lead of *The Seven Minutes*, entering the restaurant just as we were leaving. After a flurry of introductions and goodbyes, I walked into the cool night. A wooden footbridge carried me over a pond of plastic lilies, through a forest of trees and giant tikis looming over this Polynesian paradise. Driving home I listened as my tape recorder recalled the evening's events. High on the joys of people and a lush tropical beverage, I read a sign as it approached on the roadway: ENTERING HOLLYWOOD.

The Seven Minutes
Review Analysis from Film Facts

When a book dealer is arrested on obscenity charges for selling a novel titled *The Seven Minutes* (written by J. J. Jadway, who has been dead for 25 years), attorney Mike Barrett works out a tentative compromise with district attorney Elmo Duncan whereby the dealer will plead guilty in return for a fine and suspended sentence. However, a subsequent incident turns the case into a nationwide scandal: a copy of the book is found in the car of an impotent teenager,

Jerry Griffith, arrested for the sex-slaying of a young girl. Determined to run Duncan for the US Senate, Luther Yerkes, a vastly wealthy scheming political manipulator, decides to get national exposure for his candidate by prosecuting the book for inciting a decent boy to commit a sex crime. Convinced the book is *not* pornographic, Barrett visits Jerry, finds that he has attempted suicide with a drug

Meyer reads from a prop book entitled The Seven Minutes, *the namesake of his 1971 Fox production. Meyer's attempt at courtroom drama was a commercial disaster.*

overdose, and saves his life. As a result, Barrett wins an ally in the person of Jerry's cousin Maggie Russell, who reveals the address of Cassie McGraw, Jadway's mistress and, purportedly, the heroine of *The Seven Minutes*. In a Chicago sanitarium, Barrett learns that Cassie is now completely senile; but he also learns that every year she receives an elaborate floral arrangement from an Oakland flower shop. Since Maggie knows the florist, she gets the name of the sender – Constance Cumberland, a former movie star now in her middle years. At the trial, Barrett stuns the courtroom by calling Miss Cumberland to the witness stand. Revealing that she wrote *The Seven Minutes*, and that she created the fictional 'J. J. Jadway' with the aid of her secretary Cassie because she feared knowledge of her authorship might destroy her career, the actress explains that the book was written to show how a woman can use her sexuality to help the man she loves overcome his impotence. Further, she states that as a result of her meeting with Jerry, during which she was able to convince him that he can be cured since his problem is psychological, the boy has finally told the truth about the murder – it was his bullying companion who accidentally killed the girl. After a verdict of acquittal is announced, Barrett and Maggie make plans for their future.

20th Century-Fox's publicity brochure described *The Seven Minutes* as Russ Meyer's 'most restrained film in the areas of sex, nudity and violence'. But the *San Francisco Chronicle*'s John L. Wasserman replied that 'taking away sex, nudity and violence from Russ Meyer is like taking away Roget's Thesaurus from Spiro Agnew.' And according to the peeved critical majority, the result was not only a 'letdown' (*Newsday*'s Leo Seligsohn) but also 'tedious' (the *Los Angeles Times*' Kevin Thomas) and 'miserable' (Wasserman). Because the picture was 'far longer on talk than action', Thomas predicted the movie's box-office failure (Meyer's first) by writing that 'a lot of Meyer's fans are going to be disappointed.' Both the *NY Daily News*' Kathleen Carroll and *Variety*'s 'Murf' called this adaptation of Irving Wallace's novel a 'potboiler', 'Murf' blaming Meyer for reducing the book's characters into 'cardboard-caricatures', and Miss Carroll complaining that Meyer 'handles the subject in a stuffy, overbearing manner.' Similarly, *Time*'s Jay Cocks and the *NY Times*' Roger Greenspun felt that Meyer, in shifting his field of action from the bedroom to the courtroom, had met his cinematic Waterloo. In particular, Greenspun concluded that the 'parody of elemental force that is the basis for action in the Russ Meyer world' was 'most fatally lacking in *The Seven Minutes*.' And Cocks charged that even Meyer's 'usual cinematic stunts (blisteringly fast cutting) and visual diversions (actresses constructed like Goodyear blimps)' failed to salvage this 'tepid' film in which 'the leading roles are portrayed by unknowns who are likely to remain so.'

Both the *Washington Post*'s Gary Arnold and *Newsweek*'s Arthur Cooper were disturbed by Meyer's new reticence in comparison to what Cooper called his previous 'twenty E-cup epics'. Cooper claimed that Meyer's 'rigorously banning the camera from the pubic zone' proved that he was 'a sexual stick-in-the-mud who would turn back the clock on sex as Erich Segal turned it back on love.' And Arnold, after asserting that 'Meyer subdued is the squarest of square directors,' mused that 'with a handful of minor deletions *The Seven Minutes* could pass as a stodgy "G" movie, and with twenty minutes or so thrown away (in a script this plodding and talky just about any twenty would do) it could be a "world premiere" on television, which appears to be the medium it was photographed for.' In contrast, while the *Village Voice*'s Richard Corliss conceded that the movie 'has virtually no sex scenes', he nevertheless praised Meyer for delivering 'a well-wrought, highly entertaining, sensible, close adaptation of a riveting courtroom drama' that resembled 'a satisfying Seventies equivalent to the programmers of Hollywood's halcyon age.' But a nearly unanimous majority implied that Meyer should return to making his sexploitation films of yore because, as Miss Carroll put it, *The Seven Minutes* only proved that 'pornography's loss is not anybody's gain.'

The Very Breast of Russ Meyer

Sex, Violence and Drugs: All in Good Fun!

by Stan Berkowitz

Lexington Avenue runs through Hollywood between Sunset and Santa Monica Boulevards. Just west of where it crosses Highland Avenue, it traverses a district that is noted for its concentration of companies which furnish supplies and services to everyone from student filmmakers to major studio technicians. One of the newer buildings on this street is divided into two storeys of offices, few of which are larger than a bachelor apartment. Anyone who feels like it can walk up the stairs to the second floor and, without having to worry about guarded gates, card keys, or even surly secretaries, he can go down the hall to room 213. There, as often as not, will be Russ Meyer, standing in front of a Moviola near the open door.

Once Meyer basked in the exclusive trappings of a major studio, namely 20th Century Fox. Now, three years and two films later, Meyer doesn't miss any of the prestige. 'An editing room is an editing room,' he shrugs.

Meyer begins his work days with a visit to a Hollywood health club; his once paunchy frame is now almost gangling. By 8:00 AM he is at his editing room office working on his new feature. His tiny cubicle shows a few signs of the draining, time-consuming work that goes on there: a shaving kit, some other toiletries; and, tucked away in one corner, a whole case of scotch. On one occasion, Meyer ventured beyond alcohol to marijuana, but he found it lacking. 'What's the kick?' he asks. 'Nothing happened to me the time I smoked it. But anyway, who needs it? I have my films, and they're a kind of a turn-on for me.' Meyer's latest turn-on is called *Blacksnake!*

What attracted you to the story of Blacksnake!*?*
I read some legend material from the Caribbean, and I also wanted to dabble a little bit in a black film. The successful films that I've made have always been in the parody genre, so I figured I would try to come up with something that was kind of irreverent, like *All in the Family*, maybe. I didn't think about *All in the Family*, the successful TV show, to begin with, but it turned out that it has a strange similarity to it.

In films like Vixen *you've shown a liberal view on civil rights. Are you worried that this new irreverent approach might offend some blacks?*
No, I think I've made it a kind of *Joe*. I've been to a number of screenings of *Joe*, and

I like the film very much, and every audience that I've seen it with, including the blacks, enjoyed it enormously. They realised that it was a big broad-ass put-on.

When we were negotiating with the primarily black Barbadian government for cooperation in the filming of *Blacksnake!*, it finally got down to a question of what the film was all about. I went through my song and dance and explained carefully and quickly the general theme of the film. The commissioner – he was dressed like a British officer, pips, swagger stick, walking shorts, a brown belt and the lot – he asked me, 'Who wins?' I said, 'Well, the blacks,' and he said, 'Well, that's fine.' So from then on, we had no trouble about official cooperation.

This is a very liberal film, extremely so, and it's told in a manner that is forthright, and with my rambunctious style. I think there are a lot of places in the film where the blacks will get up and start cheering, particularly when they start whipping the white overseer who's been whipping them for a long time. Each slave goes up and takes one crack at him with the blacksnake whip. I think at that point, there's going to be a lot of cheering. But then again, the characters are a lot bigger than life. They're right out of an Al Capp cartoon. There are only two really sympathetic people in the picture, but for the most part, they're all terribly bad people.

Don't you also try to reflect some contemporary themes in Blacksnake!*?*
Yeah, I do that. I've often been accused of making morality plays. But I kind of like to poke fun at history and, of course, current events. When I can borrow from contemporary things, I guess I get some kind of turn-on or particular excitement. Someone might say that there's a similarity between this fellow Isaiah and Martin Luther King, or somehow Joshua reminds me of Eldridge Cleaver, and those black troopers in Napoleonic costumes and riding horses – who are they? Perhaps they're a parallel to the Ton Ton Macoutes of Haiti.

This new film seems to mark a shift in your films from sex to violence.
Sure, there's a change. If you want to compare it to *Vixen*, 60 per cent of that film dealt with matters of sex, a very small percentage had any kind of violence. But some of the others had a lot of violence: *Finders Keepers; Cherry, Harry & Raquel; Faster Pussycat*. So it's not too great a departure.

The *basis* of this film is sexual. An attractive English whore, low born, has been sold into white slavery – I don't show this in the film – by a pimp in so-called London town. And she meets old Sir Alec, who owns Blackmoor Plantation, on the mythical island of San Cristobal. He falls in love with her, and he takes her back and marries her and then she literally screws him to death. Now, again, we don't see this, but she's now gone through four husbands, and the thread that keeps our story together is the young Englishman, of the aristocracy, who calls upon an elderly lord for assistance in getting a letter of recommendation so that he may go to this island to find out what's happened to his long-lost brother Jonathan. So the story is very soapy in one way.

The Very Breast of Russ Meyer

Jonathan, who was the fourth husband of Lady Susan Walker, mysteriously disappeared. There was no more correspondence from him. We find out later in the story that brother Jonathan has been emasculated and had his tongue removed, because one hang-up that Lady Susan Walker has is that any of her men who have some sort of activity with a black girl, she shuns them very quickly, and in this instance, she really did this guy in. He is what we call a duppy, it's like a zombie, and he runs through the forest. It's a gothic thing we have there. He tries to strangle his ex-wife any chance he can, for the terrible deed she did him.

What I undertook, and I realised it afterwards, was a terribly ambitious thing. I was making a period film, *à la Captain Blood*, Warner Brothers, 1934, and we almost didn't make it.

When I was at Fox, I worked with a very large crew, and was able to delegate a lot of authority. When I went to Barbados, my associate, Jim Ryan, and I undertook the responsibility of maybe an entire studio, or a portion thereof, and put together a terribly ambitious film that would have cost at least a million dollars, had it been made by a major studio. We made it for a little over $200,000, and it's a remarkable picture.

Prior to making films at Fox – *Dolls* and *Seven Minutes* – I had gone out with four or five stalwarts and we made pictures for a very limited amount of money, and because they were made at a particular time, they were highly successful. I daresay if I were to go out and make the same kind of film today, it would not be as successful, no matter how much moxie I put in.

Why not?

Because I think that the majors on one side have hacked away at the sexual freedom that I was able to express in my early films; and the porno bunch, the hard-core people, have chipped away at the audience from the other side. So the idea of coming up with a film which showed simulated sex or eroticism, no matter how attractive or how well acted, I *know* it wouldn't be a success.

So I have to look toward newer, more ambitious projects. *Blacksnake!* was certainly ambitious, especially in view of the fact that we were making a film in a foreign land, which is not easy. It's not like dealing with a film in the United States, where there are some things you just assume. Every day there was a new staggering problem that was presented to us. We had a schedule of six weeks, but then we had a contingency of an additional week and we used that week. And then of course we were down there three weeks beforehand, Ryan and myself. Then I spent one extra week with a very limited crew, just the soundman and assistant cameraman, and we went out and shot material for a montage – which are always very prominent in my films.

Were you also the cinematographer?

No, a fellow by the name of Arthur Ornitz was. He did *The Anderson Tapes, Lillies of the Field* and some others. He's a very capable cameraman. His brother, Don Ornitz, and I were in the service together and we're very close friends. Arthur did a very capable job, although it was far more than he had anticipated. He was accustomed to working with a very large crew, but I made it clear up front that he was to be the camera operator as well and he went for it, but it was a very arduous thing, working in the cane fields, the humidity and the heat, the uncomfortableness of it, and I didn't provide all the niceties that an awful lot of these English actors expected, tea and umbrellas and folding chairs and so on. There were never enough folding chairs, there was never enough tea, never enough umbrellas. I got caught up in a kangaroo court one night, and it was kind of interesting.

Were you satisfied by all the performances?
No, two did not satisfy me, and I won't go into that except to say that one of the two will probably be the most spectacular person in the film, even though his performance left a lot to be desired. There's the area where the Moviola, the editing comes into play. I expect this one actor will probably make an enormous impact, and it'll do a lot for his career. I just regret that he could have made it easier for me, but for reasons best known to himself, he did not.

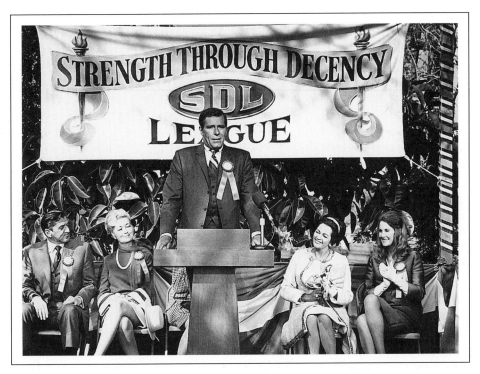

The D.A. (Philip Carey) addresses the Strength Through Decency League in The Seven Minutes
– satirising Meyer's adversaries, the Citizens for Decent Literature.

The Very Breast of Russ Meyer

Since you're the editor . . .

No, I'm not the editor per se. I have an editor, Fred Baratta, who worked with me on *The Seven Minutes*. It's just a matter of getting used to my style, and he's getting used to it. More than that, really.

Will Blacksnake! *be cut in the same style as* The Seven Minutes, *with frequent cuts, and no shot lasting longer than a few seconds?*

Pretty much so. It's a real rock 'em-sock 'em kind of thing. I find myself bored with films that are kind of pedestrian. Maybe that's a hang-up, but my cutting style seems to work. It makes the film move very quickly and informatively. Unlike *Seven Minutes* – which was a very wordy picture in which I had to try to keep this same style going – *Blacksnake!* is an action picture.

Did you have a lot of trouble casting this film?

No. The girl was a problem, because she's not the typical girl that I've had – the great cantilevered structured girl. First of all, I had to have a very good actress, which was more important than the physical characteristics. Also, I had to have someone who, like the rest of the cast, could speak with a British accent, in order to make this thing work.

I think that I selected a girl who's very . . . she's got a great ass on her, she's attractive in the same way as Brigitte Bardot. And she's a good actress. She even came up with a Cockney accent. I really went through the list in London to try to find somebody, and it's very difficult to find a really spectacular girl. Occasionally, you see someone who can't act their way out of a paper bag. In my next picture, *Foxy*, I'm very concerned about who the hell I'll use.

Do you have any idea yet?

Yes my wife, Edy Williams, will play Foxy. But I still haven't decided whether or not we can really work together. She looks great, and her acting has improved enormously. In the last six months she's been studying hard, with Estelle Harmon's Workshop, and she wants very much to do the film. She has always been associated with Fox or some other major studio, and I met her when I did *Beyond the Valley of the Dolls* for Fox. She played Edy Williams, and she did it very well. Now, she's a great admirer of this picture *Vixen*. She can see it time after time, it's a curious thing, and I think it's the basis of *Vixen's* success, because as Edy pointed out, I unwittingly made a film on behalf of Women's Lib. I didn't realise it, it was way before their time. I portrayed a woman calling all the shots. Edy's seen it fifteen times and just eats it up every time she sees it. She says, 'Christ, I'd like to do a sequel to that.' But I don't know about that yet.

Despite, or perhaps because of Vixen, *how do serious Women's Liberationists regard you?*

I don't give that Women's Lib thing a hell of a lot of thought. I get a little bit of it around home. I think that most of the people who are concerned with Women's Lib are not all that attractive, and I wonder if it isn't a crutch or a cop-out, call it whatever you want. I've been on a lot of panels with so-called Women's Libbers, I've been on a TV show with Betty Friedan. Frankly, I'm not impressed, and I don't give a goddamn what they think about *Vixen*, really. It's like Charles Keating of the Citizens for Decent Literature. He'll take umbrage with anything I do. To me that indicates a kind of inherent weakness in the individual. For want of something better to do, they will attack something that's in the public eye, in order to get themselves their own particular kind of notoriety.

Don't you think that Vixen's sexual assertiveness is one attractive aspect of Women's Lib?
I think women looked at it in a vicarious way. I think an awful lot of women would have liked to have been able to act like Vixen a few times in their lives. To have an afternoon in which they could have laid three guys, have an affair with their best girl friend, that would straighten a lot of people out. But for the most part, these women do not have the specific courage to do something of this nature, and I think they kind of lived the whole thing vicariously. One interesting thing about Vixen is that unlike *Naked Came the Stranger*, everything she touched was improved. She didn't destroy, she helped. If there was a marriage that was kind of dying on the vine, she injected something into it which made it better.

So you basically approve of what the character did?
Oh, I think that every man at one time or another would thoroughly enjoy running into an aggressive female like Vixen. I don't deny for a moment that I like aggression on the part of an attractive woman, and I don't think I'm alone in that by any means. As for the lesbian scene, it's there for entertainment, and for no other reason than entertainment. She was like a switch-hitter. You show this girl as being like a utility outfielder: she could cover all the positions.

A lot of people tend to condemn both on-screen sex and violence, considering them to be similar. How do you feel about that?
In all of my films, I've intermixed the violence and the sex. I look upon violence and sex as two highly entertaining facets of a motion picture.

In bringing these two things to the screen, have you found that they have anything else in common beside their entertainment value?
I don't know, I don't get into it that deeply. For example, maybe early in the game, when I did *Lorna*, if I did a rape scene it struck me that it was terribly erotic and exciting. Today it would not strike me the same way. I would probably treat it in a much more ludicrous fashion, more outrageous. But then again, even then I was doing that, because I always had a woman raped in the most difficult circumstances, in a swamp, or in six feet of water, or out in a sand dune. I guess my jibes at sex have been just exactly that. I've looked upon sex in a kind of a humorous, outrageous way.

The Very Breast of Russ Meyer

Are you tired of using it in your films?

No, but I don't want to get into that hard-core area, having to show explicit sex, except that I am excited by *Foxy* as a vehicle to really tax my imagination insofar as trying to portray current sex in a more explicit, outrageous way, and yet at the same time in a clever way.

Won't Foxy *also be a kind of psychological thriller?*

Yes, I don't think you could make another *Vixen* nor would I want to make another *Vixen*, just by changing the spots, or the numbers or the people. Again, I'm tuned into violence and mystery, and I came up with the idea of the so-called innocent black widow, she doesn't do it herself directly.

What happens is that she's the kind of girl who chooses her mate. Her sexual needs are gigantic, but they do not linger. She uses her male and then quickly shuns him and goes on to something else. But unfortunately for her love partner, in a very short time after he's had a relationship with her, he dies in some bizarre way.

The film's got some exciting things. I've got a sequence involving two people balling in the desert in a dry arroyo, and standing nearby are two motorcycles with brain buckets hanging on the handlebars, and the two people are attacked by a von Richtofen-type character with the square goggles and the black leather, and this individual is in a helicopter with a twelve gauge pump gun. So an interesting chase ensues with two nude people riding across the desert wearing just brain buckets, and the helicopter firing, and of course, getting the guy. They always go to great lengths to avoid shooting Foxy. One thing that I think will be significant about the film, among other things, is that she'll never get a traumatic thing about the killings. She'll never deal with the revelation that, for example, she's made it with so-and-so, and the next morning, she opens her icebox, and he's in it. So she'll go 'Agh!', but pow, she'll go into some tantalising thing, making it with a crane operator. So it will never linger, otherwise the girl would become traumatic, totally and completely wiped out. So she's just the victim of circumstance. It's got to be a light thing, and I think on the right track with a very exciting premise for a film.

You're going to try for an R rating, aren't you?

I will get one, I must get an R rating, there's no question about it. I now work in a limited partnership arrangement. I have a number of friends who participate and contribute a small amount of money, there are maybe sixteen or seventeen people. And the way things go now with X-rated films by and large, it's very limiting. And we must have an R-rated film in order to play extensively in drive-ins. So it's strictly a matter of economics.

Does it bother you to see that a basically non-violent film like Vixen *will get a stricter rating than all kinds of other, possibly more objectionable films?*

Well, you know, I take exception to people who are always hacking at violence. Violence is very much a part of our lives. But there's always that minority that will get up and scream and yell, and put down anything except Ross Hunter.

So you condemn nothing?

No, not even Ross Hunter. I'm always on TV shows with Ross Hunter. One time he lost his cool and said, 'If I had to make pictures like Russ Meyer makes, I'd go back to teaching junior high school!' He admitted that on a *Merv Griffin Show*. And then I also think he said, 'If I am ever on another television show with Russ Meyer, I think I'm gonna walk right out.' I have no axe to grind with the guy.

Who are some of the directors whose work you admire?

Peckinpah, I love Peckinpah. I like Preminger very much too. It's just unfortunate that Preminger has selected a lot of New York locale films that don't seem to go. These are two of the directors who stand out in my mind. George Roy Hill I like very much. Don Siegel, very good. He's excellent, just sensational. I thought *Dirty Harry* was a totally engrossing film. If I had cut it, I would have tried to make it move a little faster, but I admire him enormously. I think Siegel and Preminger and Peckinpah are my favourites. They're 'doer' directors. There's an action thing, a vitality about the three of them.

Isn't Vixen *an example of how you occasionally use your films for the purpose of politicising?*

Oh, that was a personal thing. We're all influenced by things. I was influenced by a couple of very good friends who kept trying to get me to join the Communist Party. They took me to a cell meeting once . . . I mean, Jesus Christ, of all people, they should have known that I wouldn't be taken by any of that garbage. Not that I was offended, but I said, 'I take it as a personal affront that you thought I had such a small degree of intelligence and dedication.' So I storehouse that stuff.

I am kind of concerned about the Democratic ticket though. I've always been a dyed-in-the-wool Democrat, but I don't feel terribly sympathetic to what they've put up at home plate. And I'm not in love with Richard Nixon by any stretch of the imagination. But I'm not about to grind any axes while I'm waiting for favourable decisions on *Vixen* from the Supreme Court, this so-called conservative court. There have been some interesting opinions handed down by a so-called conservative court that indicate no push-button thinking. There have been some very liberal opinions that have been passed down. My attorney Elmer Gertz, in Chicago, was telling me that he was very enthused about a number of opinions. So we'll see what happens. There are going to be some important decisions made in the next three or four months, I believe, about whether or not a private citizen in the privacy of his own home can look at anything. Medical photography, pornography, anything, you name it. These are terribly tough decisions that the Court has to come up with.

I'm surprised that you're still worried about that kind of thing.

Well, *Vixen's* still in the Supreme Court. It's been there for a year. No decision has been reached. Charlie Keating has been pushing this attack on 'the King of the Nudies'.

'No man escaped her island . . . or her whip.' This French Blacksnake! *(1973) poster hints at the exploitation elements undermined by casting the svelte Anouska Hempel.*

What has come and gone after *Vixen* has no bearing. If they can get a judgement against *Vixen*, literally everything else could fall. Here's a major flaw in our judicial system, letting something go on as long as this. And then, say they came out with an adverse decision. Why, there are major films that have things in them that are more explicit than *Vixen*. So it would be, as they say, a dirty shame.

You don't really expect an adverse decision, do you?
Well, I don't know. We have lost in every court with *Vixen*. We've lost on the city level, the county level, and the state level in Ohio.

In your films you've presented characters who were in the vanguard of the new morality, yet your own personal life seems to be fairly conservative, despite it all. You're married and you spend a lot of time taking care of your elderly mother. How do you reconcile that apparent contradiction?
Well, my wife thinks I'm promiscuous, but I can't convince her that I am following the straight and narrow. I have a great deal of feeling for my mother, because I think she was probably the best friend that I ever had. She was strong and long on momism and all that, but I was strong enough to circumvent that. From the moral standpoint, I would probably take exception to any friend's *wife* who might stray from the straight and narrow, and at the same time, I would take exception to *his* small or slight deviation. So I suppose in that instance I am kind of a prude, and a lot of that has to reflect back on my upbringing. Yet there's that kind of paradox with the films I've made, wherein I have glorified the swinger, as in *Vixen* – the deceit, which was kind of bland and barefaced. The perfect fool, the husband is totally believing, and totally giving, and totally good, but he's a cuckold. It's a strange thing, and I suppose my imagination has a lot to do with the whole thing.

So you see your films as being only fantasies?
That's exactly right. I can fantasise, and I think that's what the public wants to see, an hour and a half of escapism, total fantasy. I think that's what I have in *Blacksnake!* I've taken a very serious subject: intimidation of the human race, cruelty, and outrageousness, and I've treated it in a tongue-in-cheek manner. The sum total of the film will tell us whether it's going to be a successful film or not. I don't know, I'm so close to it at this point, it's difficult for me to say.

When will **Blacksnake!** *be released?*
We'll release it around Christmas time. I was just talking to the Chicago distributor, so we'll probably release it there. Uniquely this time, I have four sub-distributors who are investors in the picture, each one of them put in $15,000. I've shown them clips, and it's been very exciting for me because they've all responded in a very positive way. I'm spending an enormously long period of time cutting this, and I want to get away from

the editing because it can be a real time-consuming thing. I've got to spend more time in story development and casting, things of that nature. But I know that if I do not cut it myself, it will not have that same moxie that all the other Russ Meyer films have. And I'm just blessed by the fact that my films play and play and play, they just keep going. And I've got to make that same kind of film. Unfortunately, *Seven Minutes* was not that film.

Is there any chance that your next film, Foxy, *will fall through?*
A very few projects that I've had have really fallen through. Every time I depend upon somebody else it's not so sure, but if I depend upon myself, it's less unsure. My associate and I had two projects that did not materialise, and in each instance, those projects were dependent upon someone else raising the money. And it was just fortunate that we prepared the third property, *Blacksnake!*; we had obtained the money, just as I have obtained the money for *Foxy*, so I will make the picture. I will make it in January, no question about it. I will also do a film called *Beyond Beyond* – it's a two picture package. It will be of the *Beyond the Valley of the Dolls* genre. It will be no sequel, but it will be a similar picture. I'm going to use as my central theme a successful rock 'n' roll singer and an older advisor. And this thirtyish young man will have sampled all the fruits of life, and become a kind of recluse. But every now and then he will come out of his shell to throw an exciting party. But there's a vicious, evil basis for this whole thing. I just think it's a great vehicle to show the drug scene in a pleasant, kind of entertaining light, and sex in a pleasant, entertaining light, and violence in an unpleasant but very entertaining light, climaxed by maybe a little *Doctor Phibes* at the end. And you can guess who our man is. Is it Howard Hughes when he was 22 or is it Elvis Presley at 31? Who can say? But the basis is there, and I think the audience will associate with me and what I've done before. I think it's the basis for a very good film.

Slaves (aka Blacksnake!)
by Tom Milne

1835. Troubled by the disappearance of his brother Jonathan, Sir Charles Walker leaves England for the island of San Cristobal in the Caribbean, having secured employment at Blackmoor Plantation as a Cockney bookkeeper named Sopwith. A former Soho tart who has disposed of four husbands (including Jonathan), Lady Susan Walker now runs Blackmoor with a sadistic whip and the aid of Joxer, her brutish

Irish overseer who drives the slaves beyond endurance in the canefields, and of Captain Daladier, a black, homosexual Saint-Cyr graduate who commands her 'Ton-Ton Macoute', and ruthlessly stamps out slave rebellions. Falling foul of Joxer, who is furiously jealous when Lady Susan promptly invites him into her bed, Sir Charles stalls Daladier's amorous advances, does his best to help the suffering slaves, discovers Jonathan roaming the island feared as a zombie, and incurs the racist wrath of Lady Susan when he disobeys her command to give up Cleone, the black slave girl given to him by Joxer when he arrived. Piqued, and now aware who he is, Lady Susan delivers him to the tender mercies of Daladier, who had castrated Jonathan and cut his tongue out after having his way with him. Meanwhile, however, a slave revolt breaks out under the leadership of Isaiah, turned from his pacifist path when his militant son Joshua is crucified for putting a snake in Lady Susan's bath. Ignoring Sir Charles' appeals for law and order, the slaves hang the Ton-Ton, hack Daladier to pieces, and crucify Joxer. Attacked by Jonathan, Lady Susan shoots him but is seized by slaves and – despite Sir Charles' protests – burned alive on the cross where Joshua hangs dead.

Made before *Mandingo* and *Roots* but still timely in its parody, Russ Meyer's contribution to the slave trade ought to have been much funnier, and probably would have been with a more statuesque actress in the central role (Anouska Hempel tries hard for, but totally misses, the overripe sensual relish it requires). For about three-quarters of its length, *Slaves* seems content to raise facile laughs through melodramatic excess (with everybody overacting like mad, especially when brandishing whips which leave fierce weals painted in pretty pastel shades on the victims' backs) or through bathos ('He's so *rude!*' snarls Lady Susan, despatching an insolent slave to torture or worse), and only occasionally summoning up flights of genuine invention (the zombie arousing Stepin Fetchit reactions of terror, careering along the seashore in moonlit silhouette with his brother in fearful pursuit, but gradually lapsing into an engaging impersonation of Loopy the Loop). Suddenly, however, the film lifts itself out of the rut with the extraordinary scene mingling barbarity and blasphemy in which, with the crucified Joshua still not dead after three days, Lady Susan forces her overseer to whip him on the cross ('Do it, Joxer, he can still feel it') and Joshua expires after raising his eyes to heaven ('Father!'). Hitherto merely jocular, the characterisation of the slave leaders (Isaiah might be Martin Luther King, and Joshua any Black Panther militant) now lends a genuinely subversive quality to the final scenes: all liberal pieties about the future are swept away in a black wave of bloodshed over which one hears the dying but undaunted Lady Susan's lingering cry of 'Black and white together? Never! Never! Never!'

MEYER BOUNCES BACK!

Supervixens: Meyer Uber Alles

by T. K. McMahon

What other major filmmaker of our time can credit his films, as Russ Meyer can, as 'Produced, Directed, Written, Edited and Photographed by Russ Meyer'? The quintuple artistry of Meyer is an indication of the completely personal nature of his work, and of his obsessions. The simple fact is that Russ Meyer is the only major figure in commercial cinema today who has a total grasp of his substance as well as his form.

The substance of Meyer's *oeuvre* is well known. Gigantic women with huge breasts and insatiable, promiscuous appetites and square-jawed, lascivious supermen exclusively people his films, occasionally abetted by bizarre freaks of every description. And politics – caricatures of madly repressed Nazis and surprisingly sophisticated expositions of communist and libertarian viewpoints. A veritable stew, indeed, of modern manias stripped down to their essentials and perfectly blended with the spice of action, lust and mayhem.

Meyer's form is less attended-to, but equally important. His technique is instantly recognisable – the machine-gun editing, redolent of Dziga Vertov, interspersed with multiple repeated shots acting as touchstones or visual shorthand; lip-licking closeups of faces that embody gung-ho lust; close attention to mechanisms and appliances – closeups of radios, record players, audio speakers, candles, parts of the body, car engines, exhaust pipes, telephones, articles of clothing. Whenever sound effects or music are heard, there is sure to be a close shot of the source of sound – a technique that links Meyer with Edwin Porter and *The Life of an American Fireman*.

Meyer's entire work can be divided into two distinct categories, though there is plenty of inter-mixture between them in any one film. The two primary threads of Meyer's creative vision consist of: 1) the comedic narrative with socio-political overtones, of which *Vixen*, the masterly *Beyond the Valley of the Dolls*, and *The Seven Minutes* are prime examples; and 2) the 'film poem', less interested in the narrative than in the free-form outpouring of images and ideas, exemplified by that mad epic, *Cherry, Harry & Raquel*, with its rondo-like circularity and its 'cut-up' method of endlessly repeated and rearranged shots and sequences. Between the two main strains there is much interplay – *Vixen* is closer to the pure poetry of *Cherry, Harry* than to the almost straight narrative of *The Seven Minutes*, while Meyer's masterpiece, *Beyond the Valley of the Dolls*, superbly combines the two strains in a symphony of nuttiness.

Supervixens (1975) was Meyer's return to form – with bouncing breasts, an outlandish plot (über-sluts vs Nazi übermenschen) and the return of Harry Sledge.

The Very Breast of Russ Meyer

Meyer's newest offering, *Supervixens*, also is closer to the delirium of *Cherry, Harry*, while retaining a story-line and social comment comparable to *Vixen*, though not as tight or all-encompassing as *Valley*. The basis of the film is that old favourite of National Socialism, the concept of the 'Übermensch' (and, in this case, the 'Über-slut'). We are clued in to this right away as, over the title sequence of a tow-truck tearing through the blighted Arizona landscape of *Cherry, Harry & Raquel*, we hear the unmistakeable strains of ten thousand Storm Troopers singing a hymn to Fuehrer and Master Race on an old recording. Ensuing shots reveal it is our old pal Martin Bormann (late of *Beyond the Valley*), digging those nostalgic hits on his radio as he heads back to the service station.

Everything is super in this movie. Martin Bormann's Super Service, for example. And all the women, who are certainly super-pneumatic, append a Super to their names as prefix (Superangel, SuperHaji, SuperEula, and, of course, Supervixen herself). Clearly, we are dealing here with the Teutonic ideal, a race apart from and beyond our own, 'giants in the earth' indeed. The plot is at once super-simple and super-complex.

Easy-going young stud Clint Ramsey (Charles Pitts) pumps gas for Martin Bormann (whose workshirt name-patch identifies him as 'Marty') and is married to Superangel, a man-eating shrew of incredible proportions played by Shari Eubank. The embodiment of evil, malice and all castration anxieties, Superangel is also insanely jealous, resulting in a brawl in which she attempts to chop Clint up with an axe. Charles Napier, the quintessential Meyer lantern-jaw, once again plays Harry, a brutal cop called to the scene who roughs Clint up and dates Angel. Well-endowed as he is (Meyer here for the first time employing gigantic dildoes to put the point across), Harry is an impotent psychopath. Frustrated by Angel's vicious taunts, he stomps her to a pulp in her bathtub and drops in a hot radio for insurance, in a no-holds-barred replay of *Psycho*. Naturally, innocent hubby, who has spent the evening in SuperHaji's bar, is framed for Angel's murder.

Skipping town, Clint is picked up by a gallery of old Meyer characters, including Z-Man, SuperCherry, and the pipe-puffing Mark Trail-like forest ranger from *Vixen*. A much-needed respite, helping out a friendly farmer, ends when Clint is caught *in flagrante delicto* with the farmer's Austrian mail-order bride (the ubiquitous Uschi Digard), who rapes him in the hayloft.

Superangel is reincarnated as Supervixen, as entirely good as Superangel was wholly evil. Clint arrives at 'Supervixen's Desert Oasis' and, to the loony background chatter of ham-radio operators ('I'll chew the rag with anybody but Bruce'), agrees to stay on as 'Vix's' partner. Love blossoms and business is great until Harry shows up, captures Vix by a ruse (nobody recognises anybody else) and chains her down on a mountaintop where, clad in the black beret and fatigues of an African mercenary, Harry dares Clint to run the gauntlet of dynamite sticks launched from his 'wrist bazooka' to rescue her. I won't give away the apocalyptic finale ('your biggest bang will be your last'), but all ends happily with the patented Meyer epilogue of bareass lovers cavorting in sunny meadows.

Echoes of other films abound in Meyer's work and are rarely gratuitous. Especially clever here are the many scenes of naked super-folk running through the underbrush in evocation of the Nazi nature films and those lyrical idylls of the early Scandinavian cinema. References to Hitchcock and Antonioni will be automatic, but it should also be noted that Meyer has now incorporated the *Playgirl* aesthetic of male and female nudity in bucolic 'fantasy' surroundings.

Though *Supervixens* does not attain the sublime heights of *Beyond the Valley of the Dolls* (what does?), it is a brilliant work nevertheless. Once again Meyer has simultaneously exploited the most overblown fantasies of his audience and in exploding the terms beyond all reason underscored their essential ludicrousness. Harry and Superangel, at their complimentary extremes, deride the clichés of supermale impotence and fascistic sadism, and those of superfemale voluptuousness and shrewish cockteasing. Meyer's grotesque caricatures have acquired the status of Platonic absolutes – there is truly no 'further out' than this. Coupled with this philosophical underpinning is now a total command of all aspects of filmmaking – one particular moving shot of a breathless Supervixen pursuing Clint down an empty highway is more self-assured than are most films in their entirety. Forever on a shoestring, Russ Meyer now has a wholeness and self-sufficiency that the glamourboys of Joyce Haber's New Hollywood, with their multi-million budgets and scripts and superstars, will never achieve.

Meyer's women in Supervixens *are larger than life, as indicated by their names: SuperAngel, SuperLorna, and Uschi Digard as strapping 'Milch Fraulein' SuperSoul.*

The Very Breast of Russ Meyer

Russ Meyer's The Supervixens

In his own words

It's Horatio Alger. He was the author of a lot of books written around, I suppose, 1900, with titles like *Born to Win, Sink or Swim* and *Paddle Your Own Canoe*. They were always about a young man who was totally good and he would always set out to gain his fortune and he would always come up against terrible people. They did everything they could to do him in, but he fought fair, you know, and he always survived and succeeded in the end. So, that's just one facet of the thing.

And then I thought I would do a film that was a little bit autobiographical. Not that I'm Horatio Alger, but . . .

I borrowed liberally from a number of people I knew and it aided very well in the writing of the screenplay. And it's the first screenplay I did all myself – entirely by myself. I went to Hawaii, to a very remote resort. I made an important decision on September 19, 1973 – an important day in my life – a decision about what I had to do. And so I clambered on an airplane and went to the Mauna Kea Hotel in Hawaii and situated myself there for some eight days and totally concentrated on doing an entire screenplay. I had nine rewrites – I did them all myself, together with the actors. The actors were all very involved. They'll say, if I said this such and such a way, 'this is what I would say under the circumstances, this is more me.' And that's really what you find in a lot of screenplays that are particularly credited to the writer. I think actors contribute to the comfort of words because it's one thing to sit in a little green room somewhere and write dialogue but when you hear actors speaking it doesn't necessarily flow as well as it might.

The main female character in the film plays two roles, Superangel and Supervixen. Superangel, she's totally bad but beautiful. Supervixen, she's totally good. They're bookends. I like bookend constructions. She's in the beginning and she's also at the end. That's Shari Eubank.

What else is it? I set out to make a picture that I thought might compete favorably with today's market, in keeping with what I have done heretofore. And you know, crowded on one side by hardcore films and on the other side by major product that is very explicit. Heretofore, always, I had one super female in the film. This time, I said I was going to have *seven*. And we'd bring one in every reel, like a new linebacker. And I think it works, it really works. You don't have time to grow tired of the looks or the actions of one girl, for example.

It's not just udders that Supersoul stimulates in the cowshed. Uschi Digard was a Meyer regular, moving from supporting parts to working as a production assistant.

I felt I could make an odyssey of this. It's an odyssey about a young man who works for Martin Bormann, who is now a kindly gas station attendant in the desert. It's a film of exaggeration and great contrasts. Here's a kid who makes $70 a week, he lives in a five-room FHA house. It's an attractive little house, but it's nestled in the midst of rubble: corral, pipeyard and so on, like a little jewel. And he's living with a fantastic-looking chick who dresses in super-Frederick's finery, you know? All the time. And she's demanding as hell. She has nothing to do other than to sit home, or lay at home, in her big brass bed, thinking of ways to lure poor Clint home.

And all the girls in the film are on the make for Clint. Clint kind of stumbles through this whole movie managing to remain fairly intact, but through circumstantial evidence it would appear that he's guilty or responsible for the demise of Superangel. So he must go on the lam. And as he goes on the lam he meets the various people – SuperCherry and Cal McKinney. And all the people have names I've used in other films except the girls are all called 'Super' and they play it straight. I used John LaZar, who was Superwoman in *Beyond the Valley of the Dolls*. He plays Cal McKinney, and he and SuperCherry are a couple of muggers and they mug him. Then I had O'Luke, who was in *Mudhoney*, Stu Lancaster, married to Uschi Digard, who was an Austrian wife and giant – well, they're all giant-busted women in the picture, which I think makes the send-up. Every chick he meets is like – 'Oh Christ, here we go again!' So she's Supersoul and she speaks essentially in German and she's probably the most sexually aggressive woman in the picture, of the seven. She's just totally – she does two things, she's either milking the cow with a giant udder, or she's rapaciously taking her old man, out in the fields, wherever the case may be; and then there's a sequence where she attacks, rapes, literally consumes a young man in a manger, in a hayloft, screaming, shouting German, describing explicitly what she's doing and how it feels. Then we have a black girl who's built like the rest and she's dumb, she can't speak, she uses sign language. But she has a white father, and we never explain that . . . she's SuperEula.

Supervixen is like *The Postman Always Rings Twice*. She wears a white dress, she's good, pure. Shari Eubank. She plays both parts, it's a reincarnation thing. But, you say, did Superangel really die in that bathtub? Was she really electrocuted? And she now is on top of the mountain, with the blood streaming down, but looking beautiful and elegant, guiding the destinies of these three people: terrible, nasty, dirty, no-good Harry Sledge, policeman, former green beret, redneck, opinionated, a bum lay, sexually sick, very physical, very muscular; and Clint, clean, slim, obviously a stud but not in a pushy, forward kind of way, totally good; and Supervixen, voluptuous, pure, good, totally giving, self-sacrificing. And at the end, she says, 'Leapin' Lizards!'

Up!
Review Analysis from Film Facts

A Greek Chorus (personified by a voluptuous semi-clad young woman) announces the unfoldment of a morality tale . . . Adolph Schwartz, an aging German bearing a striking resemblance to a certain World War II dictator, uses the dungeon of his castle to practice the latest techniques of sexual bondage; assisting in the rituals are three well-endowed women and a local youth named Paul. While submitting to Adolph's sexual appetite, Paul is unaware that his wife, Sweet Li'l Alice, is having her own rendezvous in the woods with Gwendolyn, a truck driver acquaintance. Once the dungeon session is concluded, Adolph retires to his chambers; but while soaking in his tub and reading a German newspaper, he is murdered by a masked intruder who drops a piranha into his bath water. A few weeks later, an 'interpretive dancer' named Margo Winchester arrives in town and accepts a ride from a lustful driver, Leonard Box, who promptly assaults her. Margo, however, is adept at karate and she fatally disposes of her attacker with a well-placed drop-kick. The killing is observed by the sheriff, Homer Johnson, who forces Margo to become his mistress in return for covering up Leonard's death. When Margo takes a job at the cafe run by Paul and Sweet Li'l Alice, her seductive presence creates a big boom in business, so much so, in fact, that Paul and Sweet Li'l Alice open a second restaurant where Margo can perform her dance. On opening night, the house is packed, and Margo's gyrations so excite a drunken lumberjack, Rafe, that he cannot resist making physical advances. This precipitates an all-out brawl in which Paul (who has been secretly dallying with Margo) is knocked out cold. As Sheriff Johnson roars up with sirens screaming, Rafe exits – through the wall – carrying with him Margo, Sweet Li'l Alice, and his axe. The sheriff follows with a chain saw and the bloody carnage that ensues ends only when the remains of both men topple off a cliff. Following the slaughter, a shaken Margo returns to the sheriff's home to shower; suddenly she is attacked by Sweet Li'l Alice – who is actually Eva Braun Jr. As the distraught woman explains she killed Adolph because his debasement of Paul was ruining her marriage, Paul bursts in with a gun, determined to shoot both women for failing to appreciate him. But Margo gains control, and then admits that, apart from being a dancer, she is a special investigator for the government. Paul and Sweet Li'l Alice are sent to prison and Margo is commended by her commissioner for a task well done . . . The Greek Chorus attempts to explain the moral values of the tale, but is rudely interrupted by the appearance of an aggressive male . . .

With *Up!*, soft-core filmmaker Russ Meyer found himself more or less abandoned by even those reviewers who usually supported his self-rated X pictures. For example, in acknowledging that 'Russ Meyer has been roasted by the critics for his latest opus,' the *Village Voice*'s Andrew Sarris praised Meyer for his past efforts ('If he had never done anything else, *Vixen* and *Beyond the Valley of the Dolls* would remain as reminders of his power to excite and arouse'), but then added himself to the list of dissenting reviewers by concluding that '*Up!* is nowhere near that level.' Agreeing with Sarris, the *NY Daily News*' Jerry Oster (in a lowly half-star review) noted that Meyer previously 'exhibited a certain seriousness of purpose that required that his X-rated movies be treated as worthwhile undertakings.' 'But,' added Oster, '*Up!* is a dreary exercise, void of his usual good humour and imaginative photography and editing.' *The Hollywood Reporter*'s Ron Pennington disputed Oster's latter two points ('the photography is excellent' and the 'editing often provides considerable humorous punctuation'), but went on to raise two other areas of common criticism: 'The violence is extremely graphic and bloody and is likely to totally repulse a lot of viewers,' and 'the most slender suggestion of a story line' 'serves only as a feeble connective device in depicting almost every type of sex imaginable.' All in all, both Russ Meyer and his film were indeed 'roasted' – best summed up by Jerry Oster's statement that 'without wit and style, Meyer is just another pornographer.'

The Very Breast of Russ Meyer

Beyond the Big Breast: Can Russ Meyer Keep It Up?

by Dan Yakir and Bruce Davis

Russ Meyer is at once one thing and its opposite, affirming and contradicting, responsive and elusive. We tried to pin him down while growing increasingly aware that something would be lost if we succeeded too well: we would end up knowing less, precisely by discovering more. Russ Meyer is a moralist in a field where few expect to find one. His humour often makes a painful comment, reflecting a gnawing concern born decades ago. Although he is a self-professed man with no message, there is something *Up!* in his last film. What is it that is beyond the big breasts and square jaws? We found some answers and more questions.

In what category or genre would you classify your films?
Russ Meyer. There's only one Russ Meyer.

Yes, but there are several genres into which your films could fit – barely, not quite.
That's why they are strictly Russ Meyer.

Still . . .
Fun and sex, tongue-in-cheek, comedy, satire, the put-on, the send-up . . .

Many cinematic genres and clichés are subverted in Up! *Why?*
I make pictures to entertain myself. I finance them and I make them for myself, and, I suppose, one of the interesting things about my films is that people see all sorts of things, they write in different things . . . I don't give that any thought – about the subversion of any genre. I get an idea and I say: Next Tuesday at 2:45 I will make a movie. It's an idea that I have and develop as I go along, because I'm never really nailed down to anything. But I don't take umbrage or advantage or say: I think this is a take-off or play-off on anything.

It's something I'm personally turned on by. When I do my films in a very horny way: a very sensual, erotic, far-out kind of extension of my own fantasies, I don't get into a lot of heavy head-work. I get an idea – and I do it. People do write in all sorts of things, which is fine – I like that . . .

I'm interested in your cinematic taste. What directors do you like?
I like Ritt, and Siegel . . . Peckinpah.

How about people who specialise in eroticism, like Radley Metzger?
I admire him enormously. I haven't seen his hardcore pictures – I think he goes under the pseudonym of Henry Paris – I fairly enjoy pictures like *Camille 2000*. That stands in my mind as his best work. I remember *I, a Woman* and *Therese and Isabelle* . . . We were both around at the same time though I never had the pleasure of meeting him. His were usually European-oriented and mine were, what I call, shit-kicker American.

You were never interested in making hardcore films?
No.

Why not?
A lot of reasons. I'm in the mainstream of exhibition throughout the country. I have four films in the top 100 grossers of all time as reported by *Variety*. I don't know if there is another filmmaker who did it. *Beyond the Valley of the Dolls, Vixen, Cherry, Harry & Raquel* and *Supervixens*, with which I dredged myself from a lot of personal problems over the last few years and made a comeback to my old formula: big bosoms and square jaws. If you do hardcore, you're restricted outside of NY City generally to second-rate theatres.

Number two, my brand of satire, humour, doesn't normally coincide with the ultimate shot. I don't want to speak about good taste because I don't believe in that bullshit.

Thirdly, I don't think I could find young ladies like Raven [De La Croix] to do hardcore, which is important to my films: attractive, outrageously-constructed females . . .

Finally, and more important than anything else and – if I can avoid sounding corny – I don't think my mother would like it. It's very important to me. I think she would find it highly offensive. There's the primary reason.

From a purely erotic point of view . . .
I'm all for it, I think it's fine. I would try to make it outrageous. I think that the film I saw that was, probably, the most interesting of all – I haven't seen a lot of them, but I've seen several – was *Deep Throat*, because I felt that the humour came through with Reems and Lovelace.

It's just not for me, no more than doing a Disney film is for me – although Richard Schickel once said I was the Walt Disney of the skin-flicks, but I wouldn't do a Disney film or a sensitive film because I'm not that sensitive . . . I couldn't do a love story – I'd end up doing a parody of a love story. I'm very comfortable in what I do and I enjoy doing this kind of film.

I've had a little experience with a major studio, which was a nice experience – I made

This French poster for Up! *(1976) lists character names rather than cast members – including the delectable Raven De La Croix as her character Margo Winchester.*

two films, one a winner, one a loser. One X-rated, one R-rated, and I never have to go back to it. I really wouldn't be interested in doing a so-called straight film at this time of my life. I'm very happy and pleased with the results following the money, the notoriety – whatever you wish to call it. There are very few people who are that happy in what they do in life.

What sort of audience do you direct your films towards?
The Joe Gas-Stations of the world and the Joe-Colleges. In *Up!* we have – it would indicate, at least in Dallas and Houston – up to 50 per cent of our audience is women. This is the first time it's happened since *Beyond the Valley of the Dolls*. The reason for it, to a large degree, I think is because it's the first intentionally humorous film I've made – without getting laughs at the wrong places. Number two, I've always had abundant women, and now I have some abundant men . . . Learning about the reaction after the third week and the fact that they sell-out shows every Saturday night indicates that – particularly since there are couples – that women are not being dragged mercilessly into the theatre. They're there because they want to go and our observation on the scene – particularly Raven's – is that they're interested.

You say it's a funny film and yet there's extreme violence.
I like violence, but anyone who couldn't see the outrageousness of that violence should inspect their own ability to understand what is satirical or facetious or outrageous but, on the other hand, you're certainly entitled to draw any conclusion that you wish. Any man that pulls an axe out of his back and there's the sound of a champagne cork popping out or all these superficial wounds . . . I see violence in that perspective. I put

violence in my films as much as I feel my simple, feeble story needs.

Why is humour so central to your films? Is it your general attitude to life?
I take certain values. I might make some references to my mother, which I'm sure the press will have great fun with . . . Dealing with my old fantasies, it's very difficult for me to take myself very seriously. I take 'cinematic art' very seriously – the fact that it's well-exposed, well-framed and every matched-out cut works. If I don't have a matched-out cut, I go and make an insert.

Would you say you are trying to explore the various connections between sex and other spheres of life?
Maybe, subliminally. Subconsciously, I might be doing that but, again, it opens up areas . . . I like to take shots at things.

In this film, sex begins as fantasy, generally, and then, as it moves to consummation, to action, it becomes absurd and then, eventually, it leads to destruction on the part of the men.
In every one of my films someone is destroyed . . . maybe I'm influenced by retribution – one must pay for sins. In fact, in my next film, no-one will pay.

Many years ago I did a picture called *Lorna*, which was a kind of Lot's Wife, Sodom and Gomorrah and the pillar of salt, and I used a man of God, who was a Greek chorus in a frock coat. It was an important step in my films, where I – for the first time – used a script, it wasn't written on a laundry ticket. But, I had everyone pay for their deeds – the good man, who was established right off the bat as being very good, the girl – oversexed, sexually aggressive, which is my ideal of the female, anyway – is always present and, she finally realises her error and comes to her husband's rescue but, because of her sinning out in the glade, she must pay by having the ice tong buried in her mountainous bosom, perish and die. In the next one, everyone will get away scot-free.

In Up!*, only the men pay, the women don't . . . Is it just coincidental?*
This time it was different . . . My heroine is a policewoman, so she couldn't pay . . . and she stumbled, or screwed, her way through the entire community of Miranda, or so it would appear as far as the characters are concerned. The policeman had to be . . . he was in league with the devil, so to speak, by entering into this unholy alliance with Margo Winchester for carnal needs alone. So, he redeemed himself *à la* Sidney Carlton, in *A Tale of Two Cities*. But, I haven't answered your question . . . I just felt it was the best way to get rid of these two people, for future action . . . rather than just have them walk off. What the hell would I have done with Homer?

But, there were women left around at the end of the film. In fact, there was a woman who was a man: a truckdriver . . .

The Very Breast of Russ Meyer

She wasn't a man, she had the white dildo and the violin case . . . Yes, she was a husband person . . . and she went away. I must use her again, she must reappear.

Then, there was no connection between . . .
Well, I had a little male-male activity in the beginning, then I felt I would counter it with a little female-female activity. Here they are, now together as man and wife, the love in the sylvan glen in the cathedral-like forest to the strains of *Tristan and Isolde*, love and hope eternal . . . There is a little cynicism there on my part, I suppose . . . It just seemed a good idea at the time. It's me, it's how I feel and what I want to get across in the way of entertainment.

You're painting a canvas with your emotions? You're saying what you feel rather than what you think . . .
No, I give it a lot of thought. I think of the almighty dollar and the fact it's all my money. I think far beyond my emotions, let me assure you: keep the boys and the girls apart, beaver patrol, scout master . . . I give it a lot of thought, let me assure you.

The film opens with the title, 'No fairy tale this' . . .
This is not a film dealing only with matters homosexual. A lot of things that I know are hidden there [laughs] . . .

It seemed that Paul was more interested in what happened in the homosexual sequence than elsewhere . . . The expression on his face was much more . . .
Real? [laughs]

Was it also because it involved prostitution?
The hustler . . . Well, we have an inside reaction to that, and I don't want to assert myself publicly. I felt that he handled his role of the stud gracefully and with expertise.

There seems to be a trend toward sexual liberation among women . . . Do you think the outcome of this liberation will be good?
Oh, I'm looking forward. I'm experiencing nice things because of it right now.

What sort of effect will it have on the audience of your films? Do you think people are going to see your films because there isn't enough sexual liberation to satisfy them? Then, when there is, your films will no longer be . . .
By that time I'll be fishing somewhere, anyway . . . I'm heartened by the reaction of women to this film, because, heretofore, my films – with the exception of *Beyond the Valley of the Dolls* and *Vixen* – *Vixen* did attract women because she was a take-charge woman, she made her needs known and she aggressively went after them: she used men like a box of Kleenex; she threw them away when she was through . . .

There's an accusation that you're supporting women's liberation . . .
I'm not against it. I'm just against people that . . . For whom am I making my films?
I have to be against that kind of criticism that I exploit women because I don't exploit
them. My interpretation of the word 'exploit' is to force someone to work in a film
without pay . . . And I don't practice that. Everyone is paid well and, by and large,
everyone that is in one of my films comes to me to be in that film. There's a particular
kind of woman: visually, physically and mentally . . . I've never met an outright libber
who I'd use in one of my films. I couldn't put it more frankly, more straightforwardly.

I don't see how anyone could interpret Up! *as oppressing women because the women
are the heroes and victors, symbols of strength . . .*
I think it's the nudity and the intercourse . . . About that confrontation I had with
Elaine Noble, she was very polite. She'd only make a point like: 'I think these were your
adolescent fantasies,' and I'd say, 'Yes, it's true.' It degenerated into that sort of thing.
Another student asked: 'Can you conceive any kind of sexually-explicit film that would
be OK as far as your movement is concerned?' She said: 'I don't know, I'll have to ask
my mother,' that was her only retort. We must have a mother that we're both fond of.

You mentioned that in Up!, *in contrast to your previous films, you had some
superendowed males to go with the superendowed females. It's not exactly true . . . You
have superendowed females, but plastic-organ males . . .*
But I do. Leonard Box, that's his own unit . . . When he lowers his pants and turns
around . . .

Thirteen inches long? . . .
Yes, it was incredible. I had a hell of a time casting this picture. Paul's organ is real
too . . . The double-ender which Margo uses to disarm Paul is, of course, a marital-
aid, as they call them.

*Paul says to Margo: 'I loved you and I hate you.' Is this your definitive statement on
male-female relationships?*
His wife reacts to the fact. For the first time, she realises he was untrue to her. As
they're running through the fields, at the end, when she's chasing Margo with the
Alice in Deutschland knife and they're discussing the fall of the Third Reich, her
reason for doing away with her father was that Paul had his matinees with Adolf and
couldn't perform at night – to save her marriage. So, I thought I should have
something at the end to show. Finally she was willing to accept it, she says, 'For raping
my beautiful Paul' – because she raped him. Finally, he says, 'I loved you and I hate
you.' And, I wanted to get that homosexual thing . . .

That's a curious reversal of roles for a woman to say something like this about a man.

I wanted to get it in there that he wasn't all man.

This returns us to the question of who is stronger. Paul uses his gun as a substitute for his organ while Margo . . .
I just wanted to show three naked people, the guy having a Luger, which was appropriate *a propos* Alice in Deutschland . . .

Margo kicks it out of his hand with a plastic male organ . . .
I had some production problems which forced me to change the original script – I had a lot of physical karate between the girls at that point. I had the double-ender which she takes out of the violin-case – 'It's a new trick I picked up in Frisco.' And I thought that instead of having Margo throw the guy in the air . . . she could disarm him. It was thought of fifteen minutes before I shot it. It was no great conception thought of weeks before. So many things that I do in film are developed on the spot.

There's a lot of spontaneity.
Everything . . .

Do you think you communicate your fantasies better in these moments of spontaneity than when you follow a script?
I have to have a general outline to begin with. I really shine under pressure . . . really heavy pressure. If I've got a lot of problems, like my leading man didn't have a bowel movement in ten days, he's loggy and can't move around – I mean it: Homer couldn't take a crap for ten days and he's eating like a goddamn horse every night, he was really read to sink.

La Taurus Cinematografica presenta

le deliranti avventure erotiche dell'agente speciale MARGO'

con MAUREEN SPRING · JOHN SMITH · OBE WAHN · FAYE YOUNG
DIRETTO DA A. FABRITZI

This Italian poster for Up! *highlights one of Meyer's trademark 'klutzes, buffoons, clods, dopes' with an impotency problem.*

The reversal of male-female roles is a theme that goes through the film. For example: Adolf was a master, but here he's a slave while Alice herself keeps giving Paul orders, and yet she reluctantly goes to make a phone call when he orders her to – which is an exception.
Well, she lied to him in the saloon and, I think, when you lie you are defensive.

But, wouldn't you say that the characters are reversing roles?
Yes, but this is a matter of convenience. I wanted to see Alice out of the place, so she could get a proper entrance later. Thus I had her run miles to the nearest phone at the bottom of a dry river bed. Had she stayed in the saloon, I couldn't have had my little raping thing and have her stand by idly and see her husband thrown over the side. It's like an Olson-Johnson *Hellzapoppin'* – somebody rushes in, does something and then rushes out and somebody else – like room service – comes in and the guy says: 'Aha! I catch you in bed with my wife!' It just works for my kind of 'slap-dash'. Not all of it, but a lot of it is just right off the wall.

A matter of convenience?
It's convenient, but there's, I suppose, some sort of cinematic brilliance that strikes me, like a smack in the kisser, and I'm able to work it out to the advantage of the film – it makes it even more comic-strip in its concept.

To return to the relationship between men and women, all the women take some severe beatings – Margo is ferociously beaten in the stream – but then never bleed or are bruised . . .
I'm glad you observed . . .

And yet the men are brutalised . . .
Except when they get hit in the nuts – the man gets a terrible blow – and in one minute he's ready to let her have it. And I've had it in every film.

Why can't the women be hurt?
They have to be attractive; I can't have any woman who is disfigured. The blood must be in a careful area, so, in a sense, it accentuates the breast because it curves . . . All this is carefully scripted and thought-out. A woman would not have a cut lip or a black eye, according to my kind of *Playboy*-centrefold approach to cinematography. When they're screwing, it's like Rodin had happened on the scene . . . and every crevice, crack and bulge is scripted.

You mentioned Rodin, a lot of the fucking occurs on a tree-stump, which looks like a sculpture by . . .
It has that quality, like a gargoyle you'd find in Nôtre Dame . . . And always, on the sand, when he penetrates her from her rear, the tree-stump becomes like a pedestal.

The Very Breast of Russ Meyer

You use the chorus in an unusual way. The chorus traditionally presents the voice of the community and usually stands apart from the action. In Up! *the chorus begins by simply describing the action and by the film's end has joined in it.*

This is something left over from my industrial filmmaking days, when I was working for Southern Pacific Railroad. In all those films, there was always kind of a recap about, 'This is a good job.' The foreman would say, 'We make straight the curve and the river doesn't destroy the road-bend,' and I think that had a big influence on me.

Applying it to commercial films, I always at the end of the films have a recap about everybody, where they went wrong, in an epilogue. Rafe – the victim of momism and the liquor lobby, Paul – out of fellatio is its own reward, Sweet Li'l Alice – a filly ridden hard and put away wet – she's in the water and wet; I think that's funny. Margo Winchester *über alles* – the girl's having an orgasm and is encountered in a leafy glen . . . So, again, it's a style that I've evolved through the years of inter-cutting the narrator with visuals.

What was the function of the Headperson?

Well, I didn't want anyone to think that I was making a film dealing with homosexuality, and I felt that the inclusion of those heroically bosomed women added to the visual – and that would lead the audience to believe that I hadn't slipped a cog right off the bat. So, then the idea of holding him, that means: mothering him, Adolf Schwartz . . .

In the film, there are no ordinary women, there are many ordinary men in the restaurant . . .

It's the crew . . .

And no children . . .

Only in one shot. They happened to stray by. When Homer was getting head in the car, there were some schoolchildren passing by – it was shot over the trunk of a car – it was a nice shot of little children passing by, not paying any attention to what was going on.

We don't have any ordinary women . . .

Alice is kind of ordinary, normal as far as a pragmatic cantilever female. She had a great figure but was small, in contrast to Raven who is Junoesque.

Isn't that congruent with her attitude? She's not the strongest . . .

At the end she develops a pretty strong personality – she kicks the crap out of Margo . . .

Were you making any social comment in the film? It portrays people of certain professions who seem to interact – there are no real outsiders, except Margo but then

she's a policewoman – so it fits . . .
Yes, but who is she, running down the highway with a light satin suit – it's ludicrous
. . . The cop is a composite of three or four policemen I've known – my old man was
a cop and I kind of like to take umbrage with policemen. I had to counter some of
all this blue-knight crap.

*Do you think Miranda was kind of a little Peyton Place, where everything seems
pleasant and quiet and yet . . . ?*
All this seething unrest beneath the surface, yes.

Was it social comment you were making?
Oh, I suppose indirectly it existed. Again, when I perceive an idea – I look for a
location. When you ask, 'Do I think' – there's a monstrous amount of thinking – it's
the loneliest job in the world being a filmmaker: you're alone, very much of the time
even though you're surrounded by people who bust their ass for you – you still have
those moments when you're alone and you think: 'Am I really putting it together
right? Am I trying hard enough? Am I busting my ass sufficiently? Am I getting the
most out of these people?' I find always that in the morning I'm regenerated, full of
fire and brimstone – ideas come faster than I can relate them, almost.

You wouldn't say you are making message films?
I did a couple of times and I fell on my ass: *The Seven Minutes*, Irving Wallace's
supposed best-seller. I thought I should be a spokesman at the time because I was in
the courts of the State of Ohio with Citizens for Decent Literature, defending *Vixen*,
which was the *Deep Throat* of its day, and I felt I should be the one to make the
statement about freedom of expression, First Amendment rights . . . The audience was
not used to that kind of film from me – they expected the same kind of zippity-do-
da that *Beyond the Valley of the Dolls* had. That's why I ended with 30 minutes in the
courtroom. I did another message film – except that I believe that each film I make
is supposedly entertaining – I made *Blacksnake!* in Barbados on the slavery question
in the 1880s and I thought it was great, but everybody hated it – the blacks hated it,
I was three years too late, I used a foreign cast, the British had costumes, there was
this thin expert leading lady and it all came together at S.M.U. at a film festival. A
guy got up from the audience and shouted: 'Where's the broad with the big tits?' And
like 1,000 students stood up and said – 'Y-E-A-H!' It was like a James Cagney prison
epic – with the tin cups. And then, my wife was next to me at the time and she said,
'You should've used me.' Even though it would've been a pain in the ass, I probably
should've. Never work with your wife.

*Don't you think you can relate a message with big breasts and square jaws, with sex,
violence, and humour?*

The Very Breast of Russ Meyer

But, why? Why should I have a message? I purport to do nothing but entertain. Maybe it's better to have people write in all kinds of undercurrents and undertones, conclude things that I might chuckle about.

You said you emphasise form over subject-matter. Before you start working, do you have any theoretical framework about structuring the film? How does it work? What does form consist of for you? I mean, do you have a concept of the format that you want to give the film based on your idea of the plot?
I suppose so, because it's a one-man band. I look at everything like I look at you now; through a finder, through a frame . . . having had such a big background in cinematography. I deal with each sequence individually, I'm sure, as any film director would but I have an editorial concept which I think singularly is the most important contribution any filmmaker can make to a film. There is one man who puts it together – it's the editor; the man who gives the picture form. I just shoot so many – there are 2,300 to 2,800 cuts in my film, far more than in a straight film, and it's a rhythm that I have going. The form evolves out of the editing – but there's plenty of raw material to work with.

Wasn't there a time when you didn't do your own editing?
No, I've always done it. Often, I've had some weird credit for it, but I've cut every picture I've ever made.

Can you elaborate on the ending of the film?
It just occurred to me: Why not say that Adolf didn't die, but just lost his jewels? So, I put the mail box there and it fell. And, in the background you hear Martin Bormann who is saying: 'Should we hear the Horst Wessel Lied,' or, as it's more probably known, 'Die Fahne hoch' – which is banned in Germany, it's an original brown-shirt music, composed by Horst Wessel who was one of Hitler's early cohorts and we hear it and then there's a scratch of the needle and a loud slap and the guy says, 'Schmuck, I told you never to play it again.' And the guy with the high voice says, 'Jawohl, Martin.'

With which of your films are you most satisfired?
Up! and *Beyond the Valley of the Dolls.*

Do you see Up! *as a turning point in your career?*
I would hope it would further my career, because I got away from what I do best for four years for personal reasons. *Supervixens* was my getting back to what I do best and it did very well, but it didn't have the sexual content that I think it should've had. This time, I really set out to staff with a lot of horizontal activity, heroic horizontal activity.

What's the meaning of the title?

Well, I like one-word titles; could be 'up yours' or whatever's the connotation. It lends itself very well – the phallic thing – you could also call it *Ulp!* if you wanted to . . . Ebert, the newspaperman who did *Beyond the Valley of the Dolls*, and I collaborated on a film [screenplay] called *Up the Valley of the Beyond*, which was a sequel to *Beyond the Valley of the Dolls*. A lot of people have asked me why, but that really is the answer: why?

Do you tell your actors what to do?
I'm pretty specific, it's not all that complicated what they've got to do. There's not too much time wasted on expositions or dialogues.

Aren't you concerned that the ethnic references would offend some people?
Which ones?

For one, making Hitler a Jew?
Well, I thought that was the biggest joke of all. That was his ultimate disguise as Schwarz – Hitler, at 78, debauched.

When you have a final product, when you sit down and look at what you've done, do you see a theme? You begin with good, clean fun – and when you end up, is there something beyond it?
[Pause] That's a hard one to answer. I look upon the film when I finish it, as to whether or not there are areas that I find dull and wish they would go by more quickly. This is the first film that I've made that I don't feel this way. It moves fast enough and it's sufficiently accelerating and exhilarating that I don't feel any discomfiture as to whether the audience will like it. I think about what I'm going to do next. I feel like I've finished this chapter and I'm thinking of the next . . .

Then you're writing a book?
Not necessarily, but someday I will.

In terms of your films, if each film is a chapter, you're putting them together as a book – and books always have themes . . .
I can't answer. Maybe, the theme is: I did it my way. Being the maverick, expressing myself in a way that an incredible amount of people can sit down and maybe enjoy the same kind of fantasy that I had. In spite of everything else, what I do is what I really want to do and the devil take the hindmost.

The Very Breast of Russ Meyer

Rock is Sick and Living in London

by Charles M. Young

A little before midnight, my taxi arrives at a club called the Vortex. The weather is atypically dry, and the neighbourhood, like the rest of London, is a shopping district with its eye on the tourist trade. Half a block away ten or twelve teenaged boys dressed like horror-movie morticians jump up and down and hit each other. Their hair is short, either greased back or combed to stick straight out with a pomade of Vaseline and talcum powder. Periodically, one chases another out of the pack, grabs the other's arm and twists it until he screams with pain. Then they rush back laughing and leap about some more. Sitting oblivious against a building, a man dressed in a burlap bag nods gently as a large puddle of urine forms between his legs.

Shouting epithets at themselves in a loud proletarian accent, the boys finally bob down the street as another cab pulls up to the entrance. A man with curly, moderately long red hair, a pale face and an apelike black sweater gets out. It is Malcolm McLaren, manager of the Sex Pistols, the world's most notorious punk band who I have flown from New York to meet and see perform. McLaren has been avoiding me for two days. I introduce myself and suggest we get together soon. He changes the subject by introducing me to Russ Meyer, the softcore porn king of *Supervixens* and *Beyond the Valley of the Dolls* fame, who is directing the Sex Pistols' movie.

Steve Jones is by far the healthiest-looking Sex Pistol, with an I'm-a-stud-from-the-coal-mines look about him. In the taxi, I ask his impression of Russ Meyer. 'Seems like a nice bloke,' he says. 'Very aware of everything. There's going to be plenty of sex in this film, lots of birds with big tits.'

One of the things that strikes me about the punk movement, I say, is that it seems antisex – kids making themselves so ugly and mutilated that no physical attraction is possible. Sid Vicious described himself in one article as a 'sexless monster', totally bored with the whole subject.

'Sid said that?' says Jones. ''E was puttin' on.'

Russ Meyer, a grandfatherly man with a small, well-manicured moustache, shows me into his nicely furnished apartment the next day and motions to a slightly pudgy young man on the other side of the room. 'This is Roger Ebert,' he says. 'He won the Pulitzer Prize for film criticism and he's writing the movie with me. At the *Chicago Sun-Times*, he's Dr Jekyll. With me, he's Mr Hyde. He's really into tits.'

Ebert laughs and says, 'Remember, without me, there wouldn't be any mention of Bambi in this movie.'

Meyer turns around and motions to the couch behind me. 'This,' he says, 'is John.'

Sid Vicious could not have described him more accurately: all misshapen, hunchbacked, translucently pale, short hair, bright orange – undoubtedly the vilest geezer I have ever met too. He is wearing a T-shirt emblazoned with DESTROY and a swastika, black leather pants and these bizarre black shoes shaped like gunboats. His handshake is the limpest of all. 'You, uh, prefer to be called John?' I ask.

'That's right,' he says. 'I despise the name Johnny Rotten. I don't talk to anyone who calls me that.' His voice could turn 'The Lord's Prayer' into brutal sarcasm.

'You look like Mel Ferrer,' says Meyer to me. 'Has anyone ever told you that?'

'No,' I reply. 'They usually compare me to Charlie Watts.'

'We're lookin' for a journalist who looks like Mel Ferrer for the movie,' says Rotten. 'He gets murdered.' He glares at me again. This time I glare back, and we end up in an unstated contest for about ten seconds. He seems to withdraw more than lose concentration, not leaving me much of a victory. Meyer asks him about certain English slang words to give the script some authenticity. 'A tosspot is even lower than a jerk-off,' Rotten answers. 'A weed is a pansy. If you don't know that, it's just an indication of how fuckin' stupid you Americans are.'

'Just a minute, boy,' laughs Meyer. 'In '44 we saved your ass.'

'Like fuck you did . . .' Rotten trails off, suddenly realising he's put himself in the position of defending his country. 'You can slag off England all you want. There's no

Russ Meyer parodied as a leering cowboy, in the Sex Pistols movie he was originally scheduled to direct – retitled as The Great Rock'n'Roll Swindle *(1980).*

such thing as patriotism any more. I don't care if it blows up. There's more tourists in London than Londoners. You never know what accent you're going to get when you ask directions.'

'Hasn't anyone defended you from the standpoint of freedom of speech?'

'Not a one,' he replies. 'England was never free. It was always a load of bullshit. I'm surprised we aren't in jail for treason. Where's the bog?'

'Down the hall to the left,' says Meyer. 'There's ale in the refrigerator and on the counter, if you want it warm.'

'No, the *bog*, man,' says Rotten. 'You know, the shithouse, the wankhole.'

'Oh! The *bathroom*!' says Meyer. 'Straight down the hall.' Rotten trots off.

'Hmmm,' Meyer continues, 'what do you think about *Bog* for a movie title? *Bog*, with an exclamation point.'

When Rotten returns from the bog, I ask if he shares Vicious' views on love. 'Love is two minutes and 50 seconds of squelching noises,' he says. 'It shows your mind isn't clicking right.'

Meyer suggests that we go have dinner and asks Rotten what kind of food he likes. 'I don't like food.'

'Come on,' says Meyer. 'You have to eat something to survive.'

'Very little.'

'What do you eat when you eat very little?'

'Whatever is available. Food is a load of rubbish.'

Rotten finally agrees to a fish restaurant named Wheeler's Alcove and the five of us – Meyer, Ebert, Rotten, me and this roadie who showed up halfway through the talk – stuff ourselves into a subcompact that would be cramped for two. 'You can't blame him for being difficult,' whispers the roadie. 'Journalists ask the most unbelievably stupid questions. They've been calling up all day asking how he felt about [the death of] Elvis.'

On the way, we stop at a store so Rotten can pick up the following day's groceries – two six-packs and a can of beans. At the restaurant, Ebert entertains me with a joke about an elephant having his testicles crushed by two bricks until the waiter arrives.

'I'll have a filet with nothing around it and a green salad on the side, mush,' orders Rotten.

'Yes, sir, but don't call me mush,' says the waiter who appears to have just gotten off the boat from Pakistan.

Rotten leans over the table and delivers his most enraged stare. 'And I'll have a Guinness on the side, *mush*!' The waiter tries to take the orders, but Rotten insists: 'Did you hear I want nothing around the filet, *mush*?!' The waiter finally hustles off to the kitchen, much relieved to get away.

'What's a mush?' asks Meyer.

'Someone whose face is all beaten in and looks like a cunt.'

'He didn't like that. He'll spit in your salad.'

'I know it. That's why I said it. The mush couldn't take a joke.'

I ask Meyer if, as a Hollywood outcast, he feels any kinship with the punks.

'Not really,' he says. 'I don't consider myself an outcast. I'm the only independent who can compete with the major studios. I thought this would be a good transitional thing to get out of the straight bosoms-and-brawn thing. They're also paying me one per cent of the US gross.'

'You mean you don't believe in what they're saying at all?'

'Don't you know that all directors are whores? John, wouldn't you make yourself look like a cunt for a million dollars?'

'How could you make me look like a bigger cunt than I am?' says Rotten. 'The joke's on you.'

Russ Meyer on Who Killed Bambi?

by Ed Lowry and Louis Black

A few years ago, you and Roger Ebert were preparing a movie with the Sex Pistols. What happened to it?

The manager, Malcolm McLaren really overextended himself. We had the sets built and we had it cast. We shot three days and then they folded the show. Now they're bringing out a film, hopefully with the three minutes I shot, called *The Great Rock and Roll Swindle*. But they're lacking some £150,000 to complete it. I know these facts because I'm in litigation with McLaren. I guess Johnny Rotten and I have joined forces.

Did you shoot any footage of the Sex Pistols?

No, but I did a lot of rehearsing with them. Two of them are very intelligent, level-headed guys – Jones and Cook. Rotten and poor Vicious, who's no longer here, were absolutely nuts. Both had an intense hatred for McLaren. They would call me up at two in the morning to say unspeakable horrors about him. Rotten definitely had a charisma. Vicious, reputedly and in the script, was fucking his mother. Marianne Faithfull was cast for the part. Vicious embraced the sex scenes with his mother, but he objected to us showing them shooting up.

Was McLaren in the film?

No. He wanted to be. He wanted to play the huckster. We had a man who was

The Very Breast of Russ Meyer

One of the surviving pieces of footage from Who Killed Bambi?, *reproduced for a Sex Pistols album. Hiring a gamesman to shoot the deer, Meyer did indeed kill Bambi.*

emulating Mick Jagger. And we had Darth Vader, who was Little John, the chauffeur. The working title was *Who Killed Bambi?* The script was like *A Hard Day's Night*, but more on the order of *Beyond the Valley of the Dolls*. Instead of four girls, I had four boys. It was about this supposedly ageing rock star who was prone to go out into the Queen's Reserve, shoot a deer, and then give it to the poor. He was dressed in livery and had a convertible Rolls Royce. This Mick Jagger character used a crossbow. We went out to a game reserve and were permitted to kill a small deer, because they multiply so. Anyway, they strap the deer to the hood of the Rolls, and it careens through the countryside. And finally the Jagger character says, 'Stop here. It looks like those folks over there could stand a square meal.' So Darth Vader runs over with the deer on his shoulder and throws it on the porch. And a pretty little girl comes out as they drive away and says, 'Look, Mommy. Someone's killed Bambi.'

And at the end of the film she would have appeared again, when Johnny Rotten is trying to emulate Mick Jagger, dressed like him and in makeup. There's a big rock concert, and she comes forward and at the last moment we see her raise a magnum pistol – a twelve-year old girl – and murder Johnny Rotten, saying, 'That's for Bambi.' Too bad it couldn't have been made. Probably Vicious would still be living.

What kind of budget did you have on the film?
They never really knew, because McLaren had no conception of what it would cost. We did some eight versions of the script. And then, when they sat down and figured out the shooting days, they said, 'What are you doing here? This is too complicated.' So I'd say, 'Well, take this out or take that out.' And they'd say, 'Oh, no. You can't do that. You'll destroy it.'

The conception from the beginning was based on a lack of knowledge. And I have to include myself in that. Originally McLaren had committed no more than £150,000, with no expense for the Sex Pistols, who wanted a big salary, of course. We just couldn't do one-quarter of the film as it was conceived. Then the Sex Pistols got hot, so

McLaren got Warners to advance another $300,000 and then 20th Century-Fox in England put up another sum of money. Together he got what appeared to be about $1 million. But the budget was like $1.7 million. Everyone was pulling their hair. And then, I understand, Princess Grace got involved in it. She despises me, and she's an important stockholder at Fox. She was going to pull out all support of Fox in Europe.

Anyway we cast the picture. We literally built every set on stages, shot three days, and then McLaren blew the whistle. He realised, I would guess, that the picture couldn't be made. But to get in that situation where you're just the director and not the producer where you can call the shots – it's a very frustrating experience. McLaren was sincere. He was really a zealot. He had fire in his eyes. But he was unaware of the Sex Pistols' potential. I think if we'd made the film, they'd have been an important commodity in the States. But instead he determined that he would bring them over and that the young people in the States would assume the same attitude that the young people in England had.

Portrait of the Pornographer with his Ass to the Wall

by Tony Rayns

Russ Meyer had heard just that afternoon that *Time Out* had rejected the ad for *Ultravixens* (for reasons to do with the ad's sadistic pose, not the film's arguably satirical contents.) He was all set to write my piece for me: 'He was crestfallen. He couldn't eat his dinner; they served him the pasta and he pushed it aside, ordering some Perrier water instead, totally depressed as he left England with his coat-tails flapping . . .'

I wasn't around to verify the latter part of this account (though I know that he went off to West Germany in search of a lady called Dolly Dollar with a 47-inch bust), but it occurred to me that this wasn't the first time that Meyer had left England in high dudgeon. Two years ago, he'd been approached by Malcolm McLaren (a fan of *Beyond the Valley of the Dolls* and *Supervixens*) to direct a feature with the Sex Pistols. He'd come to London to talk through the project. McLaren wasn't happy with Johnny Speight's script, and so Meyer recommended two friends as possible replacements: first a Dutchman called Rene Dalder (whose script proved unusably depressing, but who became McLaren's soulmate), then Roger Ebert, the *Chicago Sun*

The Very Breast of Russ Meyer

Times critic who'd written *Dolls* for Meyer.

Everything went fine. McLaren gave Meyer and Ebert a crash course in 'punk'; Ebert came over and wrote a new first draft in four days flat, based on McLaren's suggestions (wholly fictional, the lawyer would like us to indicate) about members of the group – Sid Vicious reputedly fucking his mother, Johnny Rotten's fondness for the IRA and hatred of the English and Americans, Steve Jones' whole life being hamburgers and whores, that kind of thing. Meyer was taken on to the pay-roll: 'They agreed to pay me a sizeable sum every week, gave me walking-around money of £300, a flat in Chelsea and a car, I felt that I could do it. I would never undertake anything that was "sensitive" or "personal", but I felt that this was my cup of tea.'

So it was that *Who Killed Bambi?* started shooting. The sets were built, the costumes were made, the roles were cast. The Pistols were to play themselves. Their rise was to be counterpointed with the decline of a rockstar (identified in the script as 'MJ'), who carried on in his private life like Robin Hood. MJ was to kill a deer in one of the opening scenes, and hand it over as food to the inhabitants of a thatched cottage in the countryside. A little girl who lived in the cottage was to nurse vengeance in her heart for the duration of the movie, and assassinate Rotten onstage at the end, mistaking him for MJ. The deer-hunt and the thatched cottage were in fact filmed, on location in Wales, and will probably figure in *The Great Rock 'n' Roll Swindle* when it's released next year. But when Meyer got back to London from location, nothing else happened. 'There was silence. McLaren didn't ask to see the rushes, in fact he was nowhere to be found. Jeremy Thomas, the executive producer, disappeared on a honeymoon to the South of France. To this day, it has never been explained to me why the film wasn't made. If it came down to a money problem, then the financiers should have taken the bull by the horns and made the film, despite the fact that they might not have had enough money to finish it. That's the very kind of situation I thrive on. I specialise in what's called "off-the-wall" film-making, you know, making do.'

Meyer returned to America 'in a tremendous depression'. It took him two months to pull himself together sufficiently to get to work on *Ultravixens*. There was already a script (co-written with Ebert under pseudonyms), and one scene had been shot before the McLaren project ever came up. 'I told myself that I couldn't just lie there dormant, I had to get going on something. Once I did get going, I was, so to speak, able to hurl myself into it. *Supervixens* was the same thing – I was coming off a bad marriage, to Edy Williams, and then, too, I had to get back to what I did best: big bosoms and square jaws. I find that every time my ass is to the wall, I really do my best work.

'Basically, my films are outrageous, with cantilevered, pneumatic women as aggressors (that happens to be my taste) and a kind, dumb, industrious, muscular male with an IQ of around 38 who, by and large, has some kind of sex problem. In *Ultravixens*, I set out to make a film of unrelenting sex, screwing in every way I could possibly portray it. I used the most abundant women and the most klutzy-looking men I could find, and worked in the genre in which I'm most comfortable. The elements were: shitkickers, beautiful people living in squalor, voracious sexual appetites, menial labour for the men, pompous deliveries about Pontiacs giving way to Polarises and suchlike. All mixed with a story that never gets in the way of the action, a "problem" and a knock at what I can call commercial religion. I went into it just wanting to see what would happen.'

What has happened is that he has had a big success, especially in the American West. 'We're now in our 27th week in Portland, Oregon, with the film; we're playing in a triplex – often not the best kind of theatre to play in – but films like *China Syndrome* and *Hanover Street* have come and gone and we're still there. It must be partly because the city has the exact right mix of people: rednecks, loggers, Gothic types, the raincoat brigade, and college film buffs. Also there's a critic there who digs my stuff, has fun with it. But it's also because I went there with my star and mounted a stunt at Portland State for the opening. We were front-page news, and that had them hanging from the ceiling.

'Nowadays, it's not enough just to make a film and throw it in a theatre and expect people to come see it. I have to go out to generate publicity, talking to the press and giving the impression that I'm debauched or evil. I have seven or eight speeches that I use. After a while you feel like you're a fundamentalist preacher. I'm convinced that I could go out someday and renounce my sins. "Here I am, standing before you my flock, an avowed pornographer, high-class, but never the less a pornographer. I have thrown the shackles off, I now condemn pornography as an opiate, as an evil! I have now seen the light! The Book says, thou shalt not spill thy seed in the belly of a whore."

'What a platform! I could be a great political force, if I weren't assassinated. More retreaded than reborn.'

Beneath the Valley of the Ultravixens

by Tony Rayns

A resident of a small town in the American South-west narrates the activities of other members of his community. Lamar Shedd, a young man of small intellect but large frame, works by day in 'Junk-yard' Sal's wrecked-car lot and tries to study at night, when not distracted by the sexual demands of his wife Lavonia, who none the less resents the fact that he is incapable of anything but anal intercourse. Emigré German Martin Bormann indulges an elaborate necrophiliac fetish nightly in his home. Radio evangelist Eufaula Roop preaches her own distinctive variety of salvation over the airwaves. Lavonia enjoys more conventional

The Very Breast of Russ Meyer

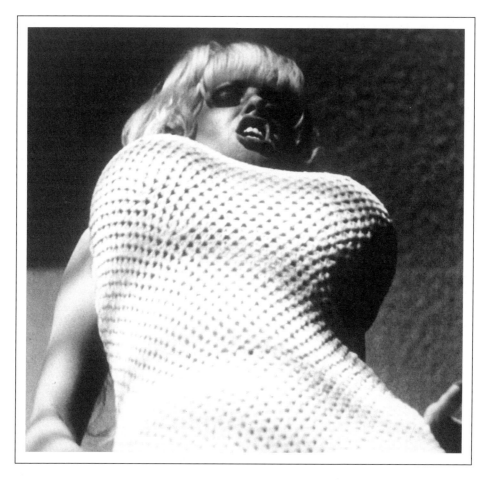

With 69-inch bosoms, Anne Marie jiggled her way thorugh Beneath the Valley of the Ultravixens *(1979). She later appeared in the softcore video* For Your Breasts Only.

sexual relations with frequent visitor Mr Peterbuilt, and also seduces virginal student Rhett when she catches him bathing naked in the river. Lamar, meanwhile, reluctantly goes to bed with his employer Sal, but loses his job when his idiosyncrasy asserts itself. A visit from underwear salesman Semper Fidelis convinces Lavonia that she should devote her energies to 'straightening out' Lamar's sexual technique. She poses as the stripper Lola Langusta and tries to drug Lamar into submission; she then takes him to marriage counsellor Asa Lavender, who promptly tries to seduce Lamar himself; finally, she drags him to visit Eufaula Roop, whose live-on-air immersion technique does the trick. The narrator returns home to his wife Supersoul (in bed with their son, as usual), while Russ Meyer sums up the moral lessons to be learned from this portrait of small-town life.

Beneath the Valley of the Ultravixens effectively picks up where *Supervixens* left off, with another breathlessly parodic saga of dumb men and huge-breasted women in search of bliss, connubial or otherwise. Pseudonymous co-writers Meyer and Roger Ebert (the latter by now as regular a fixture in the Meyer family as Henry Rowland's Martin Bormann) this time come up with an extended pastiche of the *Peyton Place* format, with a down-home narrator taking us into the typical living rooms, bedrooms and consulting rooms of Small Town, USA, to discover an average profusion of sodomy, adultery, homosexual and lesbian rapes, incest and so on, all garnished with acts of coitus at 60 m.p.h. The result is funnier and more consistent than *Supervixens*, but limited by the decision to centre the plot on sex to the exclusion of almost all else: the joke stereotypes pall well before the ending (which turns out to be another of Meyer's mock-moral summings-up, here performed by the director in person) and no amount of Meyer's primary-colour visual flair and sleek, fetishistic cross-cutting can disguise the fundamental insufficiency. It may be that Meyer, certainly one of the American cinema's true mavericks in his total independence, will never recapture the freedom of invention that he discovered during his brief sojourn at 20th Century-Fox, but will condemn himself to endless variations on the formula he pioneered in *Vixen* in 1968: the present film concludes with a fleeting trailer for his next project, *The Jaws of Vixen*, and that could easily be followed by *Megavixens* and so on, ad infinitum. Still, there is plenty to enjoy in *Beneath the Valley of the Ultravixens*, from the almost Jacobean conceit of having the characters bleed emblematic colours (the Uncle Tom-ish Negro labourer Zebulon bleeds white; the gay dentist-cum-marriage counsellor bleeds pink) to the torrent of purple rhetoric on the soundtrack (most notably in Eufaula Roop's radio patter, which would be hard to beat for sustained *double entendre*). And the spectacle of Meyer repeating himself is still many times livelier than much of the rest of contemporary American cinema.

A CLEAN BREAST

Return of the Ultravixens!

by Jessica Berens

Buxomatically breastastic. That is how Russ Meyer used to describe Miss Kitten Natividad. His love. His Ultravixen. His girl with the gravity-defying giganzos. Miss Kitten. She always knew she wanted to go places – ever since she worked as a maid in a movie star's house and saw the pools and Warren Beatty and all those Hollywood things, she wanted to go places. The giganzos helped. She didn't have many other advantages. She was short, poor and Mexican, for a start. The eldest of nine, she did not speak English until she was nearly ten. Then her mother married an American and they all moved over the border.

She met Meyer when she was 27. She was stripping at the Classic Cat, a club on Sunset, and one of her friends was Shari Eubank who had starred in *Supervixens*. Meyer likes big tits, Shari said. He will like you. And he did. Kitten turned on the charm – she has a lot of charm, 25 years later, you can see that; she has a lot of charm, because she is kind and she laughs a lot. She wanted to be in a Meyer movie. It was 1975. He was quite well-known by then, having made 21 films and established himself as one of the most controversial film directors in America.

The Immoral Mr. Teas, his 1959 comedy for unashamed adults, had enjoyed record-breaking box-office success and opened the way for a genre of saucy nudie flicks that were the precursors of porn as we know it. *Mr. Teas* featured a man on a bicycle secretly enjoying the sight of various naked ladies. It owed a lot to Monsieur Hulot and it established Meyer's personal burlesque of pop-eyed men and Amazonian women. *Lorna* in 1964 and *Vixen!* in 1968, both seized by the police in various states, had ignited debates about censorship and made millions of dollars. This last fact did not go unnoticed at 20th Century Fox, who bankrolled Meyer to make *Beyond the Valley of the Dolls*. Described, variously, as 'insanely funny' and 'completely repulsive', it was followed by *Blacksnake!*, a commercial failure starring Anouska Hempel as the whip-wielding Lady Susan Walker.

Hempel (now better known as Lady Weinberg, the owner of London's Blake's Hotel) joined the cast at a late stage when the original actress suffered a drug overdose. Hempel was not 'buxomatic' and the failure of the film everywhere except Barbados, where it was made, confirmed Meyer's belief that acting ability must never

In Beneath the Valley of the Ultravixens, *Junk Yard Sal (June Mack) scolds the anally-fixated hero who 'can't look a good fuck in the face'.*

take precedence over anatomical consideration. *Supervixens* had seen a return to formula and was a commercial success, reaping more than $17m on a $221,000 investment. There were some who thought that Meyer had 'genuine comic vision' and there were some who thought he was a 'Neanderthal hack'.

Meyer was 53. He was rich thanks to years of making low-budget movies with enormous returns, and he was alone, having split from his third wife, actress Edy Williams. The romance had begun happily enough with Meyer filming Williams for a nude water-skiing scene, but had ended acrimoniously. She told the *Hollywood Reporter* that it was not going to be easy to move 134 bikinis out of their Beverly Hills mansion. He, meanwhile, told the *Toronto Sun* that she was a 'thoroughly unpleasant person' who had married him to 'further her own career'. The exploiter had, apparently, been exploited. Tit for tat, in every meaning of the words.

So Kitten was stripping at the Classic Cat, and Shari Eubank was right. Meyer liked her tits. They were quite big because when she was 21 she had gone to Tijuana to get silicone implants. She had won Miss Nude Universe and wanted to do topless work, but her agent, Sparky, told her she must be bigger. Go to Tijuana, he said. It's legal there. So she did. It was not until she contracted cancer and her breasts were removed that they discovered the silicone used was industrial, not pharmaceutical.

Her tits were big, and then they got bigger, because Meyer paid for implants so that she could play Lola Langusta ('hotter than a Mexican's lunch!') in *Beneath the Valley of the Ultravixens*. So this was ironic. Meyer paid for the implants then, 25 years later, he helped to pay for the double mastectomy.

Kitten's husband George, a wig importer, encouraged her to be nice to Meyer, which was a mistake as it turned out because she left George and moved in with the director.

Even in the breastalicious world of Mr Russ Meyer, there were few actresses as willing to 'go nood' as Miss Kitten Natividad. She was noodtastic. She had been raised a Catholic; the entire family were in the back seat of the car when she went on her first dates to LA drive-ins, but jeez was she uninhibited. Still is.

Meyer hired a dialect coach at $100 an hour to help her lose the Mexican accent that she hadn't minded that much anyway and made her the star in *Beneath the Valley of the Ultravixens*, where she was all mouth and giganzos that looked as if they could leap clean off her body and order their own coffee to go.

After this she modelled for girlie magazines, became a name dancer in the strip clubs and developed an act, stolen from the burlesque queen Lili St. Cyr, where she bathed in a giant glass of champagne to the tune of 'Splish Splash' by Bobby Darin. In 1981, she split from Meyer, married a mechanic and then separated from him in 1987. She appeared in films such as *Thanks for the Mammaries*, *Fresh Tits of Bel Air* and *Zombie Ninja Gangbangers*, and she danced at Sean Penn's bachelor party. Harry Dean Stanton was late for it. 'Here,' said Penn, shoving Stanton's face into her chest. 'Look what you missed.'

She lives alone now, Miss Kitten. She is 53. 'I don't want to be taking care of men, making the dinner. It's just terrible! I feel like it's fun for a week, then, go and get your own meals, do your own laundry.'

Her apartment is right down the bottom of Melrose Avenue, way into an Hispanic neighbourhood. There is her cat and her memorabilia. Nowadays, the money arrives from selling her porn videos, which she owns, and from telephone sex, for which she charges 30 bucks for ten minutes. The telephone rings a lot. When I was there, a man rang her long-distance from London. There was a lot of ooh baby ooh. Big Boy.

'I have a metal cast of my fanny,' she says. 'It's really good. I just sold one to a doctor in Madrid. I only have two left. My God, I had fifteen. I must reorder! Some guy in the Valley made it.'

The priorities have changed. Last year, she started going to Alcoholics Anonymous. When she talks about going to meetings, she does not mean with producers. 'I drank everything. Beer, vodka, wine . . . If I got sick of them, I drank Jack Daniel's. I would stay home, get a video, and pass out. The next morning, I would vomit and start the whole thing again. When I was nine months sober, I still wanted to drink. It was very difficult. Sometimes I had to pray.

'I stopped doing porn in my forties. I did it for 30 years. There are other things

Meyer's top squeeze in his latter filmmaking days, Kitten Natividad had just the right combination of campness and playful sexuality for the cartoon world of Ultravixens.

The Very Breast of Russ Meyer

you can do. Anyway, I don't care if I don't have to do anything. I'm fine with my life. I have family and friends. I just want to take care of my health, take care of being sober, just be happy. That's a big enough job.'

Kitten's relationship with Meyer was volatile and complicated, and, though she remembers fondly that he paid for her grandmother's false teeth ('She lived with us for a bit'), he was a perfectionist. 'Picky about everything,' as she puts it.

'People always say that he loves women, makes them the heroes,' she says, 'but it would make him look very bad if he had not. He was still using women's bodies – to make them the heroes was a way of covering his ass.'

It is difficult, one might imagine, to be an ageing voluptuary. One minute you are big and busty and paid, the next you are middle-aged – all you have is your family, your personality and your inner strength, and boy do you need them.

The Ultravixens seem to have survived with their wit and wits intact. Lori Williams (a lead in 1966's *Faster Pussycat! Kill! Kill!*) is a happily married grandmother living in Brentwood. She went on to appear in *Charlie's Angels* and *Baretta*. 'I wasn't always the hooker,' she smiles. When she was 40, her agent kept sending her up for twenty-year-old characters, so she stopped acting and went into real estate. 'I was good at it,' she says.

Haji, who appeared in several Meyer movies and subsequently worked backstage on others, lives happily (alone) in Malibu. She has had a nose job ('The doctor gave me a cute one even though I do not have a cute personality!') and her morale is intact. Asked how old she is, she says she does not know, but she knows that she is still attractive. 'A lot of men like older women, they really do,' she says. 'Would I get a face-lift? If I came into a lot of money now, I probably would get one, but if I met an older man, I probably wouldn't.' Times have changed, though. 'Look at the talk shows!' she exclaims. 'Jay Leno brings on these beautiful women, but their hair! They look as if they didn't wash it! Where is the beauty and glamour?'

Haji's own hair is dyed red and quite big, as are her breasts, which, she says, destroyed her posture because she was so embarrassed. Then she took up dancing, became a show-girl in Vegas, and enjoyed it. At the age of sixteen, she had an illegitimate daughter to support. She liked the night life. Her brother taught her how to do headlocks. She could look after herself.

She was one of Meyer's favourites, particularly memorable as Rosie, snarling and demonic in *Faster Pussycat*. She does not work as often as she used to, though she and Kitten and Raven De La Croix (who starred in *Up!*) were recently paid around $2,500 to appear in William Winckler's *The Double D Avenger*. Winkler, 36, a fan of Meyer, set out to make a homage. His plotline sees Kitten, in the lead, as a 'super-stacked costumed crime fighter in booby battles of gigantic proportions'.

Some remember their experiences as Meyer's cantilevered cartoons with more affection than others. Erica Gavin came to dislike her role as the busty bisexual temptress in *Vixen*. The 1968 film came with the tag-line 'Is she woman or animal?', grossed more than $15m on a $72,000 budget and caused more legal problems than

Haji, Lori Williams and Tura Satana are the original Scary Spice x 3. Scary played a Tura parody named 'Blazin' Bad Zula' in the video for the Spice Girls' second hit record.

any other Meyer movie. Gavin, disaffected by Hollywood, dropped out of sight for years until (now 51) she was tracked down by a fan, Siouxzan Perry, who offered to manage her and persuaded her to appear at conventions where, to Gavin's amazement, fans remembered who she was and where an autographed poster of *Vixen* could be sold for hundreds of dollars.

'I do not think that Meyer was nice to work for,' says Perry. 'And I don't think he really likes women, judging from the way he treated some of the actresses and from the way that they are cast as evil in his films.'

'He is,' Haji observes, 'a very odd man.' *Beneath the Valley of the Ultravixens*, released in 1979, was Meyer's last film. Despite continuous criticism from women's organisations (which he tended to welcome as a useful promotional tool), his work has received many honourable accolades (including a retrospective at the National Film Theatre in 1983). He has even been called a 'radical structuralist' and compared to Jean-Luc Godard. His films are easily available on video and, as they continue to circulate, so the 'buxotic cohorts' of his vision have taken their place as revered deities among the bloodsucking freaks and vampire mermaids loved (and immortalised) by the B-movie brotherhood.

This French poster for Faster Pussycat, Kill! Kil! *features a sharp-clawed Varla – as cartoonishly voluptuous, but nowhere near as formidable, as Tura Satana.*

Respected director John Waters, in particular, assured them long-term cult credibility when, in his 1981 book *Shock Value*, he said that *Faster Pussycat! Kill! Kill!* was the best film that had ever been made. Which brings us to a demented lesbian named Varla.

For every argument that can be made against Meyer (sexist, adolescent, vulgar, dated) there is one that can be made for his representation of women as having a sexual appetite and physical strength equal to men. The Vixens are rarely victims. They do not cower. They cavort. And they have a lot more simple sexual fun than anybody Candace Bushell ever created.

Varla has taken her place in the collective post-fem consciousness as a psycho go-go gang girl made enormous by Meyer's characteristic low angles. Varla, dressed in black, a demonic dyke in a fast car, uses her sexual charisma to fulfil her ghastly desires and, by so doing, has become an admired icon. An American band named themselves after Tura Satana, the actress who played her, and in New York night clubs there are theme nights in her honour.

Tura Satana is now 61 – a big woman with long, dyed black hair. She, like Lori Williams, is a proud grandmother. 'I get fan letters from all over the world,' she says. 'It seems the older I get, the more popular I get.'

Raised in Chicago, her father, a Filipino, worked on the railroad while her American mother performed in a circus. As a ten-year-old child, Satana was endowed with mesmerising Oriental beauty and a pair of 34C breasts that arrived far too early.

'There was always somebody coming up hands first who wanted to see if the bumps were mine or if they came with the sweater.' The unwelcome attention did not stop there. At the age of ten, walking to the bakery, she was gang-raped by five men in an alley.

'The youngest was seventeen, the oldest 21. All Italian. They put me in the back of the car. I crawled home bleeding and my father went ballistic. Eventually they were arrested, but at that time you could buy a judge in Illinois,' she says. 'So they did, and I went to a juvenile detention centre for three years – they said I was enticing them. If it wasn't for my father, I would have hated men all my life. He sat down and he talked to me and he listened.'

Over the next ten years or so, Satana says, she tracked the rapists down and exerted her personal revenge. How? 'Put it this way,' she smiles. 'They talk in high voices now.'

She was married at the age of thirteen to a friend of the family. 'Mississippi was the only state that allowed it – we weren't in love, but we had been friends all our lives.' Destined, then, to be different, Tura started dancing in nightclubs when she was fifteen. 'I got the acrobatics from my mom,' she says. 'But learned the tassel

From Motor Psycho! *to* Supervixens, *Haji was a Meyer stalwart. She is seen here in her finest moment, as Mexican hellcat Rosie in* Faster Pussycat.

twirling on my own . . . I still have the tassels. Most girls could wear them as bras.'

So were the giganzos an advantage or a disadvantage, I wonder?

'In some ways, they have been an advantage because they helped me earn a living and support my children – they were an asset – but nine times out of ten, people couldn't tell what colour eyes I had.'

She met Meyer in 1965 when she was 26. She was dancing at the Pink Pussycat, a strip joint in West Hollywood. Filming in the desert for four weeks, Tura bought her personal anger to Varla, as well as the martial arts which her father had taught her after she was raped. Varla is required to karate-chop various men to death. 'Russ would always listen to my suggestions,' she says. She subsequently starred in *The Astro-Zombies*, but she did not work with Meyer again. 'I felt I had too much talent for the other films,' she says. 'They were just tits and ass.'

Now she lives in Reno, a widow, but surrounded by a huge family. She works as a uniformed security woman at the local Hilton, wearing a badge and handcuffs. Like

The Very Breast of Russ Meyer

Varla, she can look after herself, particularly after her late husband Eddie, a former policeman, taught her how to use a gun. 'I have a licence to carry a concealed weapon,' she says. 'And he gave me a .38 special for my birthday.'

Satana remains one of the most famous of the Meyer icons, but she, like all the women involved in his work, receives no residuals from the sales of the films which still sell in high numbers all over the world, because she, like the others, accepted a flat fee.

'When you think what we could have made off *Faster Pussycat*, it's frightening,' says Williams. 'We were all dumb, and we all signed off. I was twenty. I got $350 a week. I thought that was pretty good at the time.'

Now 79, Russ Meyer is suffering from senile dementia. He lives in his house in Hollywood where he is attended by a caretaker, a secretary and various attorneys who look after his business, Russ Meyer Films International Inc. He is ill, and he is isolated.

'It is very difficult to get to see him,' says Haji. 'And that is sad.'

'His house used to be a museum full of memorabilia,' says Kitten. 'Then everything was taken down. He started writing obscenities on things and destroying them. Now he has a cardboard table and chair.'

Meyer, always the *auteur*, controlled the production of most of his movies and reaped the financial benefits from them. He applied the same policy to the publication of his autobiography, *A Clean Breast*, which runs to three thick volumes and which he published himself. The price, £200, is prohibitive to loyal fans and unlikely to attract any new ones.

'I was told I was going to be given one,' says Haji. 'But I'm not going to hold my breath, you know?'

The man they called King Leer is not thought to have any family to whom to leave his strange kingdom, but Kitten insists he has an illegitimate son. 'There is a picture of the mother in his book,' she says. 'The caption does not give her real name. But I remember him telling me that the kid looked like his [Meyer's] mother. So, somewhere out there, there is a legal heir.'

The 'breastman extraordinaire' used to answer his office telephone himself, but now he can't run his own show. His place in film history is assured; the arguments about whether he is an unsettling genius or inane pornographer will continue, but it is the goddesses that he created who breathe life into the legend. It is they who have the websites, who attend the conventions, sign the autographs, give the interviews. There is some money in these things, but not a lot. Russ Meyer Films International Inc. holds control over most of the breastastic images. It is ironic that their efforts are not always encouraged by the businessmen who now run the director's affairs.

Tura Satana recently received a letter from Meyer's attorneys informing her she could not sell the *Faster Pussycat* T-shirts. 'That is not Russ,' she says loyally. 'He was always very generous to me.' But Tura is Varla and without Varla the Meyer myth is minus one very important buxomatic babe. It is a very delicate balance and the Ultravixens are bristling.

'We love Russ,' says Kitten. 'He is sitting there waiting to be put in a box in the ground. This man has so much money! He could have had a great exit.'

Russ Meyer at the NFT

Interviewed by Jonathan Ross

The National Film Theatre, London, 17 February, 1995

Mr. Russ Meyer, Ladies, and Gentlemen.

We just all watched and enjoyed Faster Pussycat – *a movie from back in 1966, makes it about 29 years old. It has always amazed me, not only as a film itself, but the title: I always thought it was the most fantastic title of a movie that I've encountered in my entire life. Where did you get that from?*
It came from Jack Moran – he was a child star who did a number of films. I met him through a friend of mine, who was in jail for writing bad cheques and Moran was in the same situation. He told me, if you ever need some narration, Jack Moran has got

TV presenter Jonathan Ross first paid tribute to Meyer in his Incredibly Strange Film Show. *This is the transcript of their extensive 1995 interview at London's National Film Theatre.*

a lot of time on his hands. [Laughter] So he wrote the narration for the picture *Wild Gals of the Naked West,* and we became good friends. Charming guy, but regrettably he's gone. He had a thing with writing *Pussycat,* he wanted to be paid every day, he wanted a quart of Jack Daniel's whiskey every day, wanted a brown bag lunch that would take care of breakfast, lunch and supper – those were his demands. He did a number of screenplays for me.

And that one, in particular, is fine. I'd forgotten how wonderful the dialogue at the dinner table is, and [it] got a great response as always. Let me ask you about the story, that you supplied for Jack.
Well I don't want to take too much credit, I had some ideas . . .

Well you take credit on screen, Russ, so you might as well. [Laughter] Bit late to change your tune now.
There's a little space on the card to put your name down.

It strikes me that the middle period of your work, the black and white period, the 'roughies' I guess they've been called since then, they were quite deranged stories, they were really wild, melodramatic pieces of work.
Well that was not by choice, I didn't have enough money to buy colour film, so I made them in black and white. A lot of people think now today that it was a very special idea of Meyer's to do it in glorious black and blue.

Let me ask you about Tura Satana, who is just the most remarkable screen presence, and the performance she delivers is remarkable as well . . .
Without her it would not have worked, there is nobody else that could have played the role.

I was always curious as to why you didn't work with her again, because she made movies after this and . . .
Well, she caught herself up with another gentleman, who made films that were a little more sick than films that I made.

Are these Ted Mikels' films? Or was that before you?
Well, you said it, I didn't.

Was she in Astro Zombies? *I think she was . . .*
Well, one of the things she did with Mr. Mikels, and she doesn't mind me saying this, he liked to be stomped on, particularly with high heels.

Let's go back to your career, Russ, as Ted can't be with us this evening – he's tied up at the moment. [Laughter] But here you have Tura, who is this fantastic character . . . I know

that you weren't keen that your cast, when you were filming, actually enjoyed themselves sexually in the evening. You wanted them to save all that vim and vigour for the movies.
I wanted the hunger, the unbridled hunger . . .

And yet Tura managed to persuade you otherwise . . .
Well, she collared me down there on the lake and she said, 'I know that you got an attitude about connubial bliss amongst the actors, and I can't deal with it for two or three weeks.' I said, 'Yes,' I knew that she had me by the short hairs. There was no one else that could take the place of Tura. So I said, 'Who you got in mind?', and she said, 'Well, the assistant cameraman, he's dirty looking, I think he'd probably work out alright.' He was not aware of this conversation. I said, 'Well, the important thing is that he has to hustle this big BMC Mitchell around. I want to make it clear to you – or rather, I *beseech* you – to have sex only once in a given evening.' She kind of smirked at me. Years later, I asked her and this fellow at a reunion party, 'Is it true that you and Tura had connubial bliss once a night?' He said, 'She was on my case all night.'

It's a technical thing, but I always notice in your movies a very short credit list at the end. I know that you worked with very small teams, was this just a financial thing or was it more of a control thing?
You hit it right on the head!

Financial?
Yeah, it was my bankroll, my wife's bankroll, and I always liked to do a lot of arduous work. I always felt the picture would be better if I really broke my ass. My wife always contributed as well, she was a bookkeeper, legal secretary, and she was always honoured. A great lady. By the way, she was the first official Playmate, which has been clarified in Hefner's new book *40 Years* [*of Playboy*]. There were others beforehand, but they were pictures that were purchased as pin-up things.

But these were the first purpose-shot photographs for a [men's] magazine, which you took of Eve? . . .
Yeah.

Back to the cost: when you were actually shooting, say, **Faster Pussycat,** *where would people stay? Were they put up in motels?*
We had a production manager, Fred Horns, who would always find the cheapest motel. I think this one was called the Amigo Motel. We would eat in a couple of restaurants, they were really vomitoriums. There was really no other place around, so I didn't have to take any crap. The only thing was 'the Vegetable' – he drank an incredible amount of orange juice. The production manager used to say, 'Do you have to drink so much? 55 cents a glass!'

The Very Breast of Russ Meyer

So he was 'the Vegetable' off-screen as well as on – a pet name that you had for him at all times? Someone told me that, on one of your shoots, you actually had them staying in tents. They had to put the tents up, then work for you, and they'd cook for you, then they'd sleep in the tents and then give you another day's work. Is that just fabrication?
Well, that was *Motor Psycho!*

So that happened? . . .
Yeah, we had a couple of trailers, and we pulled in water so that people could bathe. We had some difficulty the first night, Haji and one of the actors disappeared into the desert. There was a terrible venomous snake called the Mojave green, there was no anti-toxin, and we ran around and finally ripped them out of this fart-sack. Afterwards, I made it clear that all of the girls would be in one trailer and I would sit up front with an axe handle. You have to do these things. All this unbridled sex just burst forth sometimes. They were doing all this simulated sex, I suppose this created the problem.

We'll come back to Faster Pussycat *in a while, but I want to go back a little bit and just touch on the basics. How did you actually get into filmmaking in the first place? You were a unit photographer in the Second World War and you returned to Los Angeles, how did you make the leap into movies from there?*
Well, I tried to get a job at one of the major studios and they said, 'Forget it.' So I got

Gang member, go-go dancer and all-round bad girl Billie (Lori Williams)
finds something lacking in 'the Vegetable' (Dennis Busch). From Faster Pussycat.

involved with industrial films. It was the best training ground I had. I also learned how to use an expense account.

And the first movie, which I've never seen . . .
The Immoral Mr. Teas.

Well no, before that: **The French Peep Show** *in 1950.*
For Pete DeCenzie. Well, that was before I was married. I was terribly taken up with a girl by the name of Tempest Storm. She had tremendous credentials. [Laughter]

I don't think you need to say that about any of your women, I think we'll take that as a given, Russ, if that's okay with you. But Tempest was an incredibly famous burlesque performer.
She became after that, yeah.

And this film, I don't think it exists anymore . . .
No, we just shot a burlesque show. Myself and a soundman would sleep there at night, and then shoot in the afternoon after we'd finished doing something for Standard Oil like *Safe and Good-Looking*, *Dipstick*, *How to Be a Proper Salesman*, selling the product and so on. We used our producer's equipment, he never knew he had an extra deduction.

So **The Immoral Mr. Teas** *is the first proper Russ Meyer movie, and this was the first Eve production – you and your wife . . .*
Well no . . . Pete DeCenzie was my partner. We made this film in a very short period of time, and we planned to open up in San Diego, but a problem occurred. The picture was playing with a Gary Cooper picture, *The Hanging Tree*. It'd played already, but the problem was that nobody had come up with a 'patch' – this is a term whereby you bribed the police, like with a hundred-dollar bill. We forgot all about it, and so they blew the whistle and pulled out the film and it didn't play for like a year.

So this was to show a movie that would perhaps be risky, would encounter some opposition from moral groups and PTAs and that kind of thing?
Yeah, I think that most everybody found something wrong [with it] when it was pinched. The product was very pleasing to the 'one-armed reader'. [Laughter]

I don't know how many people have actually seen **Mr. Teas**, *but perhaps you could fill us in [on] exactly what it entails. It was the first of its kind, wasn't it?*
Yes, it was about a man who was capable of visualising certain things in his imagination and found himself in circumstances and situations with these very voluptuous girls, or at least as voluptuous as I could find at the time. Mr. Teas, I think about him a great deal, he passed away recently, but he was a very special friend of

mine. He was a very courageous man in World War Two; he did a lot of sport with General De Gaulle and was in Paris on Liberation Day.

This was Bill Teas, your war buddy . . .
Yeah. Anyway, I don't want to be morbid about this, let's go on . . .

Mr. Teas *spawned a plethora of imitators, it actually started the genre of what we now call the 'Nudie-Cudie'.*
Yeah, I even got in on that with *Eve and the Handyman*, with my wife and another army buddy, and then I did *Erotica*, *Wild Gals of the Naked West*, *Heavenly Bodies* . . .

I notice that you control the distribution of your movies on video in America . . .
Well, there was no video at that given time.

This exotic dancer adds a note of fetishism to Europe in the Raw *(1962). Despite its claim to be an undercover documentary, Meyer later admitted it was partly faked.*

But today you can get **Mr. Teas** *from you, I believe, but I don't think any of the others are available, are they?*
Eve and the Handyman.

And the others, you're not keen on them?
Well, *Europe in the Raw* was a fakeroo.

So it was like an early mondo movie?
I had a great friend who was a very fine Dutch photographer, and he was also the Queen [of Holland]'s photographer. There was a big hooker that I wanted to photograph, but it was hard to get to her, because this was in Les Halles or somewhere like that. Anyway, she was always so busy, and I had very limited French, so I asked my friend if he would accompany me and act as a translator – which he misunderstood, he thought I wanted

to take pictures of him and this big, blonde hooker. He said, 'The Queen would not take much of a liking to this kind of activity on my part, I must refuse.'

So, after that you make **Heavenly Bodies** *which, I assume, was more of the same . . .*
That was a cheat, an out-and-out cheat. I made it for a ham sandwich, but we needed the money.

And then came **Lorna** *. . .*
Lorna was important, it was a real breakthrough film. It was found to be very difficult in the Amish part of the United States. [Laughter] They didn't go for it, you know. We had a couple of real bad busts there – a bust is not a *bust*. We were facing a little jail time there.

They don't like zippers either, so what do they know? But the movie marked a great change for you, [after] you'd been making these coloured movies: they were basically films that had novel ways of showing women with very little clothing, with a little comedy and some light music perhaps, but essentially they were peep shows on film. Then you moved to this entirely different type of film: black and white, melodramatic, with violence mixed with the sexual nature, so it must have been quite a risk for you?
Well, I couldn't afford the colour film, that's why I used black and white . . . it's that simple.

But I mean to actually change from the kind of light-hearted nudie movie . . .
Yeah, I thought I had to come up with something that was kind of interpretive and off-the-wall, and I had Lorna Maitland, who was rather spectacular. She was pregnant, that accounted for this big overhang, big overbite, and she had a lot of zip-and-go. She really threw herself into the water and I have the feeling that she was trying to lose the job. That sounds kind of morbid, but she did end up with an abortion. But anyway, she participated, and made some money. I haven't seen her in years.

And you didn't work with her again, but that was obviously a very successful movie. Why was that?
I used her again. In *Mudhoney* – she and Rena Horten.

Oh of course, I'm sorry.
Two hookers, yeah.

Before we go on to **Lorna**, *let me ask you about the legal problems you'd faced. You mentioned the Amish, but even back with* **The Immoral Mr. Teas** *I believe you faced litigation?*
Yeah, we couldn't play it for a year. Finally, Pete, my partner, was travelling with a roadshow, *Pictures and Poses*, a couple of girls and they would compare them to

Lorna Maitland, the original pneumatic, cantilevered female. Despite a role in Mudhoney, *and the* Lorna *outtakes in* Mondo Topless, *she soon returned to obscurity.*

certain paintings and so forth. They ran into another partisan, turned out to be a member of the censor board in Seattle. The police don't like to bust films but they'd often have to, as they did early in the game with *Mr. Teas.* But in this instance we'd not been able to play the film, simply because it frightened exhibitors. So Pete said, 'Look, I've got a 16mm print and a projector, and I wonder if we can get the whole board inside my suite?' Well, he didn't have a suite, but he went out and rented one. He got a lot of Italian take-out food, and a lot of dago red, and he presented the film to the censor board, which was kind of unheard of, and they passed it. I see nothing wrong [with it], it's a very pleasant little film. From then on it was like a licensed seal, [the film] played and played. Sorry if I keep mentioning names, or amounts of money, 'cos I've been so much without it and it was kind of comforting that there'd be an opportunity to make another film, simply because it was successful.

Let me just ask you about the different laws in the States, because presumably you'd have a movie that was cleared by the censors in one state, but that wouldn't carry elsewhere. I know that Chicago has caused problems for you sometimes . . .
Well, you see, Seattle really opened the floodgates. They hear about it and they realise, 'We'd better not touch it.' There are places in the South that are really uptight, they would come after you, the Baptists.

Did you spend a lot of money fighting these battles?
Well, I spent a lot of money after *Vixen*, that was Charles Keating, the one that bilked all of those little old ladies out of their savings. He was on my case, there was no question about it, he wanted to put me in 'the iron hotel' forever. I got a good lawyer, Elmer Gertz, who represented [infamous thrill killer] Nathan Leopold, but he was also a special, special man, very close.

Charles Keating, we should clarify, he was in charge of some kind of censorship body, the League of Decency . . .
Yeah, the little old ladies in tennis shoes, that's him.

And wasn't there a famous quote that he made about you, that you were thinking of having on your gravestone?
Well, [Roger] Ebert came up with it, it simply said, 'I was glad to do it.'

So what did Keating say? 'If there is one man responsible for . . .
Yeah, 'the undermining of the morals of the people of the United States, Meyer has to assume that responsibility.' 'Course, he's now in the iron hotel himself for bilking those old ladies. I spent $100 for my book [*A Clean Breast: The Life and Loves of Russ Meyer*] just to buy a picture of him holding up a sign that said 'LA District Attorney'. Best hundred dollars I've ever spent.

So **Lorna** *then, there's a risk involved in making this movie, but you make this black-and-white, melodramatic, sexy, violent film, and it was successful for you.*
Very much so. Very successful, went very well.

So did you then go into **Mudhoney***?*
I went [on] to *Mudhoney* and made a mistake. It just didn't have enough of the contents that *Lorna* had. People were disappointed. Later on, it became a very popular film. I made a[nother] mistake too, I got involved with a girl in Germany, brought her over, and it was kind of shoddy. My wife didn't know about it, she put up half the bankroll – but we made a picture that just didn't have the guts that the other picture had. I've done a number of things in my life I'm not all that proud of. Not to be reported here at this given time.

What about **Fanny Hill** *then, how did that come about? You went to Germany to make this film . . .*
Well, the German producer and the American producer were keen to make the picture, and they'd seen *Lorna* and they thought that I'd be a worthwhile director, but I was just like someone who was pushing pins and keys. Fortunately, I had Miriam Hopkins [in the cast], she was married to Fritz Lang, and she'd call me aside and say, 'Sonny, look, I've got an idea about this scene,' and everything she had to say made a lot of sense. She'd be lonely

at night and I'd have to break away from something that was pleasant, and I'd drive her around the Tear Garden and she'd tell me about all her experiences. It was fascinating.

Now this will be the first time that you're just a director for hire, as opposed to something that was your own project . . .
Well, I was promised some money. I had some difficulty collecting it.

Did you find it difficult working for other people?
Oh, [producer Albert] Zugsmith was a monster, no question about him. I managed through her [Hopkins'] help, she wielded a lot of power 'cos they had to pay her a lot of money. She'd say, 'Leave the young boy alone!' [Meyer was in his early forties at the time.] She'd tell these two producers, 'He's doing his best and I'm sure we'll come up with a film that'll make some money.' Great lady.

I've never seen Fanny Hill, *I don't know whether it's been shown over here . . .*
Well, it was the one film released in the United States that they literally turned every [video] cassette back, as being a terrible result.

And why was this?
It just didn't have any steam, you know. It was a very bland movie.

So you returned to the States and went on to Motor Psycho!
Well, I went home to face the music. But my wife gave me some money and I bought a Porsche, because the cameraman had one and I thought I should have one. We did a tour of duty, it's another one of those shortcomings I have – any opportunity that presents itself, a determination to grab life by the throat and shake it and get the most out of it. I just want to create the impression that I'm not a particularly nice guy!

Motor Psycho!, *if I remember correctly, is the story of some hoods who are terrorising a small community, on what appear to be very small scooters.*
We couldn't afford the big motorcycles. [Laughter] And secondly, no one knew how to ride a bike.

Now where you were then faced with those two barriers, didn't you think, 'Maybe I'll write a different script here'?
Sometimes it gets to be too late and you do it and it works. People liked the picture . . .

A successful film?
Yeah, very successful.

Which brings us on to Faster Pussycat. *Which . . .*

Not successful. Fell on its ass.

It was commercially a failure?
People didn't understand it. Distributors used to say, 'What is this thing with women and women?' Not that there was anything particularly graphic, but the film really dumped. Not until years later did it come off.

So you re-released it, or did it get picked up on its own?
No, no, my wife and I always kept the film, we didn't let it go. It wasn't a big loser but it wasn't successful. But in later years, it's become a salaciously successful film.

I think now, probably apart from **Beyond the Valley of the Dolls***, it's the film that you're best known for . . .*
That's nice, isn't it? *The Dolls* represents my going to the mountain. That was very important to me. Now with this thing, what was great about *Pussycat* is that women discovered the film. Women bought cassettes; they liked the idea of Tura Satana not being goaded into attacking somebody. She did it for the very sheer pleasure of it. [Laughter] It's her show, without any question. I don't want to make less of other people's contributions, but without Tura it wouldn't have scored.

A couple of years ago, when I was talking to you, you were very keen on the idea of remaking **Faster Pussycat***. You were ready to go, you had the money in place, you had the cast in mind, you were ready to go to the desert . . .*
It's not a matter of the money, I had the money to promote or make films of a certain nature, but it would have been wrong to do it. It would always be compared.

So, what fired you up in the first place, why did you want to do it?
Well, I felt that if I did it in colour and found a girl that knew martial arts and so on, used the same locations, same scenes, exact angles, that it would always be compared to Tura. I don't think anybody could have matched that.

You were going to cast Pandora Peaks, is that correct?
Yes! [Laughter] She has awesome credentials.

And will you be working with her again?
Yeah, she was in Britain here for a while. I've done a video with her which is about to be finished: *Pandora Peaks – A Tale of Two* Titties! [Laughter] It's a good documentary, very good.

So would it be that the commercial failure of **Faster Pussycat** *made you change style? Because it's harder to imagine a more different movie from* **Faster Pussycat** *than* **Mondo**

The Very Breast of Russ Meyer

Topless. *There's no narrative, it's basically just reportage on the topless phenomenon.*
It was a desperate move. The girl I got, her name was Vivian Cournoyer, she came
from Maidenhead, England. *Awesome girl.* [Laughter] I mean a traffic stopper. I don't
know where she is now. Then I used Babette Bardot and a number of other people.
It was a silly little movie, but it made a lot of money.

*I'm sure a lot of people are thinking this, how do you find these women? Do they find
you, or do you have scouts out there?*
Well, one girl will always . . . Haji was a great source.

Was that her first movie, Faster Pussycat, *with you?*

In Heavenly Bodies *(1963), Meyer shows his love of the fuller form. This Junoesque figure would
fall foul of the modern bias toward 'some skinny, emaciated young girl'.*

AUDIENCE (shouts): No, it was *Motor Psycho!*.
No, she was in *Motor Psycho!*, right. Thank you.

Thanks for nothing. [Laughter] *Essentially then it's word-of-mouth and people know
that you're looking for abundantly-proportioned women who can act enough . . .*
Well no, I would tour the strip clubs and things like that and run into people that way.

Oh, life's a bitch. [Laughter]
Then one girl would recommend another . . .

*So **Mondo Topless**, which I'm very fond of, I think it's a fine movie . . .*
That was made on a ham sandwich.

You describe it as mere 'bosom mania', that's what you once told me it was.
Not *mere*, but . . . [Laughter] it's a big seller now.

*So basically, I don't know how you'd see the next phase of your filmmaking career, whether you felt there was a pattern at the time, but it strikes me that they were more colourful pictures than the **Lorna** period. But they went back to a melodramatic thing and they were slightly more comic-strip, like **Common Law Cabin**.*
Yeah, that wasn't a great film by any means. *Good Morning . . . Goodbye* was a fine film, I thought it was well done . . .

And these movies, generally, were more successful for you once again?
Every one of them was successful from there on out, yeah.

How did you distribute them, presumably you couldn't get them in the major chain theatres, so where would they play?
No, they would play in drive-ins, would play in major theatres.

It strikes me that although the movies obviously had a built-in audience, I think you described them as the 'one-armed reader' earlier on, at the same time they did begin to pick up critical praise from, shall we say, 'more respected' fans of cinema . . .
I had one review for *Faster Pussycat* that wasn't bad, it was just kind of here and there. But, every now and then, I'd catch something pretty good: *Lorna* would get it; *Mudhoney* was looked upon with considerable interest, but it just didn't have all the steam that the others had.

Which movie was it [for] that you were given the title 'the Tennessee Truffaut', by a critic? Can you remember that? I know that you've picked up 'the rural Fellini'.
That's mine, 'the rural Fellini'.

*But 'the Tennessee Truffaut' was actually in a review, I think it might have been **Common Law Cabin** or **Good Morning . . . and Goodbye!**. Let's go on to **Vixen**: **Vixen** was the most successful movie that you've ever had, I believe, is that correct?*
Well, by and large. I made it with very little money and I invited my wife to be a partner in it – at first, she didn't care for that. Nevertheless, she did come in and we made the film for very, very little money. We lucked out with an exhibitor in Chicago, who had

a theatre that played art films, things like that. I went back and did a lot of promo – Roger Ebert, that was where I first met him, and he was helpful, very much so, gave it a good review, it was the first time that he had ever involved himself with . . .

Roger Ebert, who is now a phenomenal, very, very important figure in American review circles . . .
It played for a year in this theatre and grossed over $850,000. That was when tickets were a dollar, so you got a lot of asses on the seats there, I'll tell you that.

So what was the appeal of that specific movie, because when you break it down and put it on paper, it seems a very simple, very straightforward piece of work?
Well, Erica Gavin, she had a quality about her, no question about that. She was really greedy for the male member. Yeah – how was that, did I put it honestly? [Laughter]

I know actually where she works in Los Angeles, so I'm now armed with this information . . .
Yeah, she runs a clothing store.

She works at Fred Segal's, I believe, I've been there many times, never seen her. Loitered for hours sometimes. [Laughter] Vixen *also, I get the feeling, knowing you a little better now as I do, there's more of you in than the early movies. I mean at the end when the draft dodger and the communist are getting their comeuppance . . .*
Well yeah, I had to have that song going, about blacks being taking advantage of. It worked, it worked very well. It played well in Europe; it played in Japan and continues to play. It's a very successful film video-wise.

Were there imitators, 'cos there was a film from Canada, The Fox *. . . ?*
Well that was before, if anything I might have done a little imitation there. And of course it didn't have nearly the outrageousness. Of course, *Vixen* created a lot of problems in court; Mr Keating wanted to put me in the iron hotel in the worst possible way.

It's strange, 'cos we're talking about 1969 now, which was only a couple of years before the mainstream hardcore movies appeared, before Deep Throat, *which I think was '71 or '72, and [Behind]* the Green Door, *and it was something that you never strayed into. Did you feel after* Vixen *there was something you should push, that you should go into more explicit sex and graphic sex on-screen?*
No, I didn't want to hit the toilet. I figured that there were enough raps that I got as it was. But *Vixen* permitted me to go to the majors. I know Abe Burrows and [Richard] Zanuck suggested that they [20th Century Fox] look at *Vixen*, we were playing in 197 theatres in New York City. Generally, with someone who's a producer, you give them a print to look at out of courtesy. We didn't have any, so they decided to look at it in one of the houses down on 42nd Street, they chose that purposely.

Burrows was a noted playwright – he came out of the theatre, and supposedly said, 'You've done *Tora! Tora! Tora!* and you've done *Cleopatra*, you really need somebody, why don't you pick up on this guy and have him make a film? Look at the money this film's made, you might come up with a very successful result.' So I was introduced to young Zanuck and he gave me $5,000, and said, 'Why don't you write a treatment?', 'cos they wanted a sequel to *Valley of the Dolls*. That's when I got involved with Ebert, he had much the same taste as I did in the female form. I talked him into it: he wasn't very difficult to talk into it. He did a very good job and we sent the treatment to them, Cardinal [David] Brown and Prince Richard,

In Vixen, *wood nymph Vincence Wallace is seduced by bisexual Erica Gavin – adding to legal problems caused by sibling incest and interracial sex scenes.*

and they looked at it and they said, 'Great. You've now reached the second plateau, we're gonna give you $25,000.' Ebert got off for about 30 days and we turned this thing out.

You made two movies at 20th Century Fox, there was Beyond the Valley of the Dolls *and* The Seven Minutes.
The Seven Minutes was a mistake.

Well, before we go into that, I can see what's in it for 20th Century Fox, because of course they had had Tora! Tora! Tora!, Cleopatra, *and also* Star!, *the film with Julie Andrews. All of which were huge commercial disasters, so they needed someone like you. But what was in it for you, you'd just come from* Vixen, *your most successful movie, you were presumably by then a millionaire, you could make movies as and when you chose, why go to 20th Century Fox?*
Because I always wanted to get into the mainstream, it's very important, I never had

an opportunity before. And that was the whole point, I wanted to make a film for Fox and be part of the establishment.

So it legitimised what you were doing . . .
Never really did, but people were rather awestruck by the fact it made so much money. I know when I showed the film to the powers that be, the head of production, a man by the name of Myers, immediately detested me, because, simply, I was cutting into his bailiwick. But, when they looked at it, Zanuck and the rest of 'em, they didn't know what that picture was all about.

They didn't get it?
Yeah, and Zanuck said to his distribution man, 'What are we going to do?' He said, 'Well, I think what we should do is put it in wide, 50 theatres, and play it, get all the money we can 'cos we need it.' And then I got up and said, 'That's the wrong way to go.' Alienated the other Myers. I said, 'What we need is a very important theatre right on Hollywood Boulevard.' So Zanuck then went to the distributor and he said, 'Well, what's wrong with that?' He said, 'There's no theatres available.' Zanuck got up, and in his proudest moment he said, 'Go out and buy one.' We got the Panteges, you know. It was up and running.

And then word of mouth helped to sell the movie from there?
I'd say so, yeah. And great reviews, really great, positive reviews.

Let me ask you about The Seven Minutes, *the least recognisable of your movies in terms of it being a Russ Meyer picture. It's a film based on the Irving Wallace novel on the subject of censorship, which obviously has a certain personal resonance for you, but I've never seen this film and I've never been able to get hold of a copy – I think it shows occasionally on TV. But it's a very talky kind of movie, a courtroom drama.*
Yeah, we spend all of that time in the courtroom and not enough time in the bedroom.

Is there nudity in it? . . .
Very, very little, no. It was a mistake, I should have continued with what I was doing, *Beyond the Valley of the Dolls Number Two* or something of that nature.

So was it a commercial failure?
Yeah, it was a big failure.

So is that why you parted company with Fox?
Well, no. They kicked Zanuck out and they kicked out [David] Brown, and I went along with them. I went over to Warner Brothers, and they gave me $50,000, got a writer by the name of Jerome Kilty, he did [the Broadway play] *Dear Liar*. He wrote a very good screenplay. But there was another vice president of production and he had

the good fortune of doing a picture called *Klute*. Well, you know, I had to go. They didn't need two chiefs of production, so Zanuck went, they went out and painted my name out of the parking lot, [we] got all of our stuff together, and left.

So would you like to have stayed at Fox?
Oh sure, I have hopes of going back again, yeah.

And do you still have hopes that you could maybe go back and work for them again?
Yeah, I think there's a pretty good shot at it, yeah. Particularly if they do this film with me, based on the book [*A Clean Breast*].

It's interesting at the moment, looking at the movies that come out now from the mainstream Hollywood studios, such as Sliver or Disclosure, these kinds of movies are probably just as explicit as some of your stuff. And they're coming from majors and no one looks twice. Whereas, when Beyond the Valley of the Dolls came out at the same time as Myra Breckenridge, people were saying, 'The studios have no moral values anymore and it's a disgrace.' Do you find it redeeming, what's coming out of studios now, or are you upset that you're not part of it all and you're not doing it?
No, I don't give much thought to that. I think *Dolls* came along at the right time and it was bold, and did big business, a lot of asses on the seats. It's my proudest achievement as far as films are concerned. I really dig seeing that, sitting in the theatres as I did last night, and seeing the audience reacting exactly the same way. It's just like this picture you saw tonight [*Faster Pussycat*], people clapping at the end of a picture – it's universal.

I didn't realise before that there's a link between the two: both have wheelchair jokes in them. Here [Faster Pussycat] we have Stuart Lancaster being knocked out of the chair and falling out of the van, it always gets a big laugh. On Beyond the Valley of the Dolls I can't remember the man's name, but of course he falls out the chair at the end – you're a very sick man! [Laughter] But ahead of your time in your sickness, I'm proud of you!
Let's talk about Blacksnake! very quickly, purely because you're not happy with it and I like the way you talk about not being happy with it. Anouska Hempel was the star of it . . .
Is Anouska here?

She runs the very lovely, expensive Blake's Hotel here in town, but you're not a fan of Anouska?
No, there is no real warmth that exists in that area.

But, once again, she doesn't have the look of a Russ Meyer woman . . .
Well no, we had no choice, the girl we'd selected had taken some sort of drug and she was unavailable, and I'd signed everybody else.

The Very Breast of Russ Meyer

Was this for recreational purposes or medicinal?
I have no idea, she just couldn't work. So I had to take the second choice, and there was Anouska Hempel and she's built like a hoe handle. [Laughter] I had no choice whatsoever; I had to use her. She agreed to a lot of stuff, but her figure didn't really lend itself to my enlarging of the whole thing. She was a good actress, very good, excellent, but she just didn't have the qualifications to make it a Russ Meyer movie. She got really pissed off with me because we needed some intercuts in a scene with Percy Herbert and Dave Prowse. And she was being dealt with in a carnal manner and Dave was trying to do her in because she had had his tongue cut out, right? So there were a lot of things going on there, but I do a lot of post-production stuff and I needed some close-ups of breasts and I couldn't find anybody who had breasts as small as Anouska Hempel. And, I found someone just a little bit larger, and she really got uptight about that.

Let's just say hello to Dave Prowse.
Hello Dave.

Lovely to see Dave. We know he was almost in Who Killed Bambi?, Blacksnake!, *he was Darth Vader, and, of course, let us not forget the Green Cross Code Man [British kids' road safety information films], so let's hear it for Dave . . . [Applause.]*
So after Blacksnake! *we have the final three movies that you ever released, we have* Supervixens, *we have* Up! *and we have* Beneath the Valley of the Ultravixens.
Supervixens was a saviour film. It had Charles Napier, the man with seven more teeth than Burt Lancaster. [Applause] He was great.

He became a star, quite a mainsteam star . . .
Yeah, Jonathan Demme, he's done that stuff with him. But he also worked on *Cherry, Harry & Raquel,* played the sheriff.

But these movies, they're more overblown, the comedy is broader, they're more extravagant . . .
Well, more cartoonish, yes. And the girls were much more substantial.

'Cos you hit your stride with Kitten Natividad.
Wasn't she fine, huh?

I believe you had a relationship that lasted many years as well.
Yes, we're close friends.

When I first met you, I was terrified of you, as everybody is when they first meet you, and I was walking around your kitchen. Russ has a house which is decorated with memorabilia. It's a shrine to the movies, and there are wooden plaques with mementos on. There's the straw boater worn by Bill Teas in The Immoral Mr. Teas *and all this kind of stuff, and then you have a blue plastic case, and I'd no idea what it was. I said, 'Russ, what item of cinema technology would be contained within the case?', and the answer was . . .*

Her diaphragm.

Preserved for film fans to come [Laughter] – and the plaque underneath, remind me, what does that say?

The little Formica thing?

Yes, what does it say on it? Something about body fluids?

Oh, that's right – it had to do with body fluids, yes.

Oh, I was hoping for the full thing, but that'll do. I don't know how many people here have seen up the film Up!, *but even now when I watch it, I still can't work out what the hell is going on. What's the plot of* Up!*?*

Well, it has to do with a man that resembles Adolf – and I was always pretty good at

Boob-heavy Shari Eubank in Supervixens. *Despite her impact in Meyer's hit, her only other screen credit is* Chesty Anderson, US Navy *– a sex comedy without nudity.*

dealing with that subject. I found a dead ringer for him, he was a caddy, and he spoke a little German! His genitals were taken away by a piranha fish that had been dumped in the bathtub with him.

This is in the movie, and not in real life, I figure. [Laughter] And Up!*, was that a success for you?*
Yes, very much so. We had Raven De La Croix, marvellous, incredible lady.

And Kitten was in Up! *as well, was she?*
She was kind of like a Greek chorus. She should not be dealt with lightly.

I had no intention of dealing with her lightly, Russ. Do you have, looking back, a physical preference, or do you have a particular favourite actress of the women you've worked with?
It's hard to put 'em in line. I have a nice home where I think I've done something interesting: have you ever heard of 'there were ten little Indians, and then there were nine, and then there were eight'? There were six girls that were very *co-operative* – very nice to me. And I helped them. But I've left the home, a really elegant home, to the six ladies.

This is your home in Hollywood or in the desert?
In the desert. The whole thing is that no husband can be substituted, and the one who lives the longest gets the house, which is worth about a million bucks.

That is an awful and manipulative thing to do.
It's a great thing, it's a basis of a film, isn't it?

From beyond the grave, you're controlling these poor women's destiny. What's the address of this house again, Russ? [Laughter]
The address? 72550 Sundown Lane.

Beneath the Valley of the Ultravixens *is a marvellous film, but it's your last theatrically-released feature film.*
It's my favourite too, I would guess. We had a lot of good things in there, Kitten was marvellous and Anne Marie played that evangelist.

Wonderful, incredible looking woman.
Selling pillows, and things of that nature: 'Send in one dollar.'

Once again, was that Ebert working on the script as well?
Yeah, he wrote the script, we had to keep changing names because [Gene] Siskel [Ebert's film critic partner on the long-running *Siskel and Ebert* TV series] would be

after him. I think he wrote the script under the name Eric Rheinhold Timme.

I was going to ask how you paid him – was it a similar thing to your earlier one [screenwriter], Jack [Moran]? . . .
No, he got paid writer's scale, it was okay. And he had other requirements, he was into drink a little bit there at that time, and he needed a certain amount of Jack Daniel's.

This is not Ebert?
Yeah, we're talking about Ebert. He had to be paid to scale and it was important that he have a girl of substantial proportions at the end of the day. He knew a lot of girls, knew a heck of a lot of girls!

Was this in his contract? . . .
No, it was just a handshake, you know. [Laughter] Anyway, he'd finished the script, we were cooking a great meal and Kitten had acquired a large Scandinavian blonde. And they'd repaired upstairs, okay. My friend, who was the production manager on my films, he says, 'Meyer, you're the perfect host. While your buddy Ebert is upstairs gettin' laid, you're down here cookin' for 'im!'

And Junk Yard Sal, in the movie, was a favourite of Roger's as well . . .
Oh, yeah, they had great connubial bliss, no question of that. I remember Napier watching her walk away, she was so curvaceous, and he turned to Ebert and said, 'You got your night cut out for you, Ebert.'

So let's very briefly talk about what you're doing now. You have another film project lined up . . .
Yeah, Ebert wrote a treatment that's called *The Bra of God* and I photographed a girl who is remarkable, Stacy Keith. I did a layout for German *Playboy*, they go for more upholstered girls than the American *Playboy*, and I'd consider using her as God's wife.

And so the plot for **The Bra of God** *is . . .*
It's a kind of backward reverse of *Supervixens*, it's about a man who's gone out and done a lot of terrible things to women, and he shows up in these bizarre circumstances that I'd consider to be Heaven, and he meets the wife of God. It sounds sacrilegious, but it's not meant to be that way. She says, 'Well, my husband is off getting his car fixed. What we've done here is make a mistake, you were supposed to go down there and here you are in Heaven. Something has to be done about this.' And she says, 'The only thing I can say is that you have to go out and really re-do all those things, and treat those women the way they should be treated and I'll tell you this, that if you do the job completely and fully, when you come up you got a fair chance of making purgatory.' I'll draw some fire, probably from the Baptists in Alabama and so forth.

The Very Breast of Russ Meyer

Meyer's mistress for several years, Kitten Natividad later appeared in hardcore films like Bodacious Ta-Ta's *and* Titilation *– her own sex scenes being strictly simulated.*

[Laughter]

So where does 'the bra of God' or 'God's wife' come into it? Is it sort of like the Holy Grail? Her brassiere, where does that feature?
Well, it's called *The Bra of God*.

Oh, it's just the title – I'm just too literal-minded, Russ.
This girl doesn't need a bra.

The other thing I wanted to ask you about was the book. You've been working on the book now, A Clean Breast – *the life story, two volumes . . .*
No, three volumes now, 2,500 photographs . . .

When will it ever see the light?
I'm going to Hong Kong to supervise it. It's a 'fuck-and-tell' book, I'll get right down to the point, it's not 'kiss-and-tell'. Everybody that I've had anything to do with, it's laudatory, not negative, but it's told in the most intimate way, and [on] every page, if I'm talking about a certain lady, there she is and there's her text. You have the movie on one side; you got your imagination [on the other]. This'll get you through the night, I'll tell you that. [Laughter/Applause]

Aren't there potential legal nightmares involved in doing this?
I don't think they would [sue]. I think they were pleasant. I used their stage names, [as] a couple of them were married . . .

What about those early ones, do you have a photograph of the woman to whom you lost your virginity? I believe that Hemingway was involved in that particular . . .

No, I had to use a drawing by Jack Ward, he was a famous cartoonist. I had about 25 women that I wouldn't dare put in the book if I had pictures, but he enlarged them . . . Jack Ward, great cartoonist, drawing girls, very pneumatic.

I dropped in the name Hemingway seemingly arbitrarily, but he was around when you . . .
This is a good little anecdote: Paris was about to fall and we were attached to the Second French Armoured Division and a very heroic division that was brought about by De Gaulle. But they were primarily interested in cooking chickens and drinking wine, there was nothing to do, the Hun was on the retreat and so forth. So we were all a little depressed and went over to a town called Rambouillet, which was about 25 miles outside of Paris. There was Hemingway holding forth, and he really was into fisticuffs at night, and a few press people there, but we were the only three GIs at that given time. He thought it would be good if we were to be rewarded with some sort of liaison with the girls in the local notcherie. So everybody was agreed, I had four mates with me, and I was the only virgin in the bunch. There was one guy, he had a couple of children, so I knew he'd been to the post. And then there was another guy about 35 years of age, then I was maybe twenty, and then my friend Charlie Sumners, they called him 'Slick' – I didn't dare tell any of these people that I had had no relationship with a woman. And it worried the hell out of me, but I asked my friend, I said, 'Charlie, did you ever make love to somebody?' And he said, 'Yes.' I said, 'How old were you?' He said, ' I was eleven years old.' 'Eleven years old?' He said, 'It wasn't that, it was with a chicken.' [Laughter] 'A chicken?' He said, 'Well, a chicken can lay an egg, can't it?'

I won't ask you what came first, Russ.

AUDIENCE: *Stu Lancaster, who was wonderfully sleazy, has been in quite a few of your films. Could you tell me something about him?*
Stuart Lancaster was heir to the Ringling fortune, his mother left him something like $4,000,000. But it was in such a way that he could get $4,000 a month, because she knew that he'd run and out produce 400 bad plays, he was very much into the theatre. Stuart, even to this day, manages on the 4,000, but then he runs out and contacts me and I lend him a couple of hundred. He and his wife never cook . . . [Stuart Lancaster died, aged 80, on 29 December 2000.]

Stuart Lancaster, he was the crippled father in Faster Pussycat *. . .*
Yeah, and he was in essence the dirty old man in real life too. I remember Haji worked on *Supervixens* and she was a make-up girl and I was always into body make-up, it really made a nice smell, even Stuart smelled good in it. So, she was making him up and I remember one time [she] had to do an all-over make-up job, so I said, 'Be sure and make-up Stuart completely.' And she yelled out, 'Even his berry?'

The Very Breast of Russ Meyer

At the time I met Haji, she told me a story about you, that she was making up Kitten in the trailer, it was an early morning shoot, and you were obviously in your element, you had your troops rallied and you were ready for a fine day's film-making. And you walked in and smelled the body make-up being applied, inhaled and said, 'Ah, the smell of breasts!'
Well no, that was with Raven De La Croix.

Oh well, there you go. Same smell though.
Well, you know, I had Miss Natividad, and she always had full body make-up. And then she was ever-anxious for some kind of relief. And I knew that I'd catch hell from her if I didn't supply some of that relief. People were eating, but we'd eat really fast and I'd go into this big four-poster bed and we'd have a pretty good time. She'd always come out of the bed with all of the make-up eaten off her centre section. Haji would look at me like . . . [reproachful look].

AUDIENCE: *Jonathan alluded to* Who Killed Bambi? *– it seems to be a very important event in your life.* Who Killed Bambi? *eventually became* The Great Rock 'n' Roll Swindle *with the Sex Pistols.*
It didn't become a great picture.

AUDIENCE: *Can you tell us about your working relationship in England with the Sex Pistols, and particularly with Jeremy Thomas and Malcolm McLaren?*
Well the two people responsible for the film not being made are Malcolm McLaren and Jeremy Thomas, who I think is involved with this wonderful edifice [the National Film Theatre] – surprising he would let me in here . . . You know, when you can't get people on the phone, both of these guys . . . Malcolm McLaren, right? [Laughter]

That's all you have to say on the subject, is it Russ? You met with all the Pistols, I believe? . . .
Well, you know, Jones and Cook were fine. They wanted to end up owning Cadillacs, they were serious guys, but Vicious and Rotten were difficult. Really difficult. Rotten particularly disliked me because I was an American, and I was often on his case because he was generally uncooperative. I'd been out with him when he was getting a square meal. He hated the idea of eating what McLaren gave him – McLaren would give them a case of 57 Van Camps kind of pork and beans and a case of Guinness, and that was their allotment for food. He was kind of tough to deal with, he had a lot of dandruff, and at the table he'd rake his scalp – it was like one of those little balls that you have for Christmas, you know? Then he had a lot of tartar on his teeth; he'd give that a work-over. Kind of tough to deal with, I tell you. We went to this one place and he liked to put on the waiters, he had a guy, he called him 'Mush', and I'd say he was an Iranian or something. He said, 'Begging your pardon sir, my name isn't Mush.' And he'd [Rotten would] say, 'Okay Mush.' And to make the story short, they had to pin him down in the kitchen, he was ready with a butcher knife

to go out and deal Rotten a deadly blow to the solar plexus.

You actually shot some footage, didn't you, with Dave Prowse . . .
Dave Prowse played Little John and carried the little lamb . . . we shot the lamb.
[Actually a deer.]

You killed Bambi.
Yeah, but not in that sense. We had a proper gamesman who shot the animal.

So what was the story, what was the plot you were working on, 'cos it was very different to The Great Rock 'n' Roll Swindle, *I believe?*
Oh, *Rock 'n' Roll Swindle* had nothing to do with this, this was very good. It was about a little girl who looked like Shirley Temple with brunette hair. Dave Prowse comes with this little deer on his back, puts it down on the hearth, and the man who was playing Mick Jagger, guy by the name of Andrews, says, 'Jones Cottage. Looks like they could use a square meal.' Dave picks up the animal and runs through with his delivery, puts it down on the porch, all of a sudden they drive off, and 'Who is it?' And she says, 'Mummy, someone's killed Bambi.' But she watched the car go away, and she appears at the end of the film, which was the best thing of all, I think. There's a big, big thing on the wharf, massive thing [on] which the Sex Pistols are now performing. Right towards the end, the camera zooms in on a girl's face, and it's this girl, and she gets up and walks towards Johnny Rotten, putting out. She lifts a .357 Magnum and shoots him right in the face. [Laughter] And she says, 'And that's for Bambi!' That was the end of the film. I left out all the stuff in the middle.

Did you actually like the music, were you indifferent, did you have a feeling for their particular brand of . . . ?
I didn't care. I don't care what it is. If I don't like it, [I can] play Strauss or whatever. We had to have that kind of music, and I was very friendly with Cook and Jones.

AUDIENCE: *I was wondering where* Lorna *was filmed, what location you used?*
It was up on the Sacramento River. I went up there with a friend, got one of those rum-runner boats, and we found this location, nice hotel, an old shack. Took Lorna up there and the rest of the cast. We did it in two weeks. It was a strong film for its time.

Would that be an average shooting time that you spend on a movie, two weeks?
Well, if it got up to be around four weeks that was it. But not when I was at Fox when I did *Beyond the Valley of the Dolls*, I think it was about three months.

It's still a remarkable amount of time, four weeks, 'cos if you look at Ultravixens, *the number of shots there are in certain sequences, you really must work at some pace.*

The Very Breast of Russ Meyer

Well, I'm an editor too and I think that's the most important contribution one can make to a film, as a technician. I like it tighter than the bands of your shorts, I'm telling you. Got to go.

Didn't you appear in a movie for John Landis, **Amazon Women on the Moon***?*
Well, that was the blandest part. That was supposed to be a rough guy dealing with someone coming in to rent a cassette. Poorly done, but some people think it's great.

You mean the movie was poorly done, or the performance was poorly done?
I don't know, it was dumb. I did it and contributed the money to the American Cancer Fund! I figured that nobody could complain about that.

So you're not keen on being in front of the camera?
Oh no, I'm no actor. *Not at all.* Good director and filmmaker . . .

Is it **Supervixens** *or* **Up!** *when you appear at the end with your camera?*
I was narrating, but I [also] had my friend, the man of a thousand voices, John Furlong. He could mimic a lot of people. When we had the casket rocking back and forth, we had about 60 motorcyclists [watching], and Kitten was supposedly inside the casket with Martin Bormann. He had his molars in the casket, holding them up so that they could supposedly air. They weren't in it, but I had a man behind rocking it, and these motorcyclists all applauded.

It's a nice thought that, if somebody turned up late and walked in just as you were saying, 'Kitten was in the casket with Martin Bormann,' they wouldn't know what the hell was going on, would they?

AUDIENCE: *You have quite a large role in* **Motor Psycho***!*
Yeah, I was a cop because the actor couldn't do it, there was nobody else. And I had that good line: 'Well, nothing a woman ain't built for' . . . [she's] been raped soundly.

So you only appear if you can't avoid it?
Oh yeah, what are you gonna do, you can't fold up the show, and in Blythe, California, there's not many actors.

AUDIENCE: *How would you have made* **Basic Instinct***?*
Well first of all, I'd have had [Michael] Douglas take off his shorts. [Laughter] Pretty damn hard to do a number on this girl, with his shorts on. That was bad . . . that was a big mistake.

Did you like the film though? . . .
Yeah, I liked it, I liked Douglas very much. She's [Sharon Stone's] good, very good,

In 1999 (at a party in his honour), aged 77, with his health starting to fail, tits and ass still came Russ Meyer's way.

but she's not pneumatic, I couldn't use her in a film now. [Laughter]

She's streamlined, it's the modern look, Russ, that's what it is.
Wafer-thin.

Have you seen Michael Douglas in Disclosure, the new Michael Crichton thing?
No, but the ad looks kind of funny: he's turned around looking at this girl, and I get the feeling she might have had her thumb up his rear end. [Laughter] He's got that look. Next time you see the ad, you'll think of that line.

AUDIENCE: *Are we ever going to see* The Breast of Russ Meyer?
Well, it's about fifteen hours long. I've taken some of the girls out of it and put 'em in this Pandora Peaks thing. Candy Samples is a remarkable lady.

Let's just fill people in, this was a cinematic look back at your life . . .
Yeah, World War II, it's just too much to deal with. It'd take the rest of my life to put it together, and sound effects and all that. No, I want to make a film every year, without dealing with that.

Could you delegate, give it to some young hopeful filmmakers to . . .
Well, what do they know about me?

The Very Breast of Russ Meyer

Well, you might be pleasantly surprised.
No, I don't think so, I don't think it would work. The amount of money involved in doing it . . . it's best to leave it alone. The book does a better job.

There's talk, I believe, of a mainstream studio making a film of your life, is that right?
Yeah, it looks pretty good. New Line Cinema's interest was displayed to my agent. The book might be a good vehicle. I want Robin Williams to play me. [Laughter] I'm serious. You don't need somebody to look like me, but I've got to direct it, 'cos nobody knows more about Russ Meyer than myself. Can you imagine Scorsese or someone given this assignment? He'd see it like working in a whorehouse or something.

Presumably the film would be, as we've seen this evening, as honest as you are about your life. I remember from when you allowed me to read your book, way back when, there's a scene in one of your films where somebody's making love to someone's wife and her husband returns and kicks down the door, and one minute he's inside the man's wife and then they're having a fist-fight. This is based on a scene in your life, I believe?
Yes, there was a lady in a town called Vallejo. She was a spectacular waitress and she sold so much coffee 'cos the truck drivers always came in there and she always wore a white dress, like a nurse's dress a couple of sizes too small. So I talked to her and gave her that old pitch about shooting still pictures and it worked. So we became friendly, she lived in a town called Martinez, had a big house out front, then she had a big kind of silo, and on top was this little house. Without any delay, she invited me up there and I joined her in close connubial bliss. There was an awful racket downstairs, I said, 'Who's that?' She said, 'Go down and get rid of him.' I tell you, when you're naked and you're fist-fighting, it's not the best way to do it. Anyway, when I got there, he kicked the whole bottom of the door out, and I opened the door, which was dumb, and he hit me right in the mush. Smackdab. And I had no choice other than to run out there and attack him. This great ring that my mother gave me put a good dent in his forehead. My feet were bloodied, and it was an even thing, except the police came, and all of the neighbours were up on the fence, and I was going though a divorce so it was the last thing I needed. And the girl came out with a giant pot bottle and she wanted to finish him off. So anyway, the police said, 'What's your name?', and I said, 'My name is Bill Teas.' [Laughter] They wrote it, I said, 'I don't have any identification on me, as you can see.' [Meyer laughs] They marched this guy off and put him in the iron hotel, alright. So I went upstairs with her, and she said, 'Let's see if it was all worth it.' So we did a little number on each other, it was very good. I woke up in the morning and I couldn't put my shoes on because my feet were so bloodied, then I had to find my car and I didn't know where it was. But we became quite friendly . . .

When I was married to Eve, we were very close and so forth. But I was driving past this off-shoot road, [in] Dublin, California, that's where this lady lived, and I thought, 'God, I've just got to go and say hello.' Well, I tell you, she'd really put on a little weight in the right places. She was very friendly and invited me in and she said, 'I understand that you married this blonde bimbo?' and I said, 'Yeah, it's true.' [Laughter] She said, 'Why don't you go out and get a six-pack and we'll have something to drink.' Well, all of a sudden I got aroused, there was something about her that was . . . Totally naked, you know, just ohhh wow! So I went and got a six-pack, ran back, she was sitting on the couch there, and she said, 'Why don't we do something about this?' Then all of a sudden, I thought about my wife. I said, 'I can't do this.' I'm like you; you're British, you don't break up with your wives.

Well, some members of my family do . . .
Well anyway, I said, 'I can't do it.' She said, 'You no good so and so and so and so, you no good . . .' She called me a homosexual; she just couldn't handle that. So, I got out of there in the nick of the quick, got in my car and drove off. I felt very proud about the whole thing, but, at times, I thought that I should have maybe taken a shot at it. [Laughter]

AUDIENCE: *Why did you stop producing films after* Beneath the Valley of the Ultravixens?
Well, let's see . . . I had this thing with damn [Malcolm] McLaren . . .

Wasn't that before . . . ?
It wasn't finished, no I never finished it. If anybody was responsible for that film [*Who Killed Bambi?*] not working it was McLaren. Very definitely.

Why did you not have . . . ?
He didn't have enough money, is what it amounted to.

But there was no other project . . . ?
I didn't have any other project, it just wiped me out. I went to Australia and went fishing, I sold my films and so forth, and then I came back and finished that picture [*Ultravixens*]. McLaren should have done that film, no matter what: beg, borrow or steal . . .

I think he feels that way . . .
We could have made a hell of a picture. He was okay, he'd leave you alone, you know. Sometimes it's bad to be left too much alone, but in the case of this he just didn't have the bundle.

But I suppose working on The Breast of, *which we've never seen, that must have taken some time as well?*
I was involved in that too, yeah . . . It was criminal that we didn't make that picture [*Bambi*].

The Very Breast of Russ Meyer

AUDIENCE: *Was there a key film that you saw when you were a kid that really made you want to be involved with movies?*
That would not be it, I was into Tom Mix and Ken Maynard [cowboy film stars], things of that nature.

What about the Al Capp cartoons?
Well, I was influenced by Al Capp, *Li'l Abner*. I'd emulate the cartoons and I'd make the girls' bosoms much larger. There was a girl in school, by the name of Polly, she was something: always dropping her pencils and giving this gaping cleavage out.

So there was no one director or series of movies that inspired and influenced you?
No, I had all that good background doing industrial films. Then having to do with people I've made reference to. That's it.

AUDIENCE: *I wanted to ask you a question on censorship, but before I do can I tell you a quick anecdote? There was this marvellous club cinema in London, called the Scala . . .*
Oh yeah, the man I met today who was interviewing me, he did [*Interview with*] *the Vampire . . .*

[Producer] Steve Woolley [former co-owner of the Scala Cinema/Scala Films].
Nice guy. He reminded me about the fact that the films were often played there. One thing that bothered me, they had a projector that was produced by International Harvester – that's a threshing machine. Those pictures really got a bad going-over.

Well I'm sure that's where a lot of us saw our first Russ Meyer movie in this country. You were going to tell us something about it? . . .

AUDIENCE: *I saw* Up! *as part of a triple bill and enjoyed the film greatly. So much so that the next time it was on, I thought, 'I've got to go again.' So I went along one afternoon and the film was in a terrible state. I thought, 'I'm sure this has been cut, something happened here and it's not there anymore.' Anyway, the film ended and the projectionist came out and he said, 'I'm sorry ladies and gentlemen, this was all I could get hold of for this afternoon, but if you want to stay on, for no fee, you can see the uncut version.' So the question is, have you had problems in this country with the British Board of Film Classification and James Ferman in particular?*
Who is Ferman?[Laughter] I have sealed lips here with my dear friend. He's made it clear to me to keep my mouth shut about it.

So we mustn't talk about that, that's pending the video release[s] in this country and we have to unfortunately sit on it.
But if he fails it'll be an altogether different matter. [Laughter] Don't fail.

AUDIENCE: *You mentioned problems with censorship, you've mentioned your problems with Baptists, you've mentioned your problems with the Amish, but you haven't mentioned any problems with the feminist lobby, whose rise coincided with your career, or with political correctness in any way . . .*

Now with *Faster Pussycat*, the women are very much involved with this picture, they like it very much. There were fourteen women recently [who] showed their films as part of the Academy [of Motion Picture Arts], and each one of them agreed they would show the trailer of *Faster Pussycat*. Yeah, how about that?

Sounds good to me. So you didn't have people picketing the cinema, there were never protest groups? . . .

No, well, the only one time was in Sacramento. I was up there with a newspaperman. We were driving through town, there was this nice theatre, and the women were out with signs and placards, saying, 'Meyer condones rape,' things like that. So I stopped the car and I said, 'Set the camera up there,' as I wanted some footage on this. So I eased down there and got in line and I got one of the signs, marching with the women. The woman's looked at me: 'You *son-of-a-bitch*.'

Speaking of you grabbing shots, you used to travel considerable distances just to capture, for inclusion in whatever project you were involved in, any road signs, street signs or park signs that were alluding to breasts in some way . . .

Paris Match had a sign, and *Paris Match* are very bold. It said *Defense de Penetrer* ['No Entry'], and it's on the headboard of my bed.

So they gave it to you, they made a gift of it?
I said, 'Give it to me.'

AUDIENCE: *You mentioned Candy Samples just now. I hear you've had a walk-on part in one of her films. I wonder if you can tell us some facts about it?*
I never had any personal relationship with her – but she was very co-operative working with me, in films of herself, and had an ability to carry Dom Perignon around. Just open it up, put the jug here [between her breasts] – and *boing!* It all came back up together. And that was a full bottle of Dom Perignon. [Laughter]

A magnum. I don't know whether any of the women you'll work with in the future [will have them], but certainly with surgery, with implants, the look that you sought out and had such a difficult time finding can now be achieved medically. I wonder whether you'll favour that, whether you'd rather not work with people who aren't naturally enhanced in that way?
No, there's things done now that are very safe. But the silicone was dangerous, very dangerous; it got into the bloodstream. Having a saline solution, and it's now

anchored to the back of the breast, is perfectly safe.

You've looked into this, haven't you? I can tell. [Laughter]
I've investigated.

But the fact that it's not real *real . . .*
No, no, I have no argument about that. A breast is a breast is a breast!

AUDIENCE: *What do your family make of your films?*
Well, I just have a sister. She doesn't understand, she's been ill for a long time. My mother just approved of everything I did, except that when I wasn't in earshot she'd say to a friend, 'I wish Russ wouldn't make those kinds of films.' But, if I were to accost her with this, she'd say, 'Oh, it's quite alright, it's wonderful. Lovely girls, what lovely women!' Bless her.

AUDIENCE: *You're quite well known for your montage. What kind of approach do you have before you shoot?*
Well, they are trims from the scenes, by and large. Cut scenes that would be out-takes. And I'd shoot a lot of inserts, I'm big on signs, things of that nature.

Which film is it in which you intercut your bodies slamming together in the swimming pool with the stock-car crashes, is that Finders . . . Lovers?
Yeah, my friend Jim Ryan's mother presented an interesting question: we used demolition derby, then I had these two people shot underwater and we would intercut with the cars. I was intending to have that, the sound effects and the whole thing. It worked well. His [Ryan's] mother, this lovely little old lady, she's looking at the two bodies that are nude whacking together and the cars crashing. She said, 'Jimmy, how did Russ get the cars in the pool?' [Laughter]

AUDIENCE: *Can you tell us something about the planned sequel to* Vixen, Foxy, *which was to star Edy Williams?*
Yeah. Ebert wrote it.

You shot a trailer for it as well, didn't you?
Yeah, it was a good trailer. But Edy didn't want [Charles] Napier in it. She said, 'Who's interested in seeing this guy?' I said, 'He's a great actor.' 'Well, he's a big klutz, all they want to do is see me.' Well, I knew then and there we had difficult problems. Edy was a remarkable lady, I can say a lot of very exciting things about her. She almost had a child, she had a miscarriage . . . she got upset and lost the child. She wanted very much for me to star [her] in every movie, it was difficult to think about that possibility. She did a great job in *Dolls*, she played Edy Williams to the teeth, it was

excellent. Her idea of sexuality was the flaring of the nostrils; it really was an important part of her thing. She just played herself.

She's still sort of pretty . . . she's got a reasonable profile on the Hollywood scene, she always turns up in an outrageous outfit at Oscar time and gets snapped . . .
She was a real looker, great lady. I remember, I didn't use her in *Blacksnake!*, and when we got back she carried on in the customs area with about 500 people, referring to me as 'a real son-of-a-bitch . . . cheap, tight, doesn't give me any money.' 'Here, take this' – I had $500 – 'Please leave me alone.' She figured that I might give in with this kind of thing, get down on my knees, 'I'll put you in my next film, you'll be the star; you can select everybody else you're going to work with.' But I think it would have been better than to deal with Anouska Hempel, without a doubt, except that she'd always interfere with a male actor having too many lines: 'Why do you have to have that?' Probably the only part she wouldn't intrude in is yours, David. All he [Dave Prowse] did was 'uuuhhh'. [caricature mute noises] The woman in the picture, she had him castrated.

[To the audience] The woman at the back there.

AUDIENCE: *I would like to ask you, Mr. Meyer, if is there any parallel between your movie-making career and sexual prowess, and perhaps that's why you haven't released a complete movie in the past fifteen years? [Uproar/Laughter]*
That's fighting talk!
What is this now?

I think maybe she should say it again, it would lose a lot of its resonance if it came from me . . . She wants to see if there's a parallel between your sexual prowess, your sex life, and your movie career, and if indeed that will explain why you haven't released or completed a movie in the last fifteen years. And I'll be over there if you want me! [Laughter]
What can I say? It's not true. I didn't make any more movies simply because I had a lot of disappointments that I've run through tonight. I had something that I wanted to do very much and it's not that simple to go off and come up with a new idea.

But the sex life continues at full speed ahead?
I have pretty good luck in that area, it still works.

Are you still seeing Melissa Mounds . . . ?
We're at a disadvantage at the moment, my dog bit her. [Laughter] It's not funny . . .

Well it is funny, but it's maybe not right that we laugh.
She's a great lady. Any woman that will call out while you're working on a smoking

movieola and she'll say, 'I just washed it out, it's all nice and clean; why don't you come upstairs and do a number on me?' Well, that's pretty hard to resist, I'm doing four stairs at a time. It's hard to pass up on something like that, huh?

AUDIENCE: *Do you think that your films would have had more impact if the Wonderbra had been around at the time?*
No, these girls, as a rule, don't need a bra, they are bra-less.

Are you familiar with the Wonderbra?
No, I'm aware of it . . . [Laughter] You would have to have something made by the Bay City Tech Company in way of a Wonderbra, you know.

AUDIENCE: *Who crocheted Anne Marie's one-piece in* Beneath the Valley of the Ultravixens*?*

Good question, Anne Marie's crocheted, white flared number . . .
Oh yeah, it was a big job to pack her into that.

Where did that come from, that was obviously a speciality order I would have thought?
Yeah, she and her husband lived out front in a trailer, there were people living all over the place, but she and her husband liked to have *pleasant evenings*. That old trailer was going like this. [rocking motion] Nice lady, nice lady.

That was the knitting, that's why it was going like that. An industrial-size knitting machine.
AUDIENCE: *What's your favourite Charles Napier anecdote?*
Gotta come up with something good then.

You don't have to, you'll never see him again.
No, Napier and I were good friends. I haven't seen him too much; he was disappointed that I didn't do a particular film that he wanted to be in. I think one of the better things that happened out of *Supervixens*, he was living in a car lot I had on Hollywood Boulevard in his camper, and a guy came along and pressed his face through the window. Napier had a .32 and returned the favour, and the guy says, 'Mr Hitchcock wants to see you.' And he said, 'Yeah, sure, right.' So anyway, he went along and he had an audience with Hitchcock, and Hitchcock was sitting there with a hot light, you couldn't see the detail of his face, so Napier turned around and the guy gave him a cheque for 5,000 bucks, 'Sign him up.' . . . And then *The Blues Brothers* and things of that nature came along. Then he had a piece of action in *Supervixens*. Great guy.

*'Bosomania', coined by Meyer to describe his films, also sums up his persnal fetish – on display
at this 1999 party, where the girls are alluring but not 'buxotic'.*

He was going to be in the remake of **Faster Pussycat,** *wasn't he?*
I was giving that thought. There are so many things you think about that you don't do.

It doesn't sound like there's a lot that you think about and don't do . . .

AUDIENCE: *You mentioned Tempest Storm from the early days, did you ever meet
anyone else around at that time, like Betty Page . . .*
Ah, the Betty Page question.

AUDIENCE: *. . . or Chesty Morgan?*
*Chesty Morgan was a bit later. But the sort of Fifties burlesque stars like Blaze Starr,
Tempest, Candy Barr . . . ?*
Well, we talked about Tempest, but I never was really turned on by Betty Page, she
didn't have the *accoutrements* that I most . . .

There's a big following for her now, did you meet her?
No, I never met her. More power to her.

The Very Breast of Russ Meyer

What about Lili St. Cyr, I believe you met her?
Yes, I did some work with her, she was a very attractive, successful lady. She always had somebody that was kind of her servant; she would really bedevil them. Even when I'd shoot pictures of her, stills, she would embarrass the hell out of the guy, making him do things that were sort of *tawdry*, you know.

AUDIENCE: *Where is the phallus in your films? Where is the missing phallus? Where is the missing phallus? [Laughter] I'm just the messenger, Russ.*
The *phallus* in my films? You're not talking about the big dildo? Napier use to paint the blue veins in it.

Generally, I think he's pointing to the emphasis on female sexuality and the bosom in particular, as opposed to our old friend the cock. There are some phallic scenes and symbols – if you look. [Laughter]
Yes, that's true.

But they don't tend to dominate the scene.
No, they'd want it in an erected state, see, and I'd have even more problems with so-called censors.

Are you actually talking about tumescent penises, or are you talking about symbols?
AUDIENCE: *Symbols. Well . . . no I'm not! [Laughter]*
Got a few laughs, so let's move on . . .
Well, rockets taking off, things like that.

Rockets, trains, and stations.

AUDIENCE: *Haji and Tura Satana have both stated in interviews that they've got an idea for a* Faster Pussycat, Kill! Kill! Part Two. *Would there be any chance of that?*
Not likely, no. I'll have to deal with them severely.

You're still friends with Haji, I believe?
Oh yes. They're not production people, you know. It's best to leave it like it is. It's 'good works'.

AUDIENCE: *Whatever happened to John LaZar who played Z-Man in* Beyond the Valley of the Dolls?
Oh yes, yes. I just spoke with him the other day, he said that he'd left his wife and had a new girlfriend and he said he looks remarkably well, very fit, wondered if I had some kind of work for him. That was great, that thing with him kissing [Michael] Blodgett, it was kind of a job to get him to do that. You know the scene? Lazar, and Blodgett, the Tarzan suit?

It's a fantastic scene.
They were great contributors to the film.

It's a remarkable movie. Were there moments during shooting where you came close to losing your nerve, because it is insane in places, isn't it?
No, I had it well in hand.

We're talking about the young Roger Ebert writing this. I don't mean to besmirch his character in any way, but did hallucinogenics play any part in the screenplay, do you think?
No, not at all. I say enough about Ebert without . . .

Without accusing him of dropping tabs.
His wife now begins to like me, she can handle this stuff.

AUDIENCE: *You've just been talking about Z-Man and Blodgett [as Lance Rocke]. There's a scene where Z-Man removes his [Blodgett's] head, and you used the 20th Century Fox theme music in that scene.*
We figured we would make it better for the rating board if we used the Fox logo music. Yeah, head rolling across the floor . . . Zanuck looked at me kinda strange: 'Oh, okay,' you know.

Obviously, he gave you kind of a free rein there, he really did.
They really didn't know what was going on, they left it entirely to me, and Ebert. Even when it was finished, they didn't really understand what it was all about. But, when it was shown, he said, 'People *like* this.'

AUDIENCE: *I was just curious where you got the inspiration for using the shots from underneath the empty mattress.*
In Vixen?
Oh, I like that kind of stuff with the coils, shooting straight up, yeah, that's good. It's a good idea; I've done that more than once. It's ridiculous to think about, it would be so really painful if the guy made a mistake and he got it in one of those coil springs . . . I'd have a lawsuit, right?

I think on that note, we should applaud and say thank you to possibly the greatest living American, Mr. Russ Meyer, ladies and gentlemen. [Applause]
I've never had an accolade like that in my life, it was great.

Filmography

Key

Pr	Producer
Dr	Director
Sc.	Screenplay
Ph.	Photographer
Ed.	Editor
M.	Music
Ass.Ed	Assistant Editor
ArtDr	Art Director
S.	Sound
Ass.Pr	Associate Producer
Pr.Mgr	Production Manager
Ass.Ph.	AssistantPhotographer
Sp.Ph.Effects	Special Photographic Effects
SetDr	Set Director
W'rb	Wardrobe
Pr.Crew	Production Crew

THE IMMORAL MR. TEAS aka STEAM HEAT, MR.
TEAS AND HIS PLAYTHINGS (UK) (1959). A Pad-Ram
Enterprises release, Pr: P. A. De Cenzie, Dr/Sc./Ph./Ed.: Russ
Meyer, M.: Edward Lasko, Ass.Ed.: John F. Link, ArtDr: Ken
Parker, Eric 'Mick' Nathanson, Narrator: Edward Lasko.
Cast: W. Ellis Teas (Bill Teas), Dawn Danielle, Pete De
Cenzie, Ann Peters, Michele Roberts, Marilyn Wesley, June
Wilkinson. Colour, 63 min.

EVE AND THE HANDYMAN (1960). A Pad-Ram
Enterprises release, Pr/Dr/Sc./Ph./Ed.: Russ Meyer, ArtDr:
Mel Fowler. Cast: Eve Meyer (Eve), Anthony-James Ryan
(the Handyman), Frank Bolger, Iris Bristol, Rita Day, James
Evanoff, Gigi Frost, Mildred Knezevich, Francesca Leslie,
Florence Moore, Ken Parker, Jackie Stephens, Lyle Tolefson,
Charles Vaughn. Colour, 65 min.

THE NAKED CAMERA (1960). A ten-minute colour short
directed, written, and shot by Meyer, and starring Mikki
France. It was shown as a co-feature with EVE AND THE
HANDYMAN.

EROTICA aka EROTICON (1961). A Pad-Ram Enterprises
release, Pr: P. A. De Cenzie, Russ Meyer, Dr/Sc./Ph./Ed.:
Russ Meyer, Narration by Jack Moran, Narrator: Joe
Cranston, M.: David Chudnow, Tommy Morgan. Cast:
Althea Currier, Denise Daniels, Pete De Cenzie, Elaine Jones,
Werner Kirsch, Sherry Knight, Peggy Martin, Russ Meyer,
Charles G. Schelling, Donna Townsend, Lana Young. This
film is comprised of six segments titled 'Naked Innocence',
'Beauties, Bubbles, and H2O', 'The Bear and the Bare',
'Nudists on the High Seas', 'The Nymphs', and 'The Bikini
Busters'. Colour, 65 min.

WILD GALS OF THE NAKED WEST aka THE
IMMORAL WEST AND HOW IT WAS LOST, THE
NAKED WEST AND HOW IT WAS LOST, THE
IMMORAL WEST, THE IMMORAL GIRLS OF THE
NAKED WEST, NAKED GALS OF THE GOLDEN
WEST (1962). A Pad-Ram Enterprises release, distributed by
Pacifica Productions, Pr: P. A. De Cenzie, Russ Meyer,
Dr/Ph./Ed.: Russ Meyer, Sc.: Russ Meyer, Jack Moran, S.:
Werner Kirsch, M.: Marlin Skiles, ArtDr: Mel Fowler. Cast:
Sammy Gilbert, Werner Kirsch, Nate Schwantze, Barbara

Baral, Arlyn Solomon, Rusty Taylor, Pegge Thomas, Jean
Roche, Jean Rainey, Patty McMains, Mel Fowler, Pete De
Cenzie, Janis Carter, Joyce McCord, Janette Davidson, Palva
Stano, Sandra Lind, Barney Caliendo, Russ Meyer, Jack
Moran, Teri Taylor (aka Goldie Nuggets), Princess
Livingston, the Topanga Gulch Players. Colour, 62 min.

EUROPE IN THE RAW (1962). An Eve Productions
release, Pr/Dr/Sc./Ph./Ed.: Russ Meyer, Narrators: Franklin
L. Thistle, Vic Perrin, Lynn Held, Cast: Denise Du Vall,
Heidi Richter, Yvette Le Grand, Greta Thorwald,
Abundavita, Gigi La Touche, Veronique Gabriel, Fred
Owens, 'Baby Doll' Shawn Devereaux, Donna Scott. Colour,
72 min.

HEAVENLY BODIES! aka HEAVENLY ASSIGNMENT
(1963). An Eve Productions release, Pr/Dr/Sc./Ph./Ed.: Russ
Meyer. Cast: Ken Parker, Gaby Martine, Marian Milford,
Don Cochran, Werner Kirsch, Fred Owens, Billy Newhouse,
Orville Hallberg, Bill Cummings, Althea Currier, Monica
Liljestrand, Yvonne Cortell, Paulette Firestone, Maria Andre,
Princess Livingston, Russ Meyer. Colour, 62 min.

SKYSCRAPERS AND BRASSIERES (1963). A ten-minute
colour short directed, written, and shot by Meyer, and
featuring Rochelle Kennedy. It was shown as a co-feature
with HEAVENLY BODIES!

LORNA (1964). An Eve Productions release, Pr/Dr/Ed.:
Russ Meyer, Ass.Pr: Eve Meyer, Sc: James Griffith, Russ
Meyer, Jim Nelson, Ph.: Russ Meyer, Walter Schenk, S.:
Charles G. Schelling, M.: Hal Hopper, James Griffith,
Dialogue: James Griffith, Pr.Mgr: Fred Ownes. Cast: Lorna
Maitland (Lorna), Mark Bradley (Fugitive), James Rucker
(James), Hal Hopper (Luther), Doc Scortt (Jonah), James
Griffith (Prophet). B/w, 79 min.

FANNY HILL: MEMOIRS OF A WOMAN OF
PLEASURE (1964). A Favorite Films release of a Famous
Players Corporation production, Pr: Albert Zugsmith, Dr:
Russ Meyer, Sc: Robert Hill, from the novel by John Cleland,
Ph.: Heinz Hilscher, Ed.: Alfred Srp, M.: Erwin Halletz,
Ass.Dr: Elfie Tillack. Cast: Miriam Hopkins (Mrs Maude
Brown), Letitia Roman (Fanny Hill), Walter Giller
(Hemingway), Alex D'Arcy (the Admiral), Helmut Weiss (Mr.
Dinklespieler), Chris Howland (Mr Norbert), Ulli Lommel
(Charles), Cara Garnett (Phoebe), Karin Evans (Martha), Syra
Marty (Hortense), Albert Zugsmith (Grand Duke), Renate
Hutte, aka Rena Horten (Niece). B/w, 104 min.

MUDHONEY (1965). A Delta Films release, Pr: Russ
Meyer, George Costello, Dr/Ed.: Russ Meyer, Ass.Pr: Eve
Meyer, Sc.: Raymond Friday Locke, William E. Sprague
(from Locke's novel *Streets Paved with Gold*), Ph.: Walter
Schenk, Ass.Dr: George Costello, S./Ed.: Charles G.
Schelling, M.: Henri Price. Cast: Hal Hopper (Sidney
Brenshaw), Lorna Maitland (Clara Belle), Antoinette
Christiani (Hannah Brenshaw), John Furlong (Calif
McKinney), Stu Lancaster (Lute Wade), Rena Horten (Eula),
Princess Livingston (Maggie Marie), Sam Hanna (Injoys),
Nick Wolcuff (Sheriff), Frank Bolger (Brother Hanson), Lee
Ballard (Sister Hanson), Mickey Foxx (Thurmond Pate), F.
Rufus Owens (Milton). B/w, 92 min.

MOTOR PSYCHO! (1965). An Eve Productions release, Pr/Dr/Ph./Ed.: Russ Meyer, Ass.Pr: Eve Meyer, Sc: W. E. Sprague, Russ Meyer, James Griffith, Hal Hopper, Ass.Dr: George Costello, S./Ed.: Charles G. Schelling, M.: Igo Kantor, Paul Sawtell, Bert Shefter. Cast: Stephen Oliver (Brahmin), Haji (Ruby Bonner), Alex Rocco (Cory Maddox), Holle K. Winters (Gail Maddox), Joseph Cellini (Dante), Thomas Scott (Slick), Coleman Francis (Harry Bonner), Sharon Lee (Jessica Fannin), E. E. Meyer, aka Russ Meyer (Sheriff). B/w, 74 min.

FASTER PUSSYCAT, KILL! KILL! aka PUSSYCAT, THE MANKILLERS, LEATHER GIRLS (1966). An Eve Productions release, Pr: Russ Meyer, Eve Meyer, Dr/Ed.: Russ Meyer, Ass.Pr: Fred Owens, George Costello, Pr.Mgr: Fred Owens, Sc.: Jack Moran, Ass.Dr: George Costello, Ph.: Walter Schenk, Ass.Ph.: Gil Haimson, Orville Hallberg, S.: Charles Schelling, Richard Serly Brummer, M.: Igor Kantor, theme by Paul Sawtelle, Bert Shefter and Rick Jarrard - sung by the Bostweeds, Narrator: John Furlong. Cast: Tura Satana (Varla), Haji (Rosie), Lori Williams (Billi), Susan Bernard (Linda), Stuart Lancaster (Old Man), Paul Trinka (Kirk), Dennis Busch (Boy), Ray Barlow (Tommy), Mickey Foxx (Attendant). B/w, 84 min.

MONDO TOPLESS aka MONDO GIRLS (1966). An Eve Productions release, Pr/Dr/Ph./Ed.: Russ Meyer, Ass.Pr: Eve Meyer, Fred Owens, Bill Newhouse, Richard Serly Brummer, S.: Don Minkler, M.: Russ Meyer, performed by the Alladins, Narrator: John Furlong. Cast: Babette Bardot (Bouncy), Pat Barrington (Bumptious), Sin Lenée (Luscious), Darlene Grey (Buxotic), Diane Young (Yummy), Darla Paris (Delicious), Donna X, aka Donna Scott (Xciting), Veronique Gabriel, Greta Thorwald, Denice Duval, Abundavita, Heidi Richter, Gigi La Touch, Yvette Le Grand, Lorna Maitland, Candy Morrison. Colour, 61 min.

COMMONn LAW CABIN aka HOW MUCH LOVING DOES A NORMAL COUPLE NEED? (1967). An Eve Productions release; Pr/Dr/Ed./Sc.: Russ Meyer, Ass.Pr: Eve Meyer, George Costello, Sc.: Jack Moran, Ph.: Russ Meyer, Wady Medawar, Jack Lucas, S.: Richard Serly Brummer, Irwin Cadden, Don Minkler, M.: Igo Kantor. Cast: Ken Swofford (Barney Rickert), Alaina Capri (Sheila Ross), Jack Moran (Dewey Hoople), Adele Rein (Coral Hoople), Andrew Hagara (Laurence Talbot), Frank Bolger (Cracker), Babette Bardot (Babette), John Furlong (Dr Martin Ross). Colour, 70 min.

GOOD MORNING . . . AND GOODBYE! aka THE LUST SEEKERS (UK) (1967). An Eve Productions release; Pr/Dr/Ed./Ph.: Russ Meyer, Ass.Pr: Eve Meyer, Fred Owen, Ass.Dr: George Costello, Sc.: John E. Moran, from story by Russ Meyer, Ass.Ed.: Richard Serly Brummer, Ass.Ph.: Fred Owen, Jack Lucas, Wady Medawar, S.: Richard Brummer and John E. Moran, M.: Igor Kantor, Narrator: Joe Perrin. Cast: Alaina Capri (Angel), Stuart Lancaster (Burt), Pat Wright (Stone), Haji (Wood Nymph), Karen Ciral (Lana), Don Johnson (Ray), Tom Howland (Herb), Megan Timothy (Lottie), Toby Adler (Betty), Sylvia Tedemar (Dancer), Carol Peters (Nude). Colour, 78min.

FINDER KEEPERS, LOVERS WEEPERS (1968). An Eve Productions release, Pr/Dr/Ed./Sc.: Russ Meyer, Ex.Pr: Eve Meyer, Ass.Pr: Anthony James Ryan, Ass.Dr: George Costello, Sc.: Richard Zachary, from story by Russ Meyer, Ed.: Richard Serly Brummer, S.: Richard Serly Brummer, Nikolai Volokhanovich, Bill Mumford, Don Minkler, Ph.: Russ Meyer, Wady Medawar, M.: Igo Kantor, theme by Melvin Elling with the Casuals on the Square. Cast: Anne Chapman (Kelly), Paul Lockwood (Paul), Gordon Wescourt (Ray), Duncan McLeod (Cal), Robert Rudelson (Feeny), Lavelle Roby (Claire), Jan Sinclair (Christiana), Joey Duprez (Joy), Nick Wolcuff (Nick). Colour, 73 min.

VIXEN aka RUSS MEYER'S VIXEN (1968). An Eve Productions and Coldstream Films release; Pr/Dr/Ph./Ed.: Russ Meyer, Ass.Pr: Eve Meyer, Anthony James Ryan, Richard Serly Brummer, George Costello, Ass.Dr: George Costello, Sc.: Robert Rudelson, Anthony James Ryan, from story by Russ Meyer, Ass.Ed.: Richard Serly Brummer, Ass.Ph.: Anthony James Ryan, John Koester, S.: Richard Serly Brummer, John Koester, Don Minkler, M.: Igo Kantor, William Loose, ArtDr: Wilfred Kues, Narrator: Vic Perrin. Cast: Erica Gavin (Vixen Palmer), Harrison Page (Niles), Garth Pillsbury (Tom Palmer), Michael Donovan O'Donnell (O'Bannion), Vincene Wallace (Janet King), Jon Evans (Jud), Robert Aiken (Dave King). Colour, 71 min, soundtrack on Beverly Hills Records.

CHERRY, HARRY & RAQUEL aka THREE WAYS TO LOVE (UK) (1969). An Eve release of a Panamint Film production; Pr/Dr/Ph./Ed.: Russ Meyer, Ass.Pr: Eve Meyer, Anthony James Ryan, Thomas J. McGowan, Sc.: Tom Wolfe (aka Thomas J. McGowan), Russ Meyer, from story by Russ Meyer, Ass.Ed.: Richard Serly Brummer, Robert Pergament, S.: Richard Brummer, M.: Igo Kantor, William Loose, theme by Byron Cole, James East, Stu Phillips - performed by the Jacks and Balls. Cast: Larissa Ely (Raquel), Linda Ashton (Cherry), Charles Napier (Harry), Bert Santos (Enrique), Franklin H. Bolger (Mr Franklin), Astrid Lillimor, aka Uschi Digard (Soul), Michele Grand (Millie), John Milo (Apache), Robert Aiken (Tom), Michaelani (Doctor Lee). Colour, 71 min, soundtrack on Beverly Hills Records.

BEYOND THE VALLEY OF THE DOLLS (1970). A Twentieth Century Fox release, Pr/Dr: Russ Meyer, Ass.Pr: Red Hershon, Eve Meyer, Ass.Dr: David Hall, C. E. Dismukes, Pr.Mgr: Norman Cook, Sc.: Roger Ebert, from story by Roger Ebert and Russ Meyer, Ph.: Fred J. Koenekamp, Ed.: Dann Cahn, Dick Wormel, Sp.Ph.Effects: Jack Harman, S.: Richard Overton, Don Minkler, M.: Stu Phillips, Igo Kantor, William Loose, the Strawberry Alarm Clock, the Sandpipers, ArtDr: Jack Martin Smith, Arthur Lonergan, SetDr: Walter M. Scott, Stuart A. Reiss. Cast: Dolly Read (Kelly MacNamara), Cynthia Meyers (Casey Anderson), Marcia McBroom (Petronella Danforth), John LaZar (Ronnie 'Z-Man' Barzell), Michael Blodgett (Lance Rocke), David Gurian (Harris Allsworth), Edy Williams (Ashley St Ives), Erica Gavin (Roxanne), Phyllis Davis (Susan Lake), Harrison Page (Emerson Thorne), Duncan McLeod (Porter Hall), Jim Inglehart (Randy Black), Charles Napier (Baxter Wolfe), Henry Rowland (Otto), Princess Livingston (Matron), Stan Ross (Disciple), Lavelle Roby (Tessa), Angel Ray (Girl in tub), Ian Sander (Boy in tub), Veronica Erickson (Blond date), Haji (Cat Woman) and the Strawberry Alarm Clock. Colour, 109 min, soundtrack on Twentieth Century Fox.

THE SEVEN MINUTES (1971). A Twentieth Century Fox release, Pr/Dr: Russ Meyer, Ass.Pr: Red Hershon, Eve Meyer, Ass.Dr: David Hall, Pr.Mgr: William Eckhardt, Sc.: Richard

Warren Lewis, from the novel by Irving Wallace, Ph.: Fred Mandl, Orville Hallburg, Sp.Ph.Effects: Howard A. Anderson Co., Ed.: Dick Wormel, S.: Don J. Bassman, Theodore Soderberg, M.: Stu Phillips, B.B. King, Don Reed, Merryweather and Carey, ArtDr: Rodger Maus, SetDr: Walter M. Scott, Raphael Bretton, W'rb.: Bill Thomas, Make-up: Dan Striepeke, Del Acevedo, Lynn Reynolds, Hair: Mary Keats. Cast: Wayne Maunder (Mike Barrett), Marianne McAndrew (Maggie Russell), Philip Carey (Elmo Duncan), Jay C. Flippen (Luther Yerkes), Edy Williams (Faye Osborn), Lyle Bettger (Frank Griffith), Jackie Gayle (Norman Quandt), Ron Randell (Merle Reid), Charles Drake (Kellog), John Carradine (O'Flanagan), Harold J. Stone (Judge Upshaw), Tom Selleck (Phil Sanford), James Inglehart (Clay Rutherford), John Sarno (Jerry Griffith), Stanley Adams (Irwin Blair), Billy Durkin (George Perkins), Yvonne D'Angers (Sheri Moore), Robert Moloney (Ben Fremont), Olan Soul (Harvey Underwood), Jan Shutan (Anna Lou White), Alex D'Arcy (Christian Leroux), David Brian (Cardinal McManus), Berry Kroeger (Paul Van Fleet), Ralph Story (TV Commentator), Charles Napier (Iverson), Kay Peters (Olivia St Clair), Chris Marks (Dr Erlbacher), Stuart Lancaster (Dr Trimble), Yvonne De Carlo (Constance Cumberland). Colour, 115 min, soundtrack on Twentieth Century Fox.

BLACKSNAKE! aka DUCHESS OF DOOM, SWEET SUZY, SLAVES (UK) (1973). A Signal 166 Inc. and Trident Films release, Pr/Dr/Ph./Sc.: Russ Meyer, Ass.Pr: Anthony James Ryan, Pr.Mgr: Fred Owens, Pr.Ass.: Don Dorsey, Jaqueline Ryan, Sc.: Len Neubauer, Anthony James Ryan, Ph.: Arthur Ornitz, Arthur Browne, Ed.: Russ Meyer, Fred Baratta, ArtDr: Rick Heatherly, S.: Richard Serly Brummer, Paul Laune, Sam Shaw, Producer's Sound Service, M.: Bill Loose, Al Teeter, Stunt Co-ordinator: Bob Minor, Title and Opticals: Jack Harmon, Phil Cappel, W'rb.: Elsie Gittins, Make-up: Bub Miller. Cast: Anouska Hempel (Lady Susan), David Warbeck (Sir Charles Walker/Ronald Sopwith), Percy Herbert (Joxer Tierney), Milton McCollin (Joshua), Thomas Baptiste (Isaiah), Bernard Boston (Capt. Raymond Daladier), Vikki Richards (Cleone), Jean Durand (Sgt. Pompidoo), Dave Prowse (Jonathan Walker/the Duppie), Bob Minor (Barnaby), Bloke Modisane (Bottoms), Anthony Sharpe (Lord Clive). Colour, 85 min.

SUPERVIXENS aka VIXENS (CA) (1975). A September 19 production presented by RM Films International Inc., Pr/Dr/Ed./Sc.: Russ Meyer, Ass.Pr: Wilfred Kues, Charles Napier, Fred Owens, James Parsons, ExPr: Anthony James Ryan, Ph.: Russ Meyer, Douglas Knapp, Tom Neuwirth, ArtDr: Michael Levesque, S.: Richard Serly Brummer, Producers' Sound Service, M.: Bill Loose, W'rb.:Maureen of Hollywood, Paulette, Yves Meyer, Make-up: Barbarella Catton. Cast: Shari Eubank (Superangel/Supervixen), Charles Pitts (Clint Ramsey), Charles Napier (Harry Sledge), Uschi Digard (Supersoul), Henry Rowland (Martin Bormann), Christy Hartburg (Superlorna), Sharon Kelly (Supercherry), Deborah McGuire (Supereula), Glenn Dixon (Luther), John LaZar (Cal McKinhney), Stuart Lancaster (Lute), Haji (Superhaji), 'Big Jack' Provan (Sheriff), E. E. Meyer, aka Russ Meyer (Motel Manager), Ann-Marie. Colour, 105 min.

UP! (1976). An RHM Distributors release of a Russ Meyer production; Pr/Dr/Ed.: Russ Meyer, Ass.Pr: Fred Owens, Uschi Digard, George K. Carll, Pr.Mgr: Wilburn Kluck, Sc.: B. Callum (Russ Meyer), James Ryan, Reinhold Timme

(Roger Ebert), Ph.: Russ Meyer, Master Sergeant, Pat Lennef, Fred 'Fritz' Mandl, Tom Hammel, ArtDr: Michele Levesque, S.: Dan Holland, Richard Anderson, Fred Owens, M.: Bill Loose, Paul Ruhland, Ichthyologist: Charles E. Sumners, Casting: Eddie Foy III, Samantha Mansour. Cast: Robert McLane (Paul), Edward Schaaf (Adolph Schwartz), Mary Gavin, aka Candy Samples (the Headperson), Elain Collins (Ethiopian Chief), Su Ling (Limehouse), Janet Wood (Sweet Li'l Alice), Linda Sue Ragsdale (Gwendolyn), Harry (the Nimrod), Monte Bane (Sheriff Homer Johnson), Raven De La Croix (Margo Winchester), Larry Dean (Leonard Box), Marianne Marks (Chesty Young Thing), Bob Schott (Rafe), Foxy Lae (Pocohontas), Fred Owens (Rufus), Wilburn Kluck (Kluck), Ray Reinhardt (Commissioner), Francesca 'Kitten' Natividad (Greek Chorus). Colour, 80 min.

BENEATH THE VALLEY OF THE ULTRAVIXENS (1979). An R M Films International Inc. release of a Russ Meyer production; Pr/Dr/Ph./Ed.: Russ Meyer, Ass.Pr: Fred Owens, Richard Serly Brummer, Pr.Crew: Uschi Digard, Don Oulette, Bruce Paternak, Mitch Brown, Frank Scarpitto, Sc.: R. Hyde (Roger Ebert), B. Callum (Russ Meyer), from story by Russ Meyer, ArtDr: Michael Levesque, S.: Fred Owens, M.: William Tasker, Richard Serly Brummer. Cast: Francesca 'Kitten' Natividad (Lavonia), Anne Marie (Eufaula Roop), Ken Kerr (Lamar Shedd), June Mack (Junk Yard Sal), Lola Langusta (the Stripper), Pat Wright (Mr Peterbuilt), Michael Finn (Semper Fidelis), Steve Tracy (Rhett), Sharon Hill (Flovilla Thatch), Henry Rowland (Martin Bormann), Robert E. Pearson (Dr Asa Lavender), De Forest Covan (Zebulon), Don Scarbrough (Beau Badger), Aram Katcher (Tyrone), Uschi Digard (Supersoul), Mar(c)y Gavin, aka Candy Samples (the Very Big Blond), Stuart Lancaster (the Man from Small Town USA), Russ Meyer. Colour, 93 min.